MANAGING THE
MANUFACTURING PROCESS

MANAGING THE MANUFACTURING PROCESS
A Pattern for Excellence

Ralph W. Woodgate

A Wiley-Interscience Publication

JOHN WILEY & SONS, INC.

New York / Chichester / Brisbane / Toronto / Singapore

Library of Congress Cataloging-in-Publication Data
    Woodgate, Ralph W., 1922–
      Managing the manufacturing process : a pattern for excellence /
    Ralph Woodgate.
          p.   cm.
      "A Wiley–Interscience publication."
      Includes bibliographical references.
      ISBN 0-471-50655-9
      1. Manufactures—Management.   2. Industrial management.
    I. Title.
    HD9720.5.W56   1991
    658.5—dc20   90-42385
                                                         CIP

Printed in the United States of America

10 9 8 7 6 5 4 3 2 1

To my wife Catherine, who advised, encouraged,
and put up with the many hours at the word processor.

CONTENTS

PREFACE

Management has been written about, discussed, and taught for many years. It has gone through different phases, from the authoritarian management of the 1920s to the various management styles of much more recent years. From time to time we are advised to follow the European management techniques, or the Japanese methods, to be a style "X" or a 9.9 manager, and so on. We are encouraged to implement JIT or TQC programs, to set up Quality Circles. These techniques are guaranteed to solve some or all of our production problems.

To the outside observer, and to many practicing managers, these methods appear to be of a fashionable fad that lasts for a while and then fades into oblivion. The overall results of using these techniques do not appear to permanently change the efficiency of our industry very much. There are still some companies that operate efficiently, most function adequately but not to their best level of productivity. Many stumble on from day to day, never really getting rid of their problems, always on the dividing line between success and failure. The particular management style in use, or the incorporation of one or more of the publicized management techniques does not appear to be directly related to their performance, and any changes in the form of management do not appear to have more than a very temporary effect on their long-term efficiency.

I do not wish to imply that any of these management tools are not useful, or that they should be ignored. However, I firmly believe that they cannot compensate for an inadequate understanding of the fundamental nature of the manufacturing process or the skills required of the Manufacturing Manager. If this basic knowledge is available, then the publicized techniques will be seen as examples of some aspects of the fundamental good management that is the basis of an efficient operation.

I started out in industry as a designer, but slowly began to realize that manufacturing was by far the most difficult and demanding of fields. I eventuallytransferred over to work in manufacturing, and I still believe strongly that this is the most critical part of industry and demands the highest skills of its managers.

Today I am a consultant working on the shop floor, personally involved with many companies that fall into all of the categories discussed above. I frequently see manufacturing problems that ultimately turn out to have been caused by incorrect management decisions, and I see low levels of efficiency caused by a lack of understanding of people. I also see companies that are examples of efficiency and excellence in management, second to none in the world. These variations appeared to be much more a matter of management than of technology.

Therefore, a few years ago, I wrote a magazine article entitled "A Pattern For Excellence" in which I tried to list those visible factors that appeared to be common to all the successful operations that I had seen. The response to the article far exceeded my expectations and prompted me to give a presentation on the subject at a technical seminar. I hardly expected the audience of engineers and technical managers at the meeting to be more than curious about the management aspects of manufacturing, but again the response proved to be exceptional, and suggested to me that there was a demand by many people for more practical information on the subject.

However, I first had to determine why the many books on management already in existence did not satisfy the need. Through my work on the shop floor, my lectures, and my personal observations at many companies, I eventually felt that I understood what was lacking and what was required. The practicing manager is a busy individual who has little time for information that is superfluous; it has to be applicable to the current situation and must be simply expressed. The manager needs to have the fundamental factors presented in terms of the everyday operation that he has to control. Most of the available books fell into two groups. Either they were very theoretical, using unnecessarily complex language, were written more for the student studying for an MBA than a practicing manager, or were aimed at the general public and offered little practical information that could be used in a day-to-day operation.

Because management is such a wide ranging term that no single book can possible cover every facet, I decided to concentrate on the manufacturing area which I believe to be the most complex as well as the most critical to our country's economy. It also happens to be the area with which I am personally most involved and therefore able to describe with experience and knowledge. My work is primarily with the electronics industry, and many of the examples are from this field of business. However, the same factors that are involved in the efficient manufacture of electronics can be directly applied to most other manufacturing operations.

For new or potential managers this book is intended to show the tasks ahead clearly and in considerable practical detail. It deliberately tries to avoid gobbledegook phrases, placing emphasis on the basic simplicity of management while acknowledging the complexity of dealing with people, which can be a large part of the managers' responsibility. For practicing manufacturing managers it provides an opportunity to review their present operations and determine their status. It offers suggestions for improvement and a guide to achieving excellence.

This book also has a great deal of information for managers who are at the periphery of the actual manufacturing operation. For far too long it has been assumed that manufacturing is concerned only with the shop floor, and that departments providing support, such as design, engineering, materials acquisition, and quality control, could operate in a manner that was essentially remote from the actual day-to-day struggle for product quality and cost. This assumption is of course totally incorrrect, and as our products and our manufacturing methods become more and more complex, we are compelled to recognize that these peripheral departments are as much a part of the manufacturing process as are the operators on the shop floor.

If our manufacturing is to be efficient and profitable, those who manage these peripheral departments must have as good an understanding of the management and control of the manufacturing process as anyone else who is part of the manufacturing team. In this book the effects of management decisions in these peripheral areas are considered in detail, and all managers of such departments should find the book of practical value in developing the cooperation and understanding necessary to be able to provide efficient support for manufacturing.

All of the examples in this book are factual. However, WoodCorp we believe it is important to maintain the confidentiality of our clients; thus, some of the details have been changed to avoid identifying their source. In some of the examples the manager, as well as other members of the manufacturing organization, will be shown making bad decisions, or adopting negative attitudes and generally acting in a less than effective manner. The reader should understand that these comments are not intended to characterize in any way the average manager or other employeesy. Most people want to do a good job and want to feel proud of their organization. When people perform badly it is usually because of a lack of knowledge or incomplete understanding of all of the factors involved in their job. It is my sincere hope that this book will help managers of manufacturing or any of the peripheral departments, whether established or newly appointed, to bring their operations to the degree of excellence that is necessary if we are to be successful in this highly competitive era.

Finally I want to ask for understanding from the many women in industry, especially those who are practicing or potential managers and the many with whom I have worked. I have used the terms "he," "him," and "his" throughout this book. However, this is always intended to cover both male and female managers and other workers. Unfortunately the English language does not have a simple expression to cover both sexes and I refuse to use him/her and similar clumsy and fabricated phrasing.

RALPH W. WOODGATE

Brewster, NY
September 1990

MANAGING THE
MANUFACTURING PROCESS

Chapter 1

LOOKING AT MANUFACTURING MANAGEMENT

Before the Industrial Revolution most products were handmade by an individual craftsman. He may have used some assistants or an apprentice, but he rarely worked in large groups. The lack of communications and the difficulty in transporting goods made small, local manufacturing operations economically competitive. As transportation became easier the market place for any particular product increased, machines were slowly developed to reduce costs and handle the larger volume of production, the number of employees increased, and the factory was born, together with the job of the Manufacturing Manager.

The task of controlling a manufacturing operation has, of course, changed dramatically since those early days. The products of that era were comparatively simple and the technologies used in their manufacture easily understood. This was still the age of the craftsman, who handed down his skills from one generation to another. The apprenticeship route into industry offered a way not only of learning the manual skills, but also of understanding the entire process in very practical terms. It was often possible for the general manager to run the entire operation, including the shop floor, with the help of mechanics to set up and maintain the machines and supervisors to oversee the actual work. The manager could personally control all of the activities. The manufacturing area was in fact the company, with few of the present-day large ancillary operations such as marketing, research, or procurement. Most of the materials used were locally obtained, and suppliers were usually well known and considered almost a part of the company.

Today the task has changed dramatically and the manufacturing manager can no longer expect to be able to provide all of the technical expertise necessary to operate effectively. Yet it is impossible to manage without a clear understanding of the processes and equipment used in the factory. The manager has therefore not only to be technically competent but also to be able to select excellent supervisory staff and use them in an effective manner.

The very nature of employees has also changed. Initially workers in a factory were chiefly used to carry out simple manual tasks, and the more highly skilled work was carried out by a smaller number of skilled craftsmen. The employees were tied very closely to the plant; there was no such thing as commuting, for the people who worked in a factory lived within walking distance. Because alternative work was seldom available in the immediate area there was a strong economic bond between worker and company. In a few cases the company was almost a second family, providing housing, medical treatment, and similar social needs. Jobs were frequently handed down from father to son.

Under these conditions, with employees of limited formal education and the prevailing social attitudes, an authoritarian form of management worked effectively. Today most employees are well educated, there is usually ample alternative employment and the old form of management no longer works. The social climate has also changed and attitudes that were once acceptable are now not tolerated; indeed in extreme cases managing with the old attitudes is not only totally ineffective but is also illegal.

LIVING WITH CHANGE

Thus today we find that most of the factors affecting the manager's task have changed. There is usually a choice of employment, workers are educated and the old attitudes of workers and manager no longer exist. Of course, these changes did not occur quickly but developed with the changing social and technical structure of our society. It is all too easy to assume that we have reached a status quo in our particular industry, that what exists today will continue tomorrow. But this is not so, and it is important for the manufacturing manager to recognize that change is always with us and the future requirements of the operation must be considered continuously and the organization constantly adjusted to accept these changes in an efficient manner. The only thing that is permanent in the manufacturing operation is change. In many respects the future of any business will depend on the manager's ability to cope with changing attitudes, requirements, and technologies.

We all know of companies that have failed because they either ignored changes, or were unable to accommodate them and took the necessary actions too late. It may be that the technology of the product or the manufacturing process or the worker/manager relationship changes. None of these factors is static and we fall into a serious trap if we ever become complacent and believe that what exists at this time can be carried on without change into the future. The efficient manager must always have a plan for improving the operation, and this must include an attempt to look forward and assess future requirements. It also demands an open mind that is not blinded by what is being done today and is always seeking to improve operating efficiency. He must also watch what is being done by his colleagues and his competitors. We have to get rid of the "Not invented here" syndrome, which is still prevalent throughout industry. The same tests and experiments are conducted time and time again because we do not really believe the results from someone else. The "Yes, buts" abound. Yes, I know that their results looked okay but our production is different. Yes, they are using the new process satisfactorily but our machines are not the same. Yet some very successful companies have deliberately sought out every new idea, every novel technology, anything that will improve their efficiency no matter who invented or developed it.

THE MANAGER'S OBJECTIVE

The manufacturing manager's task has changed dramatically and continues to change; however, there must be a fundamental objective that will provide a base on which we can develop an understanding of the overall task. This objective is not easy to develop and will inevitably apply only in broad terms; the details will have to be added for each individual manager. However, all manufacturing managers ultimately have to meet the following requirements.

The manufacturing manager's task is to make products of the highest quality on schedule at the lowest cost. This is achieved through the efficient control of materials, methods, tools, and labor.

The correct balance between quality, cost, and schedule is at the heart of the manager's job and can be extremely difficult to maintain (Figure 1). For example, in too many cases the schedule is considered sacrosanct and the pressure to meet the schedule forces the manager to incur additional cost and jeopardize quality. In some cases it is suggested that the quality of the product need only be adequate for the task it is to perform and not the highest that can be obtained. At first it appears there may be some truth in this comment. But, as will be seen in Chapter 16 on Quality, if we only aim to be good, it is unlikely that we will ever achieve anything but mediocrity. If we aim for excellence

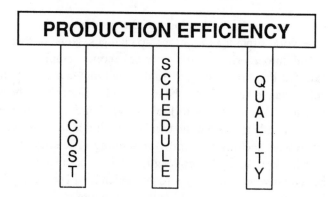

Figure 1   The manufacturing manager's constant balancing act.

we may well produce a product with good quality, and this inevitably turns out to be produced at the lowest cost.

To be capable of maintaining this balance between schedule, cost, and quality the manufacturing manager must have a thorough knowledge of the entire process, and excellent technical support in the more esoteric fields of manufacturing methods and machines. A wrong decision can so easily be made if all factors are not considered. As an example, in one factory some printed wiring boards were rejected at receiving inspection, because the through hole plating contained voids and failed the solderability test. Because of the pressure of the schedule the engineering department was asked if the boards could be used. They were signed off as usable although they did not meet the specification, were loaded with components, and then were machine soldered. The resulting joints were full of cavities due to outgassing of the base material through the voids in the plating and were rejected by quality control. The rework necessary to make the parts cosmetically acceptable to meet the final specification averaged eight hours per board and eventually some of the product had to be scrapped. The schedule was missed by three days. The product was of doubtful reliability.

When an analysis was made of these defects it was found that the initial decision was overinfluenced by the pressure of the schedule and a desire to "keep everybody busy." If the boards had been scrapped and new ones obtained, even at a premium, the product would have had a much greater long-term reliability, the high cost of the rework would have been avoided, and the schedule would have been missed only by an additional day. In this particular situation neither the manufacturing manager nor the engineer who had signed off the boards had a sufficiently clear understanding of the process to know the full ramifications of his actions.

INTERACTIONS AND TECHNICAL DECISIONS

Problems of the kind described above are part of the day-to-day responsibilities of the manufacturing manager, who must be able to make the necessary decisions quickly and correctly. He must therefore have a first rate knowledge of the process, and the tools and equipments used. In a very complex process this may not be possible, and he will have to rely on the experts in each particular field. He must therefore be able to select the right people, be able to judge their capabilities, and have the skill to use their knowledge correctly by weighing all their conclusions and then making his own decisions.

In addition to the technical aspects of the job the manufacturing manager also has to posses the skills common to every other management position. He may have to prepare budgets, control expenditure, set up and operate the organization, take care of personnel problems, and so forth. The manufacturing manager therefore has to wear many different hats and function in many different areas. Although these tasks have been discussed as if they were separate and individual responsibilities, they are closely linked and together make up the total management function. In other words, if the manager's skills are to be effective in their individual fields they must complement each other and form a single, coherent operation. This is not a simple task, and to do this effectively requires complete cooperation and coordination with all the other areas of the operation and the total support of top management.

It is this very interpersonal complexity that makes the management task so difficult to define. It also makes it difficult to break down the overall task into the various parts so that they can be considered in detail. As this book progresses we will see that each function is closely linked to many other functions and that any one cannot be considered in isolation. It is no longer possible to put a wall around manufacturing, or for that matter any other part of the operation, and consider it as a separate and isolated entity. The decisions made by the manufacturing manager will inevitably impact every other area of the company, and in the same way decisions made in any other department will affect manufacturing. One simple and obvious example is the interaction between design and manufacturing. All too often we see designs that are difficult to make, or exceed their designed cost, simply because there was not good communication between the departments during the design phase.

Developing this degree of communication is simply one action of good management and the need for it has changed little in past decades. In a very different example, the accounting department of a company had designed a method of accruing costs that was simple from the accounting point of view but did not accurately reflect the actual shop floor operations. As a result several bad decisions were made based on accounting data.

We should realize that in any manufacturing operation it is the shop floor that is the whole reason for the existence of the plant and every other part of the facility exists solely to support the manufacturing operation.

MANAGEMENT STYLES AND FASHIONS

As discussed above, management is an extremely complex task with no single format for success. Yet we are constantly being offered training programs and management philosophies that promise to produce whatever results we desire. There are certainly techniques in management that can be taught and that are effective; there are management philosophies that can provide the basis for our day to day activities. Yet there is no single management style or method that can be universally applied. The fundamental basis of management has to be understood together with the technology that applies to any particular job. The manager then has to put these together to produce an effective management style for his particular responsibilities, authorities, and organization and one that suits his own personality and ability.

There is really very little that is new in this area—only the buzz words change. Today the fashion is "Quality Circles," yesterday it was "9.9 Management," and before that it was "Participative Management." Yet when all of these fashions are looked at closely they all say the same thing. We cannot manage as dictators, we must involve everyone in the day to day running of the operation. Good managers have intuitively known this ever since managers existed. We can all look back through our careers in business and recognize these men, the boss who made things happen, the supervisor who never had complaints from his people, the manager who was instinctively recognized as a man of authority.

"Just in Time" has become a popular term in recent years, yet the good manager has always worked to reduce inventory, to turn out a high quality product. Certainly the use of the term has increased interest in this area and that alone justifies the propaganda. But the philosophy is not new nor is it universally applicable. The good manager can sort out the fashion from the truth and use that aspect of the fad or fashion which is useful and applicable to his particular operation.

The manufacturing manager is much like the old fashioned general practitioner. He has to take care of the total health of his patient, the manufacturing operation, yet he has to be prepared at times to act the part of the specialist, to operate when required, and to prescribe curative procedures.

There is no way that all of the necessary skills can be taught. Experience is the ultimate teacher, and the manager develops and expands his abilities as he works.

He needs the basic knowledge, just as the doctor has to know the workings of the human body. He needs to be able to use the latest tools of management just as the surgeon has to be able to use the latest surgical equipment. The tools change as new ones are developed, but the fundamental basic understanding stays the same. Certainly the training programs, the new ideas and techniques can be useful; they also stimulate thinking about the job. But none change the fundamental way a manager carries out his work. This will always be a very personal matter that cannot be copied or handed on to someone else. Just because every human being is different, thinks in a different way, and has different experiences and attitudes, every manager will manage in a different way. Management is not something that can be described precisely. It is not a fixed method or procedure; it is as variable as our feelings, our ideas, and our attitudes to life. What we can do is try to understand the fundamental facts of the management skills, the process that we are managing, and try to understand those that we manage. Above all we must try to understand ourselves and our own motives and ambitions. We must realize that until we can see ourselves clearly it is not likely that we will be able to motivate, lead, or manage others efficiently.

Ultimately each individual must fashion his own management style which will be as individual as his style of dressing and just as variable, depending on the occasion.

Chapter 2

THE MANUFACTURING PROCESS

At first glance the definition of the manufacturing process seems to be fairly obvious. It can be said to be the methods by which a product is made. This is certainly true, but it is far too simple and ill defined to be of use in the search for excellence in managing the process.

As has already been suggested, the extent of a process is usually far more widespread than may be recognized, and this lack of recognition is largely caused by our inability to understand the true nature of a process. Just as the task of management is easy to write in general terms but difficult to define precisely, so it is not easy to produce a definition of a process that will apply universally. The nearest idea to this objective is expressed below (see also Figure 2).

> A process is the recipe of materials, tools, labor, and methods which if applied exactly will produce a product of known quality at a repeatable cost.

However, this definition is not particularly useful except in general terms. It is on the same level as describing farming as "growing corn." A specific example is probably the best way to get into the details of the subject.

THE PROCESS OF BAKING A CAKE

Let's consider baking a cake. This is certainly a process and contains all the fundamentals of every process (Figure 3). First there has to be a written recipe. Flour, baking powder, milk, eggs, and sugar are called for in the recipe, in the

A RECIPE

Take the following ingredients...

★ ★

THE RECIPE DEFINES THE---
MATERIALS, TOOLS, EQUIPMENT,
AND METHODS
TO BE USED TO MAKE THE PRODUCT

Figure 2   If we follow the recipe exactly, the cake will always turn out right.

quantities required to make a cake of a certain size. The methods are described: for example, "Beat the eggs for ten minutes." Baking times and duration are defined: "Place on the middle shelf and bake for two hours at 375 degrees." If the entire recipe is followed exactly, the cake should come out looking like the picture on the cover of the recipe book and tasting delicious.

Yet all too often the home cook is disappointed and claims that the recipe is no good, that sometimes it works and sometime it does not. This, of course, shows a complete lack of understanding of the nature of a process. If a process is followed exactly it will perform in the same way every time. If there is a

THE PROCESS OF BAKING A CAKE

MATERIALS	METHODS	EQUIPMENT
FLOUR	WEIGH	SCALES
EGGS	MIX	BOWLS
SUGAR	FILL PANS	MIXER
FRUIT	REMOVE	OVEN
SPICES	COOL	SPATULA
MILK	PACKAGE	WORK AREA

Figure 3   Baking a cake is a process. The results will always be the same if the recipe is followed exactly in every respect.

variation in the results, no matter how small, then there must have been some variation in either the materials or the methods used. Consider some of the unexpected things that can occur: the recipe calls for large eggs but the cook has only medium-sized eggs and makes an educated guess as to the number required. The recipe calls for baking at 375 degrees but the oven thermostat is incorrect and the baking really is carried out at 325 degrees instead.

Sometimes the cook will make deliberate changes to the recipe in an attempt to change the result. For example, the cook wants the cake to be browner on the surface and increases the cooking time. This form of experimenting may be successful, but all too often there are unwanted secondary results. The cake may certainly be brown, but it may also be so hard that it cannot be eaten.

THE EXTENT OF THE PROCESS

Sometimes the cake does not turn out as expected, yet the cook is absolutely sure that he has followed the recipe exactly. It is here that the extent of the process begins to expand beyond the obvious (Figure 4). Perhaps the flour had raising ingredients added by the miller, the ratio of egg yolk to white had changed, or the mixing utensils were not absolutely clean and had contaminated the mixture. In other words, the composition of the ingredients or some other other factor had changed without the cook's knowledge.

We must now consider the manufacturer of the various ingredients used in the process, the individual who washed up the mixing bowl, and the ratio of egg yolk to egg white. To the home cook these may sound like unnecessary complications of a simple process, but to the commercial cake manufacturer who has to produce thousands of cakes every day they can be serious matters.

The process does not even stop with the manufacturer of the ingredients, for the quality of the flour may depend on the wheat from which it was ground and the fineness of that grind. If we carry our investigation to extreme limits, the farmer and the milling methods are all part of the process of making a cake. Likewise, the size and shape of the baking tin and the degree of mixing affect the end results.

Thus, in any process we first have to consider the materials to be used. It is extremely unlikely that we can control the processes used by our vendors in producing the materials, although in many parts of the manufacturing industry this is becoming the objective. The tools that are mostly used are the drawing, the standard or specification by which we attempt to define exactly all of the requirements for the particular materials, and the tests to assure compliance with these specifications. These are not always totally reliable tools and will be discussed in more detail in Chapter 10.

> # THE SCOPE OF THE PROCESS
> ★ ★ ★ ★ ★ ★ ★ ★ ★ ★ ★ ★ ★ ★ ★ ★ ★ ★
>
> ## THE QUALITY OF THE CAKE DEPENDS ON
> ## THE QUALITY OF THE FLOUR
> ## AND THEREFORE - - -
>
> *The farmer who grew the wheat*
> *The miller who ground the wheat*
> *The way the wheat was stored*
> *The way the flour was packaged*
> *The storage time and conditions*

Figure 4   The process extends far from the manufacturing floor, and this too must be controlled.

Once we control the quality of the materials used to make the cake mixture, we have to consider the way in which they will be mixed. It is probably impossible to define the exact nature of the mixed cake batter, and therefore attempting to work to a specification will not be likely to maintain consistency of the mixture. We will instead have to develop clear instructions on how the ingredients must be combined, including the tools to be used. It will be necessary to train the cooks in these methods and to monitor the work to be assured that the correct mixing methods are always used. The baking cycle must of course be defined. In addition, because the oven temperature is of great importance it will have to be controlled within the prescribed limits and the oven temperature controller will have to be checked for accuracy at regular intervals.

In summary, if every cake that we bake is to be of exactly the same quality, we have to specify in detail all the characteristics of all the ingredients and see that these requirements are met consistently. The mixing and baking steps must be developed, recorded, and taught to the cooks. Some form of control must be used to see that all of these items are followed exactly. As we can now realize, the process of baking a cake spreads far beyond the obvious tasks found in the kitchen.

Of course, it is unlikely that cakes will be the end product from our factory, and the manufacturing process will almost certainly be more complex in almost every way than that of baking a cake. There may be several individual steps that together make the total process; parts may be made in several different locations. However, the same fundamental principles apply. Although it is now obvious that defining a process is not easy, understanding the nature of a process is simple, and it is possible to list most of the requirements for this.

- It must be repeatable.
- It must not rely on the operator's decisions.
- It must be able to be recorded in complete detail.
- It must break down into simple steps.
- It must not require exceptional skills of the operator.

The human element is the most complex item in any process. Every individual is different, each person behaves in a different manner, yet in a process we are attempting to eliminate variations, and the biggest variations come from the individuals who are making the process work. The manufacturing manager must understand the way that people think and react and be able to use this knowledge in setting up and operating his organization. This, of course, is where the manufacturing manager usually has the most difficulty.

If an operation does not fall within the parameters listed above, it cannot be considered a process. For example, if the operator is required to be particularly highly skilled and make constant decisions, for example in molding clay on a potter's wheel, the results will be totally dependent on the skill of the operator and it is unlikely that the results will be consistent. If the operation is mechanized, with the pots being cast in a mold, it changes from an individual skill that cannot be totally defined to a repeatable process.

This is not to suggest that machine-molded pots are in any way superior to those made by hand; indeed, in this case it is the variations in the finished product that can make it much more attractive. However, when we consider most of the items manufactured today, especially those that are complex and of high technology, one of our aims must be to make them all exactly the same with a constant level of quality and to make them at a constant cost. These factors are not likely to be achieved unless we can set up a controllable process.

Chapter 3

SETTING UP THE MANUFACTURING PROCESS

Every manufacturing process differs in some way from every other. It is quite obvious that making sausages is not the same as fabricating refrigerators, but even comparing operations of about the same size, and manufacturing the same product, we will find some variations in the process. Most are minor, but some may be quite large. These variations come about for many reasons. It may be that the volume or mix of products varies, that the equipments used in manufacturing are different, or that management policies or organizations are not the same.

Yet even through this maze of variations there is a straight path that if followed correctly will enable us to arrive at an efficient manufacturing process no matter what the product. In order to reach this objective we must begin with the following steps.

1. The process must be fully developed and recorded in total detail.
2. The operators must be trained to follow the process exactly at all times.
3. The process should be automated wherever possible to eliminate operator decisions and variations.
4. A formal maintenance program for tools and equipment must be developed and installed.
5. Materials must be controlled at every step of the process to assure compliance with specifications, and not become damaged from incorrect handling.

6. Formal corrective and preventive action programs have to be developed and installed.
7. The correct organization must be set up to enable the process to be operated efficiently.

If the product designers have not taken into account the manufacturing capability, all of the above will be in vain and it will not be possible to develop an efficient manufacturing process. Therefore, in this chapter it is assumed that cooperation between the design and manufacturing teams has assured this compatibility.

DEVELOPING THE PROCESS

Before we can begin to even think about installing any form of process it must be completely developed. This may seem obvious but in too many cases production begins while a considerable number of factors have either not been taken into account or have not been recognized through inadequate preparation. Frequently the major part of the process development takes place during the initial period of manufacturing—timing that inevitably brings delays and overexpenditure. Indeed, no matter how much prior work is carried out on the process it seems inevitable that some small number of items are overlooked or are not recognized until the full pressure and variations of manufacturing become a reality.

It is reasonable to use the start of production as a development period, provided that it is a fully planned activity carried out without the pressure of the production schedule. It has to be provided with adequate manpower and funding, and the task must not be underestimated. It usually consumes much more time than is planned.

In one case involving a new product being assembled in a completely new, highly automated plant, the development program occupied three months and involved almost the entire staff of that particular division of the company. This development program was well planned and executed and when production was finally started there were few problems. Schedule, quality, and cost targets were achieved immediately; the cost of development was more than repaid by the ease with which the manufacturing process was able to be operated and controlled.

Compare this planned entry into production with a more usual situation in which only the minimum amount of work is done that is necessary to get production started. Although the formal development phase is eliminated, initial production is usually beset with a myriad of problems that could have been foreseen with adequate preparation. Parts do not fit correctly, operators make mistakes because of a lack of experience, tools do not work exactly as planned, and so on. In spite of these problems production schedules still have to be met. Inevitably the solution is rework, more labor, and the Bandaid approach, steps that never get to the heart of the problem. It is not unusual under these circumstances to find the same problems in existence for the entire life of the product.

In one instance, the lack of a specialized tool was responsible on one sub assembly for rework of every particular product made. The cost of this amounted to about $10.00 per sub assembly and 1,000 were made every month. As the product had been in production for just over two years, cost amounted to almost a quarter of a million dollars for reworking this part alone. At the start of production the rework had been done to "meet the schedule" because there was no time to design and make the tool. Eventually the tool had been forgotten and the rework became part of the manufacturing cycle. A simple $250.00 fixture eliminated the problem.

During the development phase every aspect of production must be examined. Experiments may be needed to be carried out to determine the effects on the production process of the tolerances permitted in the specifications of materials or parts. The acceptable limits of tool wear must be determined. During all of this work the operator must be considered at all times and included in the development program. It may be easy for the engineer to assemble one or two parts under laboratory conditions, but a completely different situation exists for the operator who has to carry out the work day in and day out in the factory environment. Wherever possible the operators should be brought into the process development at the earliest possible stage. They are the people who will be carrying out the process; they understand their own capabilities and limitations. In addition, there are advantages to be gained when the operators view the job as "their process." They have helped to develop it; they will want to make it successful.

Once developed the process must be recorded IN DETAIL (Figure 5). This step cannot be overemphasized; for example, if it is necessary to switch on a machine the record must say where the switch is, what it looks like, and what to expect when the switch is operated. If it is required to fill a reservoir with a liquid, it must define what the liquid looks like, where is it to be found, what carrying container is to be used, and to what level the reservoir is to be filled.

The argument is often put forward that this level of detail is not necessary as the operators know the process. But this assumes that the operator will never make a mistake, never needs his work to be checked, will never be absent, sick, or take a vacation. If the process is not recorded in detail there is no way that we can ever be sure that it is in fact being carried out as it was originally developed. If it is not monitored regularly against the recorded process, with

---

THE PROCESS
MUST BE RECORDED IN DETAIL
★★★★★★★★★★★★★★★★★★★★★★★★★

For example
The instruction "Switch on"
must tell the operator...

What the switch looks like
Where he finds the switch
How he turns it to "On"
What happens then
What to do if it does not work

Figure 5   If the process is to be followed exactly at all times, the record must cover every possible detail.

time there will inevitably be a drift into an out-of-control condition. It will then be extremely difficult to find the cause of that lack of control.

Nothing must be left to the operator's judgment unless this is absolutely necessary and then every factor must be completely explained and the operator trained thoroughly in making that decision. The operation will have to be monitored closely, backup operators will have to be trained to assure adequate coverage of trained people, and they must be rotated in the actual job. Problems can arise when one operator always performs an operation and the backup person only takes over when the original operator is absent. Skills are soon lost if they are not used regularly.

The record will usually be in written form but it may also be part of a computer program or be designed into a machine. Whatever the actual recording method it must be possible to go back and repeat every aspect of the process in complete detail. Recording the process details is more difficult to carry out than appears to be the case at first glance; often we do not even recognize every detail of what we do, or the importance of some factors. For example, an operator may use some previously learned technique quite subconsciously. If it is not noticed and recorded, another operator may not work in the same manner and the process will then not be repeated exactly.

In one case an operator had found, accidently, that rinsing a substrate in an acid bath, which happened to be located adjacent to his work station, improved the adhesion of a plastic film that was applied in a later process step. This acid rinse was never discovered until the operator retired, when a major problem arose with the film falling off the substrate. It is good practice therefore to repeat each process segment with several different operators, not only to avoid this type of problem but also to find out the degree of training that will be necessary.

The detailed record of the fully developed process is the basis of every well-controlled manufacturing operation. Without it, quality, cost, and schedule cannot be guaranteed, and when problems arise they will not be easily solved. It is the foundation on which everything else is built.

TRAINING

After the process is developed and recorded it is necessary to train everyone concerned in his particular task. If the operators have been involved in the development phase this is much less difficult, but the training requirement should never be underestimated. No matter how simple the job nor how highly skilled the operator, training is still necessary.

On one occasion cracked solder joints began to appear on a sub assembly. The product had been manufactured for several years and this defect had never been seen before. It was eventually found to be caused by three high school students who had been hired as help during the summer vacation. They had been given the job of cutting off the excess wire on soldered connections and had soon developed their own technique for quickly carrying out this work. Unfortunately their method also cracked the connections, which then had to be reworked. They had received no training, on the grounds that "Anyone knows how to cut wire."

During one training session some students were asked to cut wires to about one inch in length. The results were astounding: the wires varied from a quarter of an inch to over two inches. The students were then given rulers to assist in making the wires the correct length, but the results were not much better. Finally, it was found necessary to teach the class how to measure with a ruler. At first glance this seemed ridiculous but on closer examination the reason was obvious. Most of the class were married women in their forties who had spent the last twenty years looking after the home and bringing up a family. They had little time or need to become experienced in measurement. Similarly it was found necessary to instruct them in the names of tools, so that they understood what was meant when asked to use cutters or long-nosed pliers. Incidentally, they turned out to be absolutely first-class operators.

The conclusion is obvious: do not assume that anything is known or understood until it is proved, and provide adequate training for every step of the process. Adequate training means formal training under the supervision of a skilled instructor. Today the "Sit by Jimmy" or on the job training of the past is just not good enough. Inevitably it will only perpetuate the mistakes and omissions of the operator who is doing the training; in addition, while training the student he cannot give the effort and concentration to his normal work that the job deserves. Both trainee and instructor lose out in this situation, the training is inevitably less than adequate, and the productivity loss is unacceptable.

Like any other job, training requires specific skills and is most economically carried out by a properly trained instructor, working to a formal training program. Additionally some forms of retraining or review will be necessary to ensure that the skills are retained. Certification for any particular skill is recommended, with regular reclassification and retraining when necessary.

Training in any of the shop floor skills falls into three parts and all three are equally important (Figure 6).

- Teaching the theory of the job.
- Training in the necessary manual dexterity.
- Gaining experience in the operation.

The first part consists of teaching the operator the fundamental theory of the process and identifying the particular skill being taught. This step is often omitted on the grounds that either it is unnecessary or the operators will not

---

THE THREE STAGES OF TRAINING

(1) UNDERSTAND THE THEORY
(2) LEARN THE MANUAL SKILLS
(3) PRACTICE TO GAIN EXPERIENCE

Figure 6 Training is not a "One Shot" deal. It is an ongoing program and is an essential part of any efficient process control.

understand the theory because it is too complex. Both of these arguments are absurd. The first step in carrying out any job efficiently is to understand what is being done, and the operator can understand the process as well as anyone else. Of course, it may be necessary to provide the theory in some form that does not require specialized knowledge. For example, the author frequently lectures on solderability and an understanding of wetting is necessary for a full comprehension of the subject. As it is unlikely that many students will be knowledgeable in the mathematics of surface physics, which is the formal way of teaching this subject, it can be presented by relating it to everyday events such as raindrops, or water wetting a clean and a greasy plate. The skilled instructor will have no difficulty in providing this form of theoretical training on almost any subject. Without such an understanding of the job, operators will be working blind; although they may be able to perform their task, they will have no idea of what to do when problems arise. Indeed, they may not even be able to recognize a problem. In addition, the knowledgeable operator has much more interest in the job and thus invariably will carry it out more efficiently and accurately.

The next step in training is to develop the manual skills that the operator will require to perform the job, and this is usually not a difficult or long task. However, the fact that the operator can then carry out the work is not adequate. The operator is required to do the job on the shop floor where there may be numerous distractions, and to do the job consistently and at a reasonable speed.

Because all of these things will come only with experience, the next phase of any training program has to provide the opportunity to develop this experience. It must be done under the supervision of a trained instructor as this is the time when bad habits develop. During this phase it will become apparent that a few operators will never acquire the skills to do the job properly and they should be moved to other more suitable work at this time.

We should always remember that many people other than the operators will need to be trained. Everyone must understand exactly where his particular job fits into the complete process. This will be discussed in more detail in Chapter 7, where the extent of the process is considered.

PROCESS AUTOMATION

Human beings are generally ineffective at carrying out repetitive operations even when they are simple and require no decision making. Machines perform much better than people under these conditions; ideally—if we could automate the entire manufacturing process—quality, cost, and the delivery schedule would all be under perfect control. Of course, this is done in some industries where the product is suitable for such methods of manufacture and the volume justifies the capital expenditure. People, on the other hand, have tremendous flexibility in the things that they can do, and also have the ability to make complex decisions. Unfortunately we frequently tend to use people in the manufacturing process for the very tasks for which they are least efficient.

Therefore we have to recognize these limitations and attempt to minimize their effect on production. Wherever it is possible, we must eliminate the need for the operator to make continuous simple decisions, because boredom can quickly affect the accuracy of his performance. This does not necessarily mean a tremendous expenditure for machines or other equipment although this will surely be the case when it is justified. What is required is simple common sense. For example, if a part has to be placed precisely, then a jig or fixture must be provided so that it can be done automatically. If adhesives have to be used, a pneumatic applicator with an X-Y coordinate table should be considered to position the parts correctly. As an alternative, precut film adhesives may be more suitable. There are many ways to set up an operation so that it becomes difficult, if not impossible, to carry it out incorrectly. If there is confusion in identifying parts, certain systems can make it impossible for the incorrect part to be presented to the operator, or it can be clearly marked by color coding.

None of these proposals to add automation is intended to imply in any way that the operators are not efficient workers. Generally everyone wants to do a good job, but we have to recognize that repetitive work can become boring, and that some small distraction can result in the incorrect performance of an operation. Anything that can be done to prevent these errors will result in a more efficient process.

MAINTENANCE AND CALIBRATION

The moment that machines, or any forms of automation even of the simplest kind, are introduced into production, maintenance and calibration of the equipment become part of the total process, and the maintenance program has to be fully developed and recorded in the same way as that for the basic manufacturing process. It is strange how frequently maintenance is given a low priority even in companies that otherwise have their process well in control. The arguments are almost always the same, and all are equally ridiculous when considered carefully. "We are too busy to do maintenance," or "We never had a machine problem so we cut back on maintenance," or "We got behind on the schedule so we could not stop for maintenance," or "The calibration of the temperature controller never changed so we stopped checking it." At one company the philosophy was expressed as "We do not believe in preventive maintenance—we only fix machines when they break down."

All of these comments indicate a complete lack of understanding of the purpose behind a maintenance program. It is not to prevent the machines from breaking down or to fix them when they do not work. It is to keep them working consistently, producing exactly the same results all the time. In one case, a small but persistent scatter of defective parts was holding up the installation of a zero defect program. It proved to be very difficult to trace down the cause of the problem, but it was eventually found to be a machine that—from all outward appearances—was operating correctly. An intermittent variation in its performance however was enough to cause the defects. Because the machine was apparently functioning correctly, the maintenance periods had been lengthened until regular maintenance was in fact stopped altogether and work was only done on the machine when the maintenance department had some spare time.

A fully developed maintenance program must cover not only the obvious machines but also hand tools. For example, in the electronics industry it is important that soldering irons be checked for tip temperature and electrical leakage on a regular basis. One company was suffering soldering problems that had been blamed on the operators, and a program of retraining was to be initiated. However, when the soldering irons on the shop floor were checked it was found that over 70% had tip temperatures that were well outside the acceptable limits. Once they were replaced only minor retraining was found to be necessary. In a similar way we constantly see screwdrivers with worn and rounded tips, wrenches that no longer fit the bolts tightly, cutters that are blunt, pliers that do not grip—minor and simple items that can easily be forgotten if there is not a formal maintenance program.

The maintenance program must define exactly what has to be done to each machine—the tools required, the methods to be used, and the checks to be carried out after the work has been completed—to assure that the machine is correctly set up and ready to go into production. If all of these are not defined carefully, production problems can arise that may be difficult to solve. For example, the regular maintenance on a certain machine was carried out over a weekend and the machine was put back on line on Monday morning. The results were unacceptable. It seemed obvious that the problem lay with the machine but everything appeared to be correct. A careful check was made with the mechanic who carried out the work and it was found that a heater in the system had been removed for cleaning and was replaced an inch and a half farther from the processing station. But the heater was held on four long threaded rods with no indication of the correct distance. There were no maintenance instructions and no machine check was required after the work was complete. The cost of the investigation was several thousand dollars.

The intervals between maintenance will depend on the machine, the hours run, and many other variables. Each machine must be looked at individually and the schedule of work set up to assure that there will be no changes whatever in the performance of that machine. Remember that the overall objective is to guarantee repeatability of the process at all times.

MATERIALS CONTROL

As it is impossible to produce a product with a stable quality and cost if the materials used in its manufacture are not consistent, a major part of process control is to guarantee that the materials are correct for the task.

This guarantee requires four basic steps (Figure 7).

- To assure that the specifications for the materials are adequate.
- To check that the materials coming into the plant comply with the specifications.
- To recognize any storage conditions that may change the characteristics of the materials and take the necessary actions to prevent these changes.
- To prevent damage to the materials on the shop floor prior to their use.

MATERIALS CONTROL
DEMANDS

Good specifications used intelligently
Excellent vendor process control
Intelligent receiving inspection criteria,
    with authority for rejection
Excellent storage and handling in both
    stores and manufacturing areas

Figure 7   The control of the quality of incoming materials is a key factor in eliminating product defects. It demands cooperation among many departments of the organization.

The fact that the materials engineer or designer has written a specification does not mean that it will necessarily be adequate for the manufacturing process. Every specification therefore should be reviewed by manufacturing through a formal review procedure and be approved before it is released. All too often the designer does not have a good enough knowledge of the manufacturing processes and some important factors may be missed. There may be tolerances that will not allow a machine to operate consistently, or a finish that is not compatible with a particular process step. Electronic components may need to be sealed so that they can be passed through the cleaning system. Parts may be incapable of withstanding the heat developed in some steps of the process. The higher the degree of automation the larger the number of problems will be found. Although these particular items are not difficult to spot and can be corrected easily, in some cases it is extremely difficult to write a meaningful specification that covers all of the requirements, and the specification of itself is comparatively useless as a control tool without some means of testing the materials to assure compliance.

Some material specifications are impossible to check without complex and expensive equipments; for example, if the manufacturing process calls for a particular grade of stainless steel, it is practically impossible for the smaller company to determine the exact grade of metal received. Similarly, checking the exact composition of items such as paints, fluxes, and solvents requires a laboratory and a good knowledge of chemistry. Often these facilities are not available or it may be too costly to carry out the testing. In these cases the purchaser is totally at the mercy of the suppliers, and the decisions as to which vendor to use and what backup they will provide when problems arise become of concern.

After the correct materials and parts are brought in house, storage has to be considered. First of all, it has to be decided if the parts will deteriorate during storage and whether any special care has to be taken with respect to the types of packaging materials. For example, metal parts may rust or corrode and need to be protected in some way. Mechanical damage has to be a concern, especially with parts with a high finish, and appropriate measures must be taken to protect them. If parts are likely to deteriorate during storage, the purchasing and production schedules become extremely important.

Not only is damage possible during storage, it is equally possible for parts to become damaged during the actual shop floor operations. Handling, for example, can cause rusting and damage the finish of highly polished steel; it can reduce the solderability of electronic components and diminish the bond strength in many cases where adhesives are used. If adequate storage is not provided on the shop floor, parts can become damaged merely by being piled on top of each other.

CORRECTIVE AND PREVENTIVE ACTION

The fact that the process is completely defined will not guarantee that it is absolutely correct in every detail. As it is operated improvements will be found, variations that have not been considered will show deficiencies in the program, and of course problems will arise from many causes. Unless there is a formal way of correcting these problems when they arise and preventing their reoccurrence, they will stay with us for the duration of production of the product.

We should also constantly be looking to improve the process. Ideas for improvement can come from many places, but especially from the shop floor. Unless there is a a formal method of communication, these improvements can be lost, and unless the ideas are properly acknowledged the suggestions will dry up from sheer frustration. On one occasion an operator provided the solution to a rather troublesome production problem and explained that he had known of this for a long time. However as he had once proffered a similar suggestion and nothing had been done about it, it seemed pointless to him to make any other comment.

A sound corrective action program must be backed up by adequate manpower and authority to get the job done. When a problem arises there are almost always two tasks to be tackled.

- That which will keep production moving, the "Band-Aid" solution.
- That which will prevent the problem from ever occurring again.

All too often the first task is given priority because of the demands of the great god "schedule." Once the urgency of shipping the product is over, the second and most important task is usually forgotten or pushed into a low priority position. But by then another problem has cropped up, another "Band-Aid" solution has to be found, and the basic causes of the problems are never identified and eliminated. It is only when adequate manpower is made available in a formal program that defects are ever eliminated permanently.

THE ORGANIZATION

Finally, an Organization has to be set up which will provide the necessary authority and responsibility to each individual in the operation to allow the process to proceed smoothly. This is unfortunately not often carefully considered. The Organization is frequently set up for some other reason: to fit a corporate plan, to suit the accounting budget, to provide a place for the president's cousin, or some equally unfortunate reason. We often hear that so and so cannot be done because "I do not have any control over that area." Or

CORPORATE MANAGEMENT		QUALITY CONTROL	
ADVERTISING	STORES		MAINTENANCE
PURCHASING	ACCOUNTING		MARKETING
MANUFACTURING			

Figure 8 The manufacturing operation supports the entire company and the Organization must reflect this and provide the authority to get the job done efficiently.

"We have always been set up in this way." It is as if the manufacturing operation is there to suit the Organization rather than the other way round.

In any manufacturing facility it is the production department that is the whole reason for the Organization to exist, and every other department is there only to support and assist production. This is a complex subject because here we are dealing with relationships among people. It is discussed in detail later in this book, in Chapter 9.

The Organization must be developed to provide the management support and technology necessary to operate the process. It must allocate the authority necessary for each individual to be able to play his part in the overall manufacturing operation (Figure 8).

THE OVERVIEW

Managing the manufacturing process is not a simple task that can be carried out according to a prescribed method. It involves technology and science, which of course do follow strict rules and disciplines. But these are largely implemented through people and here the rules no longer apply. People are all different from one another and their particular strengths and weaknesses have to be taken into account. The manager also has to understand that everything he says or does will affect his people, their attitudes, and their reactions. He has to understand his own reactions to the everyday world of the shop floor and make conscious steps to develop an outward appearance in words and actions that will best communicate to his people his own attitudes and desires for excellence and a successful operation.

In this chapter we have taken the bare basics of managing the process and attempted to add some of the details. It would be nice if we could continue to add these in an organized manner, but as already suggested, the process is not simple. As every one of its parts is connected and related to every other part, the process does not break down into clear sections. As this book progresses we will return to the same aspects of the process, each time looking at them more closely and from different perspectives until we have exhausted all the details and—we hope—provided the practical information necessary to control the process.

Chapter 4

CONTROLLING THE PROCESS

In any process two basic methods are used to maintain control. The first is preventive; that is, to monitor the materials, tools, and methods to prevent any deviation from the developed process. The second is corrective; that is, to monitor the product for any deviation from the quality standard, determine its cause, and make any changes that are necessary to the process to bring the product quality back to the required level (Figure 9). Although they are largely separate and self-contained there will always be some overlap and one can affect the other. We will consider each in the simple example that has already been used, that of baking a cake. From this we will move on to more complex

CONTROLLING THE PROCESS

PREVENTIVE CONTROL	MONITOR THE OPERATION FOR ANY DEVIATION FROM THE STANDARD PROCESS	CORRECT ANY DEVIATIONS FROM THE RECORDED PROCESS

CORRECTIVE CONTROL	INSPECT THE PRODUCT FOR ANY DEVIATION FROM THE PERFORMANCE SPECIFICATION	DETERMINE THE CAUSE OF THE DEVIATION. DEVELOP AND IMPLEMENT A FORMAL CORRECTIVE ACTION PLAN

Figure 9 The two phases of process control. They will inevitably interact in many areas.

processes and review the changes in the complexity of the controls that become necessary to maintain product quality.

PRIMARY PREVENTIVE PROCESS CONTROL

The overall objective of any process control procedure is to make sure that the process is carried out in exactly the same way at all times. As we have seen, the first thing that has to be done is to define the process and record every detail so that it can be repeated exactly. The objective of the primary control system therefore is to manage and monitor the manufacturing process so that every step will always be repeated according to the recorded details.

This objective implies that materials, methods, tools, and machines must all fall into this area of control. We have already briefly discussed the steps to guarantee consistent materials and the need to control maintenance of tools and machines. They will be covered in detail in later chapters, together with more information on the procedures that can be used for controlling the manufacturing methods.

In the example of baking the cake, according to the overall objective we have to follow the recipe exactly at all times, we have to be sure that the ingredients are as called for in the recipe, neither less nor more in amount and of the defined quality. The mixing has to be done exactly according to the recorded process and the baking carried out precisely for the recorded time and temperature. (Figure 10). Yet even in this simple case we all know that variations can occur. The flour may have been stored too long or in a damp environment, the mixing may have been inadequate, the thermostat on the oven could be incorrect, and so on.

If these variations are not detected before the ingredients are mixed and baked, the results will probably not be noticed until the cake is taken from the oven. Of course, by then it may be too late to do anything except throw it away. Even worse is the case in which the cake looks good and appears to be just like any other cake until it is eaten and then the changes are found to have affected the taste in some way. The consumer, our customer, will have a very poor opinion of our cooking skills and will be unlikely to come back and buy another cake.

The answer to these problems of course is to avoid any such variations through excellent preventive control. Changes in the product will then not occur and we will have a perfect process. If our recipe is sound we will always produce cakes of the highest quality. In turn the cost will stay the same and we will be able to schedule our production accurately. The prevention of variations

PRIMARY
CONTROL AND
MAKING THE CAKE

★ ★

PRIMARY OR PREVENTIVE CONTROL
DEMANDS THAT WE
FOLLOW THE RECIPE
AND MONITOR THAT IT IS FOLLOWED
EXACTLY

★ ★

THE RIGHT MATERIALS
MIXED CORRECTLY
IN THE RIGHT QUANTITIES
BAKED AT THE RIGHT TEMPERATURE
FOR THE RIGHT TIME

WILL ALWAYS PRODUCE A
PERFECT CAKE

Figure 10 Primary or preventive control is the first and most important stage in producing a quality product.

in the process must always be our first line of defense against problems of quality, cost, and schedule.

PRIMARY CORRECTIVE PROCESS CONTROL

In an ideal world we could set up an effective preventive control system and all the cakes would be exactly the same. But we live in an imperfect world; inevitably there will be some variations, both large and small. Let us consider a major variation first. Suppose we find that the color and texture of the cakes vary from batch to batch, and eventually we trace these deviatons to changes in the amount of water in the cake mixture, caused by small variations in the milk quality. The result is that some batches of cakes are not as golden brown as others.

However, we find that we can compensate for this variation in milk quality by modifying the bake cycle, and if we carry this out correctly all the cakes will once more be the same color, with no affect on taste or texture.

We can then train an operator to inspect the cakes in the oven, estimate the increased baking time that is required, and modify this so that they all have the same appearance. These steps will get around the problem of variations in the milk quality, but it will increase the cost by the salary of the operator. In addition, we will have to rely on the operator's judgment, and it is inevitable that from time to time he will make a mistake and some batches will not meet the quality requirements and have to be scrapped. The baking time will also vary from batch to batch and it will be difficult to schedule exactly when the cakes will be completed (Figure 11}.

Corrective control therefore may not initially eliminate any changes in the process, although it may make it possible to continue manufacturing the product by taking some compensating actions. However, this form of correction can only be accepted as a temporary measure while the basic cause of the problem is eliminated. The real solution in this case is to find out the cause of the changes in the quality of the milk and eliminate this variation.

But what if the dairy tells us that we were very fortunate to have used milk with such a stable amount of water during our development of the process and

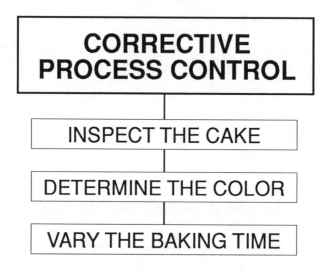

Figure 11   A simple example of a temporary correction to the process. Remember this is not a cure: the basic cause of the problem must be determined and corrected.

that it is impossible to guarantee this quality of milk consistently throughout the year? Several options are open to us and this is where the manufacturing manager has to understand clearly the full impact of his decisions.

1. We can attempt to find a supplier who can maintain a steady water content in the milk.
   - Is such a vendor available?
   - What will be the cost impact?
   - Will it be necessary to monitor the milk?
   - Will it be possible to find a second supplier to guarantee continuity of supply?
2. We can add a process step to dilute the milk with water so that it will always be consistent
   - Will this mean that the milk will have more water than the sample used to developed the process?
   - Will this affect the quality of the cake?
   - Will this require testing of the water quality?
   - Will this permanently increase the baking cycle?
   - What effect will this have on throughput?
3. We can develop an automatic scanning system to monitor the color of the cakes during baking and make the necessary changes to the baking cycle.
   - Is such a system possible?
   - What will it cost?
   - Will this system compensate for the expected range of water content?
   - Will the cake quality be acceptable over the entire range of control?
4. We can continue to use the skill of the operator to make any baking cycle changes.
   - Is the scrap cost acceptable?
   - Will the quality be satisfactory in all cases?
   - Will it be necessary to carry out some form of final inspection of the cakes?
   - Can a back up operator be trained to take over when the original operator is not available?
   - Will the results be consistent?

After a decision as to which of these alternatives will provide a permanent solution to the problem, it must be properly developed and then introduced as a change to the original process. From then on it will be controlled as part of the new, changed process and will be subject to the full primary preventive control procedures.

This example shows how a simple change in any one aspect of the process can escalate into a major problem and also demonstrates how vitally important it is to consider every possible variation when developing the process. Now let us consider a less serious problem; suppose that black specks are found on the top of some of the cakes. They are determined to be harmless particles of carbon and can be brushed off. This is the immediate solution to enable production to proceed, but investigation shows them to be pieces of burnt cake mixture falling from the top shelf of the oven. We change the maintenance routine and the problem is solved. We could merely tell the operator to blow off any black specs that are seen but this would not eliminate the problem, which would only get worse and worse until it could possibly develop into a major disaster.

Thus, corrective action must always aim to eliminate the problem as well as provide an immediate "Band-Aid" to keep production going.

We can also see that corrective action may have many solutions. In the simplest form it concerns a review of the development process to see where we have strayed. In an extreme case it may mean redeveloping some parts of the process and making the appropriate changes.

In the above examples we have considered only comparatively simple processes and it is unlikely that the manufacture of many products fall into this class. Let's consider something more complex, for example, producing television receivers.

A MORE COMPLEX PROCESS

With a complex product such as television receivers, there will be several separate process steps, and there will be processes that will be parts of other processes. In fact, the whole manufacturing operation will become much more complicated, and the control of these multiple processes much more demanding. The materials will now be many more in number and in volume. Several hundred electronic components may be purchased from a large number of vendors. Printed wiring boards must be bought from the fabricator; cabinets, metal work, parts, wires, and cathode ray tubes will have to be acquired. The task of assuring the quality of all of these materials is a major part of the procurement and quality functions. As some materials can deteriorate with storage, the time and methods of storing them have to be controlled. During the assembly operations there will be many more opportunities for error with the many different parts, each of which has to be placed in exactly the correct

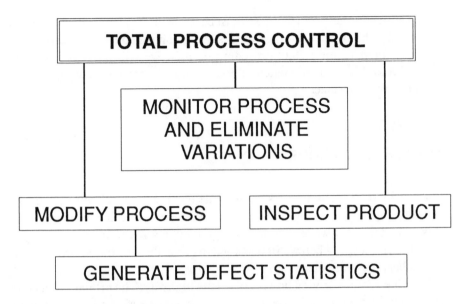

Figure 12   Total process control demands a constant drive for improvement in every area, with excellence the objective.

position. Every function can be looked upon as an individual process and every one must be controlled. Purchasing, receiving inspection, stores, assembly, and so on will each require a fully documented process and each will have to be monitored for compliance (Figure 12). However, it is vitally important that all these functions mesh together to make the single grand process of which they are each a part.

In a complex situation such as this, a failure of the process in one area may not be obvious until much later in the overall process, when it may be costly to rectify or result in the loss of production. For example, if printed wiring boards are stored for too long a time they will not solder properly, but this problem may not be discovered until the boards have been loaded with components and run over the wave solder machine. It may be possible to recover the product at this stage by the expenditure of a great deal of labor in rework, but inevitably the television receivers made from this batch of boards will have less than excellent reliability. The manufacturing manager will have to decide if this quality is acceptable or if the assembled parts must be scrapped.

Thus, a storage deficiency eventually shows up as a failure of the soldering process and the result is either scrapped materials or a considerable expenditure of labor in rework and the subsequent inspection. In either case, there will inevitably be a considerable impact on the schedule.

The corrective action in this case must be to check the stores process control document to be sure that storage time is being controlled by such methods as a sound "First In First Out" procedure. If it is, we will have to find what happened to this particular batch of boards and take the necessary actions to prevent a reoccurrence.

THE FEEDBACK LOOP

For any control system to work at all, some form of feedback must tell us the effect of any actions that we take. A good example is steering an automobile. It is something that we tend to take for granted, but if we can remember just how difficult it was when we first learned to drive, the way the control process works becomes very clear.

Imagine you are driving down a two-lane highway. The primary objective is to keep the car approximately midway between the road edge and the line down the center of the road. The car begins to veer to one side, and you make a slight movement of the wheel and correct the change in direction. A simple move, carried out automatically without any conscious thought; but a lot of things happened to make it possible. First your eyes noticed that the front of the car was no longer centered between the middle and edge of the road. They sent a signal to your brain which in turn told your hands and arms to move the steering wheel a certain amount in the correct direction. These items were in your memory from past experience and required no thought on your part. When you were learning to drive, you had to make a conscious effort to determine these factors. As the car once more approaches the correct path, your eyes signal this to your brain, you once more center the wheel, and the car proceeds safely on its way. The feedback path is from your eyes to your brain and from your brain to your hands and arms. Remove any part of that path and you cannot steer the car. Damage or weaken any part and it will not function correctly. Drunk driving is a perfect example of damaging the feedback path.

Every control system has to have this feedback. In the case of baking the cakes with a varying amount of water in the mixture, the feedback comes from the operator, who looks at the color of the cake and then adjusts the bake cycle (Figure 13). In manufacturing, the overall process control feedback is usually derived from inspecting the product for one or more features. This may be a 100% visual inspection, which as we will discover later in the book (Chapter 8) is not a very effective or efficient method. It may be an electrical or mechanical test of some or all of the product. It may be a functional test in which the product is operated under certain conditions.

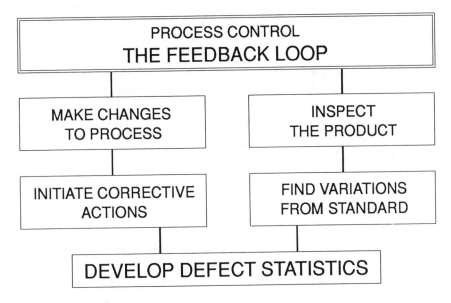

Figure 13   The detailed procedure of the feedback loop in process control.

We are now considering inspection as a tool to generate data for control purposes, to indicate if we are operating within the recorded process, and to determine if any corrective action is required. We are not considering inspection for sorting out good product from bad. If inspection is necessary for this purpose, our process is so far out of control that we should shut down our operation and immediately begin a major corrective action program.

Inspection data can, however, indicate changes in the process, and as such they are an essential part of our control procedure. The data so produced can be used in two ways.

1. They may indicate an out-of-control situation that requires immediate corrective action and possibly stopping of production until this is completed. A typical example is the soldering of the television receivers with the boards that have poor solderability. Once the first examples with defective solder joints are found, the soldering must be halted, and it may well be necessary to pull the affected lot of parts off the shop floor and carry out a detailed inspection to be sure that none is missed and shipped.

2. They may show that the process is drifting from the ideal but is still within the process limits. For example, a process control inspector looking at the solder joints on the television receivers may see that the joints are frosty. There is nothing unreliable about this condition but it can indicate that the tin content

of the solder is low and should be brought to the correct level until the joints lose their frosty appearance.

If inspection is used in this way it will not matter if there are small random errors in the information. The data will be used to show up any trends in the quality of the product, which in turn will be used to make the corrections necessary to bring the process back into line. Just like the information absorbed by our eyes when we are driving the car, inspection data will enable us to hold the process in the center of the permissible control limits.

SUMMARY

The main effort in controlling manufacturing must be to monitor every important point so that we can be assured that it complies exactly with the developed process. This has to be the basis on which our process control is built, but inevitably some variations will occur. We must set up a procedure to check for these variations, usually by inspecting the product, and then use the data collected during this checking to develop the necessary corrections to the process. Although it is essentially a simple procedure, as we will see the ramifications can make it a complex matter in some practical cases.

Chapter 5

MANAGING PROCESS DEVELOPMENT AND PREPRODUCTION

In previous chapters we have looked at the basic mechanics of developing and setting up the process, we have considered the various methods of controlling the operation, and begun to understand the philosophy of close loop control. However, we have barely mentioned the task of managing the process.

In this chapter the emphasis is on the detailed management of the development of the manufacturing process. In later chapters we will expand on many of the ideas expressed here and examine them in practical terms.

MANAGING THE PROCESS DEVELOPMENT

It is not likely that the manufacturing manager will personally develop the processes that will be used to manufacture the product. This development will usually be the task of the manufacturing engineering department, possibly with some help from the design team or other specialists. However, the manufacturing manager must be involved in this part of the program, for on it will be built the manufacturing of the future, and failure to develop the process correctly can involve unnecessary cost, quality, and schedule problems. The manufacturing manager therefore must immerse himself in the process until he is thoroughly conversant with all of the details.

USING THE SPECIALIST

It will usually be necessary to use the skills of specialists in the development of the more complex areas of a technology, but they can be biased by their own specialized expertise and sometimes fail to consider the entire process. In these circumstances the manufacturing manager must probe and question until he is certain that all possible factors have been taken into account.

As an example, a process was developed to solder connectors into an insulating base. The parts were made of brass with an electroless tin-plated finish, and initially the manufacturing went along smoothly. However, soon the operation was plagued with field failures from soldered joints that broke when cables were screwed into the connectors. The problem was eventually traced to their plated finish. The specified tin plating was too thin and the parts would not solder correctly if they were stored for more than a short time. In addition, the zinc from the brass contaminated the solder bath, which reduced the wetting action of the solder. This then had to be changed every two or three weeks at a cost of several hundred dollars. It took some time to get to the bottom of the problems, as the process had worked fine with the small quantity of fresh preproduction parts. During this time production and quality were severely affected and costs rose dramatically. The simple solution was a change to steel connectors with a hot tinned finish.

If the manufacturing manager had persisted in his original demand to carry out more testing before the process development was completed, these difficulties could have been avoided. If the manufacturing engineer had possessed a better knowledge of metallurgy or had consulted an expert in the soldering process, he would have avoided the obvious errors in the selection of materials.

LOOKING FOR VARIATIONS

It is not unusual for a process which appears to work well when checked out on small quantities to fail under the conditions of full production. Tolerances shift when parts are produced in quantity by a vendor, rather than a few at a time in the model shop. Components may become bent or suffer other damage when handled in larger numbers. To avoid this type of problem the manufacturing manager has to use his interpersonal skills to question, to weigh the various opinions, and to assure himself that every possible facet of production has been fully considered.

- Have all possible variations in the materials been considered and tested?
- Do the materials specifications adequately control these variations?

- Are there any special requirements regarding storage and handling of materials?
- Is there an adequate receiving inspection organization to assure the compliance of the materials?
- Have the machines and tools been checked using materials at both extremes of the specification?
- Are the operators properly trained to work to the process?
- Have adequate controls been established to maintain the process?
- Are all personnel trained in the corrective actions to take when a problem arises?

USING THE SPECIALIST

These are only some of the questions that the manufacturing manager must answer from his own understanding of the process and by working with the specialists. He must use his knowledge of these people to determine if their answers are correct. This is not to suggest that they will deliberately give him bad advice, but the physicist, the engineer, and the chemist are human beings and will have all of the characteristics found in any other group of people. One individual may be optimistic and believe that the process will function correctly even though there is no good evidence to confirm this belief. One may view the process in broad terms and not consider all of the many small details.

There is a tendency to believe the specialist: he is fully qualified, he has a degree, he understands all of the technical jargon, often he can prove mathematically what he is doing. We sometimes forget the man behind the expert, with all the strengths and weakness of a human being. He may be biased toward one scientific discipline or he may not like another person in the production team, and these things can sway his judgment.

The author once complained to a doctor friend that his treatment by a certain medical specialist had not been as good as was expected. He was then reminded that "Fifty percent of all doctors graduate from the bottom half of the class." The same comment can be applied to most of the experts that we meet.

It is not unusual to find that a particular design or method is discredited because "It was not designed here." "Reinventing the wheel" is a common phrase, yet this is often done because there is a desire to avoid using ideas from another company or division. Not infrequently the expert may not be such an expert in a particular detail of the process as his title or background would suggest, and he attempts to start development from scratch without adequately researching the available information. At one aerospace company a well-qualified engineer explained how he had spent several months working with a new machine to develop the optimal parameters for a particular process he was developing. If he had been really conversant with the process he would have known that there was nothing further to be researched for there was plenty of information available on the performance of that particular machine. This information was readily available, and he could have arrived at the correct settings for the machine in a few hours, not after months of experimentation.

THE SPECIALIST AND THE MAN

The tendencies described above are all perfectly understandable once we consider the nature of man and the particular attitudes and ideas of the individual. We have to work with and through these weakness and get to the strengths of individuals. The manager has to measure them and use their capabilities. He has to ask appropriate questions and sort through the answers to arrive at the truth, or to recognize that sufficient information is not available and push for more work to be carried out in the appropriate areas. We must differentiate between proved facts and opinions and be suspicious of the "hunch" or the "gut feel." This is not to suggest that opinions, especially opinions based on long experience, are not valuable; but they are usually only as good as the knowledge and experience of the individual concerned, and it may be difficult for any manager to develop an honest, unbiased knowledge of the skills of any individual. The manager in fact must recognize that he himself often makes decisions based on his own opinions. Facts are much more reliable than opinions.

The manufacturing manager must also support the efforts of these people by adequately funding both money and labor, and by providing time, the necessary facilities, and the freedom from other responsibilities so that the work can be brought to a satisfactory conclusion.

The pressure to get a new product into production quickly is understandable. Competitors are always working to be the winner in the race, and the first of any particular product on the market has an advantage that is difficult to overcome. However, if the new product is lacking in quality or is not competitive in price, it may only whet the appetite of the customer—who will eventually buy the competitor's product. The latecomer who does the job properly can sometimes end up the ultimate leader in the marketplace.

MANAGING PROTOTYPE PRODUCTION

The manufacture of prototypes is usually considered to be a step for the benefit of the design engineers, giving them the opportunity to try out their ideas and test the final product. It should also be used to initiate manufacturing people into the coming task of developing the manufacturing process. This is an excellent place to bring together design and manufacturing, and one way of doing this is to place any engineering model shop or prototype assembly area under the direct control of manufacturing engineering.

However, the manager of this area must be sympathetic to the engineering function, to the need of the designer and engineer for fast turnaround, for changes made quickly and informally. He must provide an excellent service to the designer. At the same time, having the opportunity to learn about the product, to liaise between design and manufacturing, and even to be able to influence the designer cannot be overestimated. Building the prototypes provides an opportunity to test various manufacturing methods at an early stage and begin to lay down the process that will eventually be used.

At this stage the manufacturing manager needs to go outside his normal sphere of influence. He may well have to go to a higher authority to have the organization changed to make this setup possible. Then, when it is successfully set up, he will need to use all his managerial skills to maintain the essential cooperation between design and manufacturing. For many years these two parts of the organization have tended to work in isolation, with design to some extent considering manufacturing a less skillful operation that constantly frustrates its attempt to innovate by saying "It will cost more" or "We can't do" this or that. Manufacturing, on the other hand, frequently sees design as an impractical organization with no knowledge about the difficulties of making the product. Although there is a certain amount of truth in both of these opinions, it is time to eliminate such antagonism. Cooperation will only come about with constant and free communication between both parts of the organization.

Once the protypes have been handed over to the designers for testing, it is time to consider the preproduction build. It is surprising how often the entire business of prototyping and preproduction manufacturing is either glossed over as quickly as possible or is not correctly organized and scheduled.

PREPRODUCTION

When the preproduction phase of product introduction is correctly organized, it will do much more than test the basic manufacturing process and equipments. It provides a prime opportunity to monitor the effects of the following items.

- Variations in materials.
- Machine and equipment changes with time, the number of operations performed, wear, and setup variations.

- Maintenance requirements for tools and equipment.
- Operator training and retraining needs.
- The necessary process controls, and the method of producing control data.
- Manufacturing organization development.

These factors cannot be ignored and this phase of product introduction must be planned in detail. The time span should not be underestimated, as problems invariably will arise and must be corrected before full production is started. It is too easy to view preproduction manufacturing as an expensive delay in getting the plant into full production—merely a time for engineering to "play" with the process.

Nothing could be further from the truth. A well-designed preproduction program will eventually save both time and money and will prevent any possibility that inferior products will be shipped. However, this phase must be well planned and operated strictly according to the plan. It is not a time to "play" with the process but to work in a logical, organized manner to define and refine the process so that it will function smoothly and consistently once full production is started.

Preproduction offers the best opportunity to develop the process properly in an organized, scheduled manner. As sections are completed, the documented steps can be tried out, the necessary controls set up, and any tools and equipment proved in actual practice. A clear objective must be set that by such and such a date all of the preproduction work will be completed and the plant will be ready to roll. It is only then that planned, scheduled production can begin.

SUMMARY

Managing the development of the process demands that the manager become fully acquainted with the technology of producing the product, but it also brings into play the much more complex matter of the interaction between the manager and those who report to him. The manager has to consider all of the opinions and facts brought to him, and from these he must determine the activities that he must control, their relative importance, and their possible effects on production. He must sort out and determine the accuracy of the various bits of information.

From all of this he must then develop the aims and objectives that he will eventually agree upon with his people and that will form the basis of managing the operation. He must also recognize that he has total authority and responsibility.

Chapter 6

PEOPLE AND THE PROCESS

No matter how advanced the level of automation in any manufacturing plant, people are still the single most important factor in the process. We have all heard the stories of the visitor to a Japanese factory who found the entire place in total darkness because it was completely automated and the lights were put on only for the maintenance personnel to carry out their work. In the same breath we are often told of the dozens of operators in the back room who are busy fixing those items that were incorrectly made by the machines.

The truth probably lies somewhere in between the extremes described in the story, but it shows how much people intervene in even the most highly automated facility. People are involved in designing products, ordering parts, controlling costs, scheduling production, maintaining equipment and of course managing and supervising the overall process. If or when all of these functions can be part of a completely automated installation, then we may be able to totally eliminate the human factor. When this stage is reached, however, we will also be able to eliminate the manager. We will have arrived at the time when the technologist and the mechanic will reign supreme and interpersonel skills will not be necessary.

This, however, is daydreaming. We will always have to deal with people, to work with and through people, and to recognize that the process will stay in control only as long as we have the necessary abilities to understand, communicate, and motivate the people who actually make the process work.

PEOPLE—THE COMPLICATING FACTORS

When the author was managing a particularly complex manufacturing process, the quality control department carried out a routine monitoring of the shop floor to assure compliance with the documented process instructions. The result was a twice daily report on any deficiencies that were found, which was then used to initiate corrective action.

The actual variations from the process were all quite obvious: incorrect tools being used, instructions not being followed, equipment out of tolerance, and so on. When the causes of these deficiencies were discovered, they turned out to be most illuminating and showed just how difficult it is to communicate clearly, and without ambiguity. It was a rare occasion when the operator was deliberately careless. Most often it was found that the processing instructions were unclear or ambiguous, or were being interpreted incorrectly. Sometimes the operator believed that he was following the documented process exactly but through some misunderstanding was in fact doing something quite wrong. Sometimes he had the wrong tools. On one occasion, the specified tool had been damaged and sent out for repair. It had been lost and after a few weeks was completely forgotten, and the process was carried on with a makeshift tool. In a few cases, it was found that the operator had never been trained on the process being carried out.

Yet the vast majority of the operators were carrying out their duties correctly, so the instructions were not incorrect and the training was not ineffective. This finding indicates one of the difficulties in dealing with people. Everyone thinks in a different manner, and any one communicating with people has to recognize these differences. They have little to do directly with intelligence or education, but are much more related to family, language, upbringing, and background.

RECOGNIZE THE INDIVIDUAL

It is easy to suggest that blanket rules can be applied in certain situations or to certain groups of employees. For example, in one very efficient plant in a foreign country, the manager behaved "like a father." His office door was open to everyone and he took care of every problem brought to him by his employees, even those relating to home and family. He was quite convinced that here lay the secret of his success, and that the ethnic background of his employees made this management style necessary. Yet, in fact, he did not treat every employee in the same way; to each he offered the level of concern, discipline, or encouragement that was necessary to produce the personal environment for a productive and happy working life. Without any formal training, he intuitively recognized the differences in people, he understood that each person is an individual and must be treated as such, and he modulated his management style accordingly. It is questionable whether the ethnic background of the employees made this form of management more efficient than it would have been with any other group of people. His efficiency as a manager was chiefly the result of his tremendous understanding of people.

Of course, race, upbringing, and background will certainly affect the individual, but it is not possible to lump people together and categorize them by any of these terms. People are all different and we have to accept this fact when we work with people. The chief challenge for any manager is to understand people both as individuals and as part of groups; to recognize that every action he takes and every word that he speaks can affect their attitudes, their feelings, and their goals.

MOTIVATION AND PEOPLE

Most people want to do a good job. Work occupies a large part of our life, and if our work is not satisfying, then our life seems pointless and we carry out our daily tasks with little interest, in a machine-like manner. Under these conditions we usually do as little as possible to get by and pick up our paycheck. With this attitude it is inevitable that our attention wanders, for thoughts of home, friends, and leisure activities are much happier than is our concentration on the work in hand. We then make mistakes, but any blame seems unfair because we are genuinely trying our best, our work becomes even less attractive and a deadly spiral begins.

The symptoms of this unhappy situation are everywhere in our factories. The operators wearing headphones who find that listening to the "top twenty" helps the time to pass more quickly and is in any case more interesting than their work . . . The office desks with semisarcastic cartoons. "You want it when?" "You don't have to be mad to work here but it helps." While having a cartoon on a desk does not mean much, when these and other symbols of lack of interest in the workplace abound, it suggests that there is probably something seriously wrong with the management of that area. The key word is management. It is rarely the people who are to blame; it is the environment, and the overall company policies and attitudes.

The primary cause of this problem is a feeling by the employees that they have little or no control over the work that they are doing and therefore of their future (Figure 14). It is amazing just how hard people will work and how creative they will be if they are given the chance to influence their own future. All kinds of popular programs use this philosophy, from the recent flood of Quality Circles, to the older Managerial Grid. No matter what the name given

```
┌─────────────────────────────────────────────────┐
│ ┌─────────────────────────────────────────────┐ │
│ │        EMPLOYEE INVOLVEMENT                  │ │
│ └─────────────────────────────────────────────┘ │
│     ┌───────────────────────────────────┐       │
│     │        GOOD MANAGEMENT            │       │
│     │          PROVIDES                 │       │
│     │ EMPLOYEE PARTICIPATION IN DEVELOPING │    │
│     │   AND RUNNING THE PROCESS         │       │
│     │           AND                     │       │
│     │         PRODUCES                  │       │
│ ┌───┴───────────────────────────────────┴─────┐ │
│ │   A CREATIVE AND EFFICIENT WORK             │ │
│ │              FORCE                          │ │
│ │ ★★★★★★★★★★★★★★★★★★★★★★★★★★★★★★★★★★★★★★★★★★★★  │ │
│ └─────────────────────────────────────────────┘ │
└─────────────────────────────────────────────────┘
```

Figure 14 If they are to work effectively, people must be able to affect their own future.

to the program, it is ultimately nothing more or less than good management, which has never changed and which recognizes the needs, hopes, and aspirations of the employees.

INVOLVEMENT

The people carrying out the process must be involved in the development of that process. They must understand why it is necessary to make sure that the process is followed exactly, and to see that this is their responsibility. The interest in their work must come from exercising all of their talents to be sure that no process variation occurs.

In addition, through a formal corrective action program they must have a clear and direct communication path with all of those who make decisions, whether those decisions are related to the technology of the process or the management of the operation. The communication must be fast, and the responses must be quick and guaranteed.

The employee must know that any suggestions or comments on working conditions or work improvements not only will be heard but also if of value will be implemented. This is a far cry from the ideas in the usual "Suggestion Box" that are looked at only once a week or month and then usually judged solely by the financial savings that can be achieved. Every idea must be examined immediately and replied to with the same urgency, including a full explanation for the reply. The impetus for this formal corrective action program must stem from top management, and a senior individual must take overall responsibility to see that it is implemented correctly. There is a tremendous well of knowledge on our shop floors which is often never tapped or is allowed to dry up. In one plant a recurring problem was eventually eliminated through discussion with one of the employees. He had known the cause and the solution of the problem for several years. When asked why he had not told someone earlier, he pointed out that he had filled in a suggestion form two years ago but had never received a reply, so he had not seen the point of trying again when obviously no one was interested.

PROCESS, DISCIPLINE, AND PEOPLE

At first glance it appears that we are asking for two totally opposed require-ments. The process demands excellent control, which in turn means a highly disciplined approach to work. Yet we want our employees to feel that they are part of the process and that their work, their efforts, and their ideas are important to the success of the operation. We want them to be interested in everything that they do, yet we have to define exactly what is to be done.

Sometimes the process will demand working conditions that may be unpopular, and in some cases management is reluctant to impose these on the shop floor because doing so may cause labor unrest. A case in point is the banning of eating, drinking, and smoking in areas where electronic equipment is being assembled and soldered. It is difficult to demonstrate the effects of these actions on product quality, although it is known that contamination by any of these items will increase the number of defective soldered joints. If the ban is applied without explanation, it is inevitable that people will complain. Why should they change their working habits just to comply with some rules that they see as being unnecessary?

The author frequently has to apply these restrictions, and once people understand the reasoning behind them, they are willingly accepted. Most people want to do a good job; they want to be proud of the products they make and feel part of a winning team. If hard work, rules, or restrictions are necessary to develop that winning team, most people accept them willingly provided they understand why they are necessary.

PEOPLE AND CONTROLLED CHANGES

In practice, these types of problems are minimal provided that we bring the people into the development stages of the process and also make it absolutely clear that they can change the process at any time if the change is justified and agreed upon—in other words, that the method of changing the process is in itself controlled. It is not change that is to be avoided; indeed, change must be welcomed and a part of everything that we plan. It is uncontrolled change that is dangerous.

Almost all human beings are born with curiosity and a desire to change and improve everything that they do. If these creative efforts are not channeled and controlled, they will eventually cause variations in the very process that we must hold constant. In so many cases defective products can be traced back to small changes introduced by a well-meaning operator who is attempting to make improvements. These attempts must not be stifled—they are a valuable source of new ideas. They must be directed in a formal manner through the corrective action program discussed earlier.

We must have a disciplined work force; that is, everyone must know his position in the organization, understand his responsibilities and authorities, and work in a clearly defined manner. This does not mean that people should be expected to work like machines. We must use to the fullest extent their human abilities to make decisions and to be flexible; we must also recognize that the human being has limitations when compared to the machine working in a repetitive fashion and we must tailor the work to avoid these factors.

WORKER AND MANAGER

In most plants these days, the old hierarchy has disappeared. Although there is no longer the manager's dining room or the reserved parking spots, in fact the various levels of authority still exist and always will. However, these exist not as we have seen them in the past when the manager could rule like a dictator and "Do as I say, not as I do" was the rule, but in a team approach in which every member of the team is recognized as being valuable and necessary in achieving excellence.

Because of this new approach the position and authority of the manager are often seen incorrectly. In any team the captain is still the boss. When the chips are down, it is the manager who is looked to for leadership, he is the man who has to take charge of the situation. He may consult with all those around him but ultimately he must demonstrate his willingness and ability to make the necessary decisions and accept the responsibilities for those decisions.

No matter how well a process is developed and controlled, from time to time decisions will have to be made. Should the line be shut down? Can rejected materials be used? Sometimes the decisions are hard to accept. Sales are down, should employees be laid off? Should a poorly performing employee be fired?

These decisions are the total responsibility of the manager and the way he makes these decisions can materially affect his relationship with his people.

That decisions are made decisively, fairly and even-handedly, will go a long way toward maintaining confidence among the employees. Even unpleasant decisions will be accepted when the workers know that every factor has been taken into account and the manager has made his decisions as fairly as can be expected. As a young manager the author took over a department that contained a very poorly performing engineer. Guidance and discussions had no effect on the individual's attitudes and eventually it was obvious that he would have to be fired for the overall benefit of the department. This was an agonizing action for a new manager, but eventually the deed had to be done. Far from causing any concern to the individual, he laughed at the news and commented that he had received a fair deal and in his own opinion he should have been fired weeks before.

It could be argued that we are getting away from the manufacturing process, but this is not so. If the process is to function consistently, the performance of our people is of vital importance, as are their relationships with their manager and each other. We have come a long way from the manager as a dictator, but he is still the leader and has to accept the responsibilities that come from that position. Similarly, the employee is no longer seen as simply a pair of hands but as an integral part of the whole operation. The worker and the manager are equally important if the process is to function successfully; each has a part to play and each must understand his duties, responsibilities, and authorities.

ENCOURAGEMENT, REWARDS, AND THE TEAM

Everyone enjoys the recognition that should come from doing a good job. Most of us are equally disappointed when that recognition is not given. It is easy to suggest that we should obtain satisfaction merely from knowing that we have done the job as well as we possibly can. But we are human, and it is a very human desire to want the recognition of our peers and our bosses when we have put all our efforts into doing the job well.

There are many ways in which an employee's efforts or ideas can be recognized—awards such as employee of the month, dinner with the boss, certificates, and of course hard cash. Yet, when surveys are made of workers feelings about their company, it is surprising that wages and salaries are not the most important items. Of course, we all have to make money in order to live and there is no doubt as to the importance of our income. However, once an average level of wage is reached, the recognition for work well done becomes the most important reason for working. If management does not understand this simple fact and incorporate this knowledge into the organization, one of the greatest tools for controlling the process will be missing; that is, the employees' involvement.

RECOGNITION

The formal means of recognizing an employees' performance seldom seem to work as expected. Initially the "Employee of the Month" award, with a photograph placed in the lobby, of the individual holding his check for $200, seems a good idea. After a while the same few individuals always seem to be in the running for the prize, and some mental adjustments are made by the judges so that the awards are more fairly distributed. Then grumbles begin that accuse the judges of being unfair, until slowly the entire program is seen by the employees as nothing more than a management ploy to keep people happy.

If we are honest, this is exactly what the award eventually becomes. All people do not have the same ability and in any group a few will be the leaders and have most of the bright ideas. If we accept this fact honestly, then these are the people who should receive the awards, and every one else will be ignored. If we attempt to spread the awards evenly, then we have lost the whole intent of the program and it will have become nothing more nor less than an employee pacifier.

THE TEAM

A small number of leaders, however, can do little without the remainder of the group. Indeed, when any group activity is checked, it is often the quiet plodder who holds the team together but receives little recognition. Any group has individuals of many different skills and abilities, and it is the informal manner in which they develop the team approach which makes them effective employees. The development of the team is something that cannot be forced by management. It takes individuals working together, giving and accepting ideas and attitudes until each member finds his own place.

As we all know, this development takes time whether it concerns a football team or a manufacturing line, and efficiency comes with time, experience, and coaching or training. The only fair approach is to reward the team effort rather than to recognize any particular individual. Working together, the team members will know better than anyone else the efforts put into the team by each and every member and will reward, encourage, and even discipline individuals. When implementing such a team approach, the author has frequently found that the team is much more demanding of the individual member than any supervisor or manager.

In one operation, eight people working in a team environment were responsible for assembling a piece of equipment. One worker was inefficient simply through a lack of ability, but was accepted by the rest of the team because he did his best. The team made up for his inefficiency by working harder and giving him the easiest jobs. However, when another team member slacked off and became careless the team asked that he be removed because he was not doing the best job that he could. The outsider would probably not have recognized the difference between the two individuals, but their peers could and made an accurate judgment.

The concept of the team approach of course fits in extremely well with that of process control. The team members will monitor each other for consistent operation, identify any failure to comply with the instructions, and provide informal training when necessary. All of these can occur under the umbrella control of the documented process. The effective manager will take them into consideration when setting up the organization and allocating authority and responsibility. We should consider using the team approach where this is possible, and avoid identifying individuals in that team when recognizing achievements.

Each individual should be encouraged to see himself as part of a team and the teams as part of the larger team that is the company. Competitivness between teams can be encouraged, as it adds further motivation. However, it must not reduce their cooperation with each other or affect the way that they work together

MANAGEMENT BY OBJECTIVES

Whether working as a team or individually, all our people need to know what is expected of them, and to be given some way of measuring how well they match up to the boss's expectations. Setting targets or objectives is a very effective way of doing this. It is not a new technique, for it is fundamentally nothing more than good management, but some years ago was popularized and formalized under the term Management by Objectives (MBO).

Correctly used, MBO forces the manager to sit down with each employee on a regular basis, and discuss what is expected of him and how his performance will be measured. Not only is this a good start, it also provides a wonderful opportunity to exchange ideas, to air grievances, and to get to know people as individuals. However, it requires effort, time (about half an hour per person for every session), and a genuine desire to be open with each other. Some simple rules must be applied.

- The objectives must be agreed upon by both parties, not imposed by the manager.
- The objectives must be measurable.
- The objectives must obviously fit into the total company objectives.

The author once took over the management of a quality control department that was having severe personnel problems. There was much bitterness because some people were paid more than others for what appeared to be the same jobs, there were demands for excessive salary increases, and productivity was poor. The first action was to generate some measurable objectives for the department as a whole, referenced to the products being made, number of tests carried out, processes monitored, quality defects, and so on. Then a private, no holds barred, meeting was arranged for each of the 40 or so individuals in the department. They were each asked what they thought they should be expected to know and to do, and by discussion some simple but directly measurable objectives were agreed upon.

One individual who had caused more than his share of problems was adamant that he should have a large salary increase. He agreed during the discussion that to carry out his work he needed to be able to read drawings, calculate tolerances, and measure the appropriate dimensions on the parts using a micrometer and calipers. When he was handed the measuring instruments and asked to do so, it soon became evident that he did not have the skills that he had agreed were necessary. Training was arranged, a reasonable time was given for him to become skilled, and he was told that there would be no salary increase until he had acquired the ability to carry out his work properly.

It took over two months before every person had agreed upon his objectives, but the change in the department was dramatic. People knew what was expected of them, so they could assess whether they were doing the job as expected. They knew that there would be a personal one-on-one assessment of their performance twice a year, and that to advance in the company they had to meet their agreed objectives. Once again, MBO is not a panacea for all management problems, but it is a useful tool for the manager to get to know and understand his people, to probe, to suggest, and to develop a good rapport. It takes experience and time to develop Management by Objectives into the innovative program that can be obtained from this technique, one or more years in most cases.

PEOPLE INVOLVEMENT

The formal corrective action program is an important way of involving the employee in the operation of the process. However, other forms of involvement can be extremely productive. At one company a formal weekend program was set up. People from all levels of the company were selected and put into small teams of four or five individuals. A team might have a senior manager, two or three shop floor people, and a store keeper. It might contain the president, a maintenance man, an inspector, and some operators. The team makeup was chosen to include as many areas of the company as possible.

Once each month on Friday evening, the teams were taken to a hotel, far enough from the plant to give privacy, and they first sat down together to dinner. Dinner completed, each of the ten or so teams was given a problem that was causing difficulties in the company and asked to provide a solution. They were then given a team room to work in and asked to meet on Sunday for lunch and to present their answers. They were free to set their own schedule of meetings.

Initially the results were disappointing until it was recognized that training was necessary to show people how to work together and to come up with a team approach to the task. After the training was completed and the concept had matured, it proved to be an indispensable tool for problem solving. It also provided a wonderful opportunity for individuals to get to know each other. Discussing, arguing, and even becoming very heated over a particular point of view, the team members quickly began to see each other as individuals, and to understand each others' abilities, weaknesses, hopes and fears. Time had little meaning and teams frequently worked until two and three in the morning. A few worked through the night. The solutions provided by the teams were invariably the best.

Even though there was no financial reward for working on these teams and participation was voluntary, there was never a shortage of volunteers. Three things made the program successful.

- Adequate training in the interpersonal skills.
- A careful mixture of people of all levels and abilities.
- Formal implementation of the solutions.

As a side effect the overall morale of the company rose to unexpected levels, and it became an exciting place at which to work. People at all levels not only recognized the team approach but also lived it day by day.

MANAGING PEOPLE: THE VARIABLE FACTOR

We have considered many of the possible methods of managing people in the chapter. How simple it would be if we could list all of the things to do to be effective in this most complex part of management. Unfortunately this is not possible; as we have seen, every person is an individual and must be treated as such. The problems usually start when people are lumped together and classified so that all of those in a particular class are treated in the same way.

MANAGING WITHIN THE FORMAL ORGANIZATION

In all honesty, however, this may be the only way to organize in a large operation. For example, many big companies have personnel guides that dictate almost every aspect of an employee's working life: what he can and cannot do, what benefits he is entitled to, even the furniture in his office or work place. As the manager is expected to work within this framework he has little individual freedom as to his method of management. Yet even under these conditions some managers seem to be able to produce a working environment that is conducive to an efficient manufacturing operation while others have constant problems. The efficient manager finds ways to recognize the individuals, to be in touch with all that goes on in the process, to take time to know the person not the employee number.

An aerospace company was suffering from poor quality and overexpenditure in its manufacturing operation. Because morale was poor on the shop floor a new manufacturing manager was appointed. He made two simple changes that radically changed the situation. First, he had his office moved from the executive block to an open space on the shop floor. Second, he had each manufacturing engineer moved from the engineering office to a desk alongside the supervisor of the line for which he was responsible, and given co-responsibility with the line supervisor for shipping a quality product on schedule within budget. Most of the new manager's spare time was spent on the floor—questioning, talking with the operators, finding out the problems with the process, and generally making his presence obvious. His actions presented a clear message. The shop floor was all important and it would be given maximum help in performing efficiently. The message was clear to both top management and the operators. The morale of the employees rose dramatically and within a short time productivity also indicated an efficient operation. The new manager's actions were simple but they acted as a catalyst. The feelings of the operators were clearly expressed by one individual, who said how great it was to be able to walk into the boss's office and talk to him face to face.

"The last manager was here for five years," he said ,"and I only ever saw him on the shop floor twice." Yet the new manager was operating well within the comparatively strict organizational rules that applied in that company. Just as it is impossible to manage by remote control, it is equally impossible to operate outside the organizational standards.

SUMMARY

We have looked at several examples in considering the people aspect of management and it would be wonderful to be able to end with a list of rules to follow. But as we have discussed before, the variability of the human being makes rules extremely difficult to apply. Indeed, the only rules that can be of use express these very thoughts.

- Always remember that people are human beings and each is an individual.
- No matter what general statement is made about people, we will always find the exception to the rule.
- The way that we appear to the individual can have a marked effect on his interpretation of our words.
- External influences can change the attitudes of individuals, and methods of management that work today may not work in the same way tomorrow.
- Most people want to do a good job.
- Most people want to feel proud of what they do.
- Most people need recognition.
- Most people respond positively to honest and fair criticism.

Chapter 7

TRAINING

All of the people involved in our process must be properly trained if they are to carry out their task efficiently. They must have a clear understanding of the fundamental theory behind their work and receive thorough training in the necessary manual skills. When the manufacturing process involved very simple technologies, it was common to do this by using the "Sit by Willie" technique. The new operator was put alongside an experienced individual who was already performing the work and told to copy exactly every step of the operation. This technique was rarely effective for the following reasons.

- The trainee only came to understand the actual operation being performed, and had no overall view of the total process and no clear understanding of where and how his particular part fit into the whole.
- This limited view of the total process, plus a lack of training in the theory of the operation, did not provide the knowledge required by the operator to troubleshoot the job when it did not work as expected, or even to recognize when a problem existed.
- The trainee copied all of the bad habits of the operator and inevitably developed some of his own.
- Frequently the operator doing the training did not pass on all of his knowledge because he saw the newcomer as a threat to his job.
- When the training was repeated from operator to operator, the process became diluted by various small changes that were introduced both deliberately and accidentally.

When the process became more complex or when the skills required of the operator increased, the "Sit by Willie" method of training was found to be totally inadequate. When excellent process control became the objective and deviations from the process were measured and recorded it was usually found that the operator was the major cause of variations in the end product.

It was too easy to put the blame on the operator; inefficient, careless, and lazy were terms that were often used, but the real problem was the lack of understanding and of skills, often coupled with incorrect tools and equipment. Training will take care of the first deficiencies but training of any kind must be set up and carried out correctly if it is to be truly effective.

SETTING UP A TRAINING PROGRAM

The first thing to be defined is the training requirement; that is, the subjects to be taught, the skills level required, the specifications or standards that have to be met, and the machines or tools that will have to be operated. From this basis it is possible to develop a syllabus of training, to define the necessary capabilities of instructors, the tools and equipment required, and a schedule of instruction (Figure 15).

This process step is not quite as simple as it may at first appear. When it is examined in detail it is frequently found that much more than the basic manual skills have to be taught; for example, the operator will need to know how to complete paper work, load and unload parts from bins or trays, and a host of other small but essential items. This "skills definition" must be done carefully and with the cooperation and consultation of all concerned. These requirements will be the starting point for developing the training program, plus other practical details that must be taken into account. The line supervisors, the manufacturing engineers, the quality control people, and above all the operators should be part of the team that will develop the training program. Time must be made available to reach this stage, and it must be included as part of the process development. The manufacturing manager has to make sure that the training programs are tested during the preproduction phase of process development; they cannot be left to chance. When all the requirements have been agreed upon, they must be incorporated into a training manual, which becomes the foundation on which all training is built. The skills of the trained personnel must then be monitored to guarantee that the training is consistent and does not vary from one group to another or from one instructor to another.

---TRAINING---

★★★★★★★★★★★★★★★★★★★★★★★★★★★★

DEFINE
SUBJECTS TO BE TAUGHT
SKILLS LEVELS REQUIRED
SPECIFICATIONS TO BE MET
MACHINES & TOOLS INVOLVED

DEVELOP
TRAINING SYLLABUS
INSTRUCTOR CAPABILITIES
FACILITIES TO BE SET UP
SCHEDULE OF INSTRUCTION

Figure 15   The stages involved in setting up a sound training program. These are crucial to good process control.

THE INSTRUCTOR

The instructor is the key to excellent training. All too frequently the wrong person is chosen for this work or is in turn not given adequate training to carry out the task. Not only must the instructor be able to carry out the operation that is being taught and to understand its importance in the total process, but he must also have the necessary instructional skills to be able to effectively impart the information. These teaching skills are actually much more important than the ability to perform the operation.

All too often the best operator is given the job of instructor and this frequently results in the loss of a good operator in return for a mediocre teacher. Part of the development of the training program must be finding good instructors. If necessary, people with the practical skills should be sent for training in the techniques of instructing others. These are not difficult to learn but are not likely to be developed correctly without some formal training. It is usually much easier to take someone who has teaching ability and provide the practical and theoretical knowledge of the operation to be taught. Indeed, it is not necessary for the instructor to be totally skilled in the operation to be able to teach it correctly.

In the electronics industry one of the most intensive training areas is teaching hand soldering. It is not unusual to find that the instructor is by no means as capable as some of the students, but he has the ability to demonstrate the manual dexterity necessary to make a good joint, and to identify errors in the technique and correct them without taking away the student's motivation or self-confidence.

It is not sufficient for the instructor to be able to teach the manual skills; he must also have a clear understanding of the total process and the theories on which the various operations are based. If students are taught to carry out the operation in a mechanical manner without knowing all of the basic processes, they will function with all of the failings of a robot but without its ability to repeat the process accurately at all times. If the students are given an understanding of the entire process and some knowledge of the basic physical and chemical theory on which it is based, they can function with this knowledge and understanding. They will not have the ability of the robot to repeat without variations but will have the ability of the human being to think, to accept and adapt to changes, and to make decisions. These human capabilities are frequently overlooked, but they are the very reasons for using people instead of machines. If we ignore them we are wasting some of our most precious resources.

SKILLS RECOGNITION

The fact that time and money has been spent on training an operator makes that operator a very important part of your operation. The operator in turn has given something: interest, skills, understanding, and intelligence. If the training has been done well, you will also have generated a feeling of importance, of belonging, of wanting to use the skills and do a good job. The recognition of these feelings can go a long way to reinforce them and to assure that they continue. Of course, wage and salary scales are important, but so is anything that shows the rest of the world that the person is considered to be skilled and special—a badge, a certificate, something that demonstrates that the person is important to the company.

Certification is one excellent way of doing this. On satisfactory completion of a training program the operator is certified as a skilled individual for a specific job or range of jobs, with a badge that says this clearly, containing at least the operator's photograph and the manager's and instructor's signatures.

This also provides a formal opportunity to monitor the operator's skill by requiring that each individual be retested on a routine basis in order to retain this certification.

THE PRACTICAL DETAILS

If it is to be retained, training has to be carried out correctly and repeated from time to time. Correct training implies a well-planned program content, presented by a trained instructor. The practical details must also not be forgotten. A suitable room has to be set aside for training, with adequate lighting and ventilation. It has to have the tools required for the operations that are to be taught and an adequate supply of materials. This latter rquirement is sometimes not carefully considered. A supply of rejected parts that would otherwise be scrapped is not good enough for training purposes.

The training area should simulate the production floor as far as is humanly possible. The same benches, seating, lighting, and tools should be used. The operators who are being trained should actually manufacture products as quickly as possible. They should be taught some manufacturing functions that will provide experience but will not be costly or affect product quality if carried out incorrectly. The incentive to learn quickly is much higher when the pupil understands that he is doing real work, that this is no longer a make-believe situation, that his skills are really being put to use. Of course, until the necessary level of skills is reached each operator will work under the close scrutiny of the instructor, who will stop the work at the slightest indication of an incorrect operation.

The human instructor cannot be eliminated. From practical experience it has been found that the flow of ideas between the instructor and the student is a major factor in retaining the facts presented during the training. Video and audio tapes, movies, slides, and similar aids can provide an addition to the teacher's skills and are also useful where students wish to refresh their knowledge. However, they do not provide adequate training by themselves; the personal touch of the trained instructor is indeed necessary.

When the author is commissioned to set up a training program it is not at all unusual to find that a considerable amount of money has already been spent on visual aids. Today this invariably means video tapes, which are used during the initial enthusiasm of setting up a training program with the idea that they will make it unnecessary to have an instructor properly trained in the technology that the student is to learn. This would be an excellent idea if it were possible to make tapes that are clear in every respect and answer every possible question that can arise during the instruction program. As this is extremely difficult to do, the students become bored and disenchanted with the training process. The tapes gather dust and the entire training program fizzles out.

Audiovisual aids are extremely useful in the hands of a trained instructor, who can fill in the unexplained details or use them to reinforce his own instructions. They are especially useful in teaching a process by viewing each section actually being carried out, and by showing items that would otherwise not be visible because of the danger of moving machines or other safety or practical considerations.

UNIVERSAL TRAINING

All too often training is limited to individuals at the operator level on the basis that the operator has to have the skills to do the job but everyone else can just pick up the knowledge of the task in some ill-defined way. After all, they will not be required to actually carry out the work on the shop floor. Of course, this is nonsense and does not give those on the periphery of the process the knowledge necessary to carry out their work efficiently and with total understanding. For example, it is vitally important that all supervisors and managers have the same understanding of the work to be done, or they will be unable to supervise it efficiently and will not know whether it is being correctly carried out or not. Engineers, quality people, inspectors, and other auxiliary staff must also be considered when training programs are developed. When all the people on the shop floor understand the operation, many of the day-to-day problems disappear; when everyone concerned with the process understands it in detail, the interdepartmental conflicts vanish and the entire organization will work as one team.

It is essential to train the designers in the processes and machines that will be used to manufacture the products that they design. This may appear to be an obvious fact but it is frequently not given the attention that it deserves. Serious manufacturing problems at one company were traced to certain aspects of the design of the product. The design office was situated in another building a few blocks from the manufacturing plant. In conversation with the designers it was found that some of them had been working there for over five years but had never even seen the factory floor. In fact, they had only the sketchiest idea of the process by which their designs were manufactured. A one-day visit was arranged and proved to be of tremendous value—not only because of the information that was gleaned from seeing the manufacturing operation, but also because it laid the foundations for a lasting interchange of ideas.

In another plant there was a major concern over the large number of parts that were being damaged in production. It was found that a tool was consistently being used incorrectly, but this was not discovered until an outside consultant eventually pointed it out. In addition, neither the supervisor nor the quality man on the floor had been trained in the use of the tool and had no idea that incorrect use could produce the damage.

It is not unusual to find that purchasing people have little idea how the parts or materials that they procure are used. Some time spent with them on the shop floor as they learn what is required and the way that the parts are used can materially help them in their work and avoid some of the mistakes that frequently occur.

We have seen the importance of communications between both individuals and different parts of the organization; we have also discussed some of the advantages of working as a team. To become proficient in these skills also requires an effective training program.

Training therefore must be all-encompassing: everyone who is part of the process must understand all aspects of that process. It is not necessary for everyone to be trained to the same level in every detail and determining what level of training is necessary must be considered as part of the process development.

MANAGEMENT TRAINING

We have discussed the many interpersonal difficulties that we find in the management process and the way in which they can affect the overall operation. These are skills that can be taught, knowledge that can be acquired. Although it is impossible to instruct a manager in the exact techniques to be used in every situation, it is possible for him to become skilled in the individual items that he can then apply as his growing skill and experience guide him. He needs to understand himself and his reactions to the various characters of the people who he will manage. He needs to recognize that the way in which he responds to them can in turn alter their behavior.

He also needs to become experienced in practicing these various attitudes. For example, he must understand that controlled positive criticism will result in a very different reaction from that caused by indiscriminate complaints, that praise linked directly to excellent performance is very different from overeffusive back slapping, and that the degree and direction of any of his attitudes must take into account the attitude of the individual or group concerned. As an example, one employee had for years performed well if not brilliantly and had therefore held his present position for a long time. He did not want a promotion; he just wanted to stay in his present job for the next five years until retirement. It was pointless to treat him in the same way as a new young engineer who was ambitious and eager for promotion. Within the department there were many variations in individuals between these two extremes. The manager had to recognize these differences and treat each person accordingly. While this type of attitude variation is comparatively easy to recognize, others cannot be noticed easily without experience or training.

It is rare for this type of training to be offered to the new or practicing manager, yet it can be the most powerful tool in his day-to-day operation. Some commercial business training programs have provided this experience in very simple but effective methods. Role playing offers an excellent opportunity to gain experience provided it is well thought out and practiced under the control of an experienced instructor. Some college courses introduce the psychology of business. Generally this is one of the least well-understood areas of management and yet it remains one of the most important if we are to achieve excellence. It is one of the basics on which many of the fashionable management fads are built, although they rarely recognize the fact.

Training has to be all encompassing; it is not a one-shot deal. It must be carried out in a professional manner. As we have discussed in previous chapters, change is always with us and our methods and even our organizations will change from time to time. Any change, no matter where it occurs, will require that the employees have the change explained, the effect on their work shown to them, and adequate training provided in order to perform their new roles efficiently. It may be a very simple explanation that can be given in a few minutes. It may require days or even weeks of formal classroom or shop floor training. If so, it must be carried out effectively and formally. People cannot be expected to "pick things up"; they will do so as well as possible but this is a slow, costly, and inefficient process. We must recognize the training needs, plan for them, and then train properly.

Chapter 8

INSPECTION AND THE ROLE OF QUALITY CONTROL

We have seen that by controlling the process we can consistently produce a product of the same quality at the same price. It would then be logical to suggest that inspection is unnecessary and that the term "Quality Control" is meaningless. This is basically true, yet this function and the people performing it are generally found in our operations no matter how well the manufacturing process is controlled. We must understand their purpose and the way that their objectives, authorities, and responsibilities have changed from those used in an uncontrolled process.

THE ROLE OF INSPECTION

How often have we heard the phrase "You can't inspect quality into the product"? But how many people really believe it to be true? Not too many if we look at the way most products are made. In many plants the product is inspected at several points in the production phase and almost all have a "final inspection" station. If you ask what all of this inspection is for, the answer is almost always that it assures that the product is sound and that nothing leaves the plant that is not manufactured completely according to the standards set by management. In other words, the in-line inspection is there to be sure that the correct materials are used, and that the operators do their job correctly. The final inspection is to check everything once again to be sure that both the operators and the prior inspectors carried out their tasks correctly and did not miss any errors.

64

INSPECTION ACCURACY

The answer given above cannot be accepted as anything more than wishful thinking, however, if all of the factors involved in inspection are considered carefully. The first question to be asked is whether the inspectors can consistently determine if every part of the product is correctly made and assembled. If the operators are incapable of doing their jobs properly all the time, it is illogical to suggest that the inspectors can carry out their inspection accurately all the time. As far as final inspection is concerned, once the assembly operation is complete it is usually impossible to do more than inspect the external appearance of the product. The inspector may be able to derive some idea of quality from this, but it is a far cry from checking the overall product reliability (Figure 16).

As suggested above, we have to consider whether a human inspector can consistently work to a constant standard. Again the answer is in the negative. Many studies have been carried out on this subject and all indicate the same inefficiency and inaccuracy, especially when subjective decisions have to be made. One military contractor presented the same product to the same inspec-

INSPECTION ACCURACY

Do you think visual inspection is accurate?

Visual inspection by the vain but very human inspector will inevitably involve various errors which may not be possible to verify. Very often those that violate the specification are valid, but variable, vague, and inevitably will be missed in the struggle to survive in the busy environment of a viable business operation. The value of valid inspection can vanish in the variability of the standards that involve the verification of work

COUNT THE NUMBER OF "V"s IN THE ABOVE PARAGRAPH.

NOW COUNT THEM AGAIN

DO YOU STILL THINK VISUAL INSPECTION IS ACCURATE?

Figure 16 Ask a few people to take this simple test and see how many different answers you get. If we cannot count a few letters accurately how can we rely on visual inspection to find our defective products?

tor on two separate occasions; the inspector's findings only agreed in about 45% of the defects originally indicated. When four inspectors were used in the test agreement fell to around 15%. Yet these very inspectors were the people who were deciding whether the products met the specification or whether they should be reworked or rejected. If a final inspection is necessary to check the prior work and inspection, it is logical to suggest that there should be a post-final, final inspection in case the final inspector missed a defect. Of course, this procedure can continue ad nauseam until we have more inspectors than operators. Although this is ridiculuous, it has actually occurred and is not far from what exists in some manufacturing operations.

For example, a senior member of one of the armed services pointed out that almost half the cost of some military electronics is solely to pay for the inspection that is carried out by the military inspectors, to assure that the contractor complies with the myriad specifications and standards that are imposed in the contract. We note that in these cases the words reliability and quality are rarely used; "meeting the specification" is everything. But the specification is only man's attempt to describe in words some of the product changes that may be caused by variations to the process. They can be difficult to define and describe and the specification can never be anything but imperfect.

These comments are not intended to decry the abilities of inspectors but rather to show that we expect them to do work that a normal human being is incapable of performing consistently. All too often we ask them to inspect by rote, to compare results to pictures or diagrams, or to use some other indirect measurement. If only we trained our inspectors correctly they would be able to inspect with intelligence.

Although it is true that we cannot inspect quality into the product, we attempt to do so day after day. Yet a moment's thought tells us that if the process is correct—if everything is always done in exactly the same way with exactly the same materials—the product quality will always be the same. Somehow we find great difficulty in accepting these simple truths.

INSPECTION AND THE OPERATOR

There is a far more subtle factor to be considered when inspection is used in the way described above, and that is the effect on the thinking of the operators. Whether we like it or not, it says, "There is no need to strive to do the job properly—we have arranged for someone to pick up all the mistakes that you make." This was brought home strongly to me as a young, newly appointed manufacturing manager. There were quality problems in my plant which were causing a high rate of field failures, and I did not know how to tackle the situation. Inspection had been beefed up by my predecessor to the point where there was an inspector to every five operators, but the field-failure rate of the product did not drop. Walking down the production lines one day I saw a component lying on the floor. I picked it up and gave it to the operator from whose bench it had fallen with the comment, "You will need this." "Oh, no" said the operator, "It has nothing to do with me—it's his responsibility," pointing to the inspector sitting immediately behind him. As a result of this experience I reorganized the shop floor and removed all inspection from the production lines. I also changed the role of quality control from inspection to that of process monitoring. The responsibility for quality was placed squarely back on the operators. With some other minor actions, field failures fell in a few weeks to one tenth the original figure. We did not have a quality problem: we had a management and organizational problem.

What then is the task of inspection in the well-controlled process? Certainly not to decide whether the product is good enough to ship or not, for that will be taken care of through excellent process control. Instead, inspection is needed to develop data. These data are used first to assure that the process is indeed within the control limits, and second to initiate any preventive actions that may be necessary to maintain or improve the process control.

For example, suppose that the product has a highly polished finish. In an uncontrolled process the inspector would check every item for defects in the polish, returning those that did not pass his inspection criteria for refinishing. There may well be some limit set on the number of items that can be returned without some investigation as to why these defects are being generated, but there is usually no attempt to eliminate the problem. There is "an acceptable defect level." In this case the accuracy of the inspection becomes very important. If the limit is set at 1% but the inspector is only 70% efficient, there may well be a number of products shipped that have scratches or paint dribbles. The inspector is the final arbiter; he is solely responsible for the quality of the finish and will be blamed for any defects. Yet it is impossible for him to be 100% efficient, and from the very start we know that he will miss some errors.

It is not possible to inspect quality into the product. In a well-controlled operation the process will have been properly developed to a well-defined quality level, with perfection as the ultimate goal. If everything is carried out correctly, the number of defects in the finish will be tiny, say 50 defects per million units. If the defect rate exceeds this, the operation will be halted until the cause is found and corrected. But we do not want ever to reach this level, and inspection of the product is used as the quality monitor. The difference between this form of inspection and that in the previous case, is that it accepts the inefficiencies of the inspector. We do not expect him to find each and every defect in the finish; we are not asking him to inspect every unit made. We *are* expecting him to detect changes, by carefully inspecting samples of the product. If statistically the sampling shows that the defects have gone above 50PPM, production is halted and necessary actions are taken to eliminate the basic cause, because the numbers show a totally out-of-control condition. No matter how low the defect rate there will always be some form of preventive action to reduce the defects. The aim is excellence, and inspection is used to monitor the process and to indicate the areas for improvement.

REWORK

What can be done to make the product quality right when it is found to be faulty? The product can certainly be reworked, but this is expensive and in many cases will result in nothing more than a cosmetic fix. For example, the cracked casing on a lawn mower that was dropped while it was being assembled may be found at inspection and replaced, but its bent shaft or out-of-line bearings are unlikely to be discovered and may ultimately result in a short life for the machine. In other words, rework will hide from the customer the fact that a problem existed in the product quality, because the cosmetic defects will be fixed. It will also hide the fact that problems exist in the manufacturing operation—in this particular case, the way the lawn mowers are handled and stored—which have to be reviewed and improved. Rework removes the pressure on production to fix the problems promptly because the products are eventually being shipped, but in many cases this means that the problems are never fixed. After all, if we believe that inspection can find every defect in every product and there is a group of people whose job is solely to fix products that fail inspection, why bother to prevent the problems from occurring? In many cases the rework department is nothing more than a catch-all that hides from management the fact that quality problems exist and removes any pressure to eliminate those problems.

REWORK AND RELIABILITY

It would be naive to say that no rework should ever be carried out, although some companies are in fact making this part of their overall objective. However, rework should never be carried out without a thorough understanding of what is to be done. The rework methods should be clearly defined, the operators well trained. Above all other considerations, it must be determined that the rework will not impair the life or performance of the product. Finally, rework must never be carried out lightly; we must recognize that it indicates a failure somewhere in the process and the basic cause of that failure must be found and eliminated.

Any rework, no matter how small or simple, is an unnecessary expense that demands immediate corrective action.

WHAT IS THE OBJECTIVE?

Our aim must be to make the highest quality product that we posibly can. It must perform perfectly, be completely reliable, have a superb appearance, and last forever. It is unlikely that we will ever achieve this aim, but if our objective is lower than this it is unlikely that we will ever achieve more than mediocrity. Perfection must always be the ultimate quality requirement and our overall objective.

Living in a practical world we have to consider the many factors that will determine the lowest level of product quality that can be shipped; that is, the quality level that is acceptable to the customer and produces a saleable product. This is a much more difficult level to define and requires that many facets of our business be examined closely (Figure 17).

- At the least, the product must perform properly according to its advertised claims.
- The sales price must be competative.
- The reliability must be at least as good as the competing products.
- Its appearance must attract the customer.
- It must be convenient and safe to use.

THE PRODUCT SPECIFICATION

From the above list a detailed product specification must be written which can be related to the manufacturing process, used by inspection as a standard, and to which the process must be developed. However, we must never loose sight of the fact that this specification defines the lowest possible level of quality that is permitted. It cannot be our objective or we will never get away from quality problems. Excellence must be the aim, and while the specification defines the lowest quality level we must always aim for perfection.

The specification must be clear and definitive, and as far as possible must remove any subjectivity from the various quality requirements. As this is rarely totally possible, these very areas of ambiguity cause conflict and argument. We have all seen the conflict in which the inspector argues with the operator

PERFECTION

LESS THAN PERFECTION
DEMANDS
IMMEDIATE CORRECTIVE ACTION
TO BRING THE PROCESS BACK INTO
CONTROL

SPECIFICATION

FAILURE TO MEET THE SPEC.
DEMANDS
PRODUCT REWORK, OR SCRAP

Figure 17 The quality objective must always be perfection. Anything less will inevitably result in higher costs.

that this is rejected for this reason, and the operator says that this is not so. Inevitably when this happens the defect is marginal, and each side genuinely believes that his opinion is correct. Here is another very good reason for aiming for excellence. When the quality objective is the specification we will always have a quality level that hovers around the accept/reject criteria. When we are satisfied only with perfection we will soon raise our quality level so far above the specification that the inspection criteria will rarely be invoked.

THE SPECIFICATION LEVEL

The specification level defines the absolute minimum level of acceptable quality and nothing less than this quality must ever be allowed out of our plant. We have to set our goals much higher than this or we will never get away from constant quality problems and bickering over specification requirements.

Setting such a goal is like attempting to fly over a 20,000-foot mountain range. If the pilot sets a course at 21,000 feet any minor variation in the weather or the performance of the aircraft could be disastrous. If, however, he flies at

30,000 feet, these minor variations will be a nuisance but will not affect the outcome of the flight. There is plenty of tolerance for unplanned and unexpected variables, and there will always be variable forces acting on the aircraft just as there will always be variable items in our manufacturing process. Although we must minimize these variables, they will always exist to some degree and there must be sufficient tolerance in the process to accept them without causing the product quality to deteriorate below the specified level.

There are many product specifications already in existence, ranging from those applicable to military and aerospace hardware to those developed by the various standards organizations and industry organizations. It is rarely necessary to start from scratch and write a new one. Yet most suffer from the same problems.

- They attempt to specify the barest minimum that can be accepted on the incorrect assumption that good quality will make manufacturing more expensive.
- They do not define what should be done when the product fails to comply with the specification.

The author frequently sits on committees that write product specifications, and invariably a majority of its members have one idea in mind and that is to dilute the specification to the absolute minimum quality level in an attempt to reduce the cost of manufacture. Typical is the case of the criteria for acceptable solder joints in electronics. We would all like to see that every joint is perfectly made with a complete soldered connection around 360 degrees of the lead, which would guarantee a sound reliable joint. Yet, at every meeting on the subject, the argument is put forward that 180 degrees of joining is "all right." The argument then goes on to say that if a specification calls for 360 degrees of solder around the lead, then all of the joints having a lesser amount of connecting solder will have to be reworked to make them comply with the requirement and this will push up the labor costs. Here is a case where the objective is to do the least that is necessary to get the product out, not to provide the ultimate quality and reliability. The simple fact is that it costs no more to make a good joint with a 360 degree fillet than it does to make one with a 180 degree fillet.

SPECIFICATIONS AND CORRECTIVE ACTION

There is some merit, however, in the arguments against making the specifications too tight, because nowhere in most of our requirements is there any mention of the actions to be taken when the product does not meet the specified limits, nor is there usually any quantitive limit on the deficiencies. For example, if one screw on one assembly is found to be loose should all of those assemblies be inspected, or just used as is? The answer is almost certainly that this is a minor processing problem and nothing more than an inspection of a sample of the lot is required to confirm this, plus an investigation to determine and eliminate the cause. If 0.01% of assemblies are found to have screws that are loose, then the process is so far out of control that it should be shut down until the problem is eliminated, and all products inspected and reworked as may be necessary. Only when this corrective action is completed should the line be restarted.

Yet in most specifications this problem would probably be seen as an item that merely says, "All screws shall be tightened according to the torque table in section XXX. Any screws that do not meet this requirement shall be cause for rejection." In other words, one screw found to be loose in one assembly is considered in the same terms as all the screws loose in all the assemblies, and the corrective action is inferred to be the same. This type of specification encourages inspection and rework, the objective being to get the assemblies past the inspector.

The specification must acknowledge that mistakes are made, and that elimination of the causes of these mistakes is essential and should be part of the specification. One error can be attributed to a simple mistake, two to carelessness, but more become a case of total negligence on the part of the operator, or failure of a machine or incorrect parts or some other problem. The actions to be taken must consider these factors and define the corrective actions.

In this case, perhaps the specification should say the following:

> Any screws found at the process inspection station not meeting the torque requirements of Table XXX shall be retightened and documented. If the number exceeds 25 PPM, or if their location is not random, or more than one are found in any single assembly, the line shall be stopped until the cause is found and eliminated.

Fortunately for most commercial products, the manufacturer can write his own specification, limited only by certain state and federal requirements. Military and aerospace contractors have to abide by strict and sometimes totally impractical military specifications and standards.

SPECIFICATIONS AND RELIABILITY

In practice it is strange to find that the specifications that are used appear to have little effect on the ultimate quality or reliability of the product. A good example is the case of automobile electronics compared with aerospace products. Of course, there are wide differences in complexity and volume, but the engine computer in the average American automobile is far from a simple device and operates in a very hostile environment with no preventative maintenance at all. It is made to commercial specifications without the benefit of the many in-process requirements and inspections called for by the various Military Specifications and Standards. In addition, it is made for a very small fraction of the cost of a comparable military product. The quality and reliability are superb. Perhaps the reason is obvious when we examine the history of the automobile industry. From rock bottom it has fought back to become profitable. Everyone in the industry suffered dramatically for several years; the message was loud and clear: the customer demands quality and reliability and the industry responded. As one manager told me, "We cannot afford to have one automobile break down because that customer will be lost forever and will never buy another one of our cars." Or, as I was told by one man on the shop floor, "We are going to make the best cars in the world." It is this attitude, this aiming for perfection, that produces good automobiles—not the words printed on a specification or workmanship manual.

In spite of this, we have to have some standards to which we can all agree. However, these must never be considered as the upper limit of quality, rather the rock bottom beyond which we will not even consider working. We also have to understand that it is difficult to write a specification or standard that covers every possible case. They should be considered as guides, specifying an absolute minimum quality level to be used with thought and understanding, not a rule book to be used without intelligence.

For example, some of the military specifications identify a frosty appearance of the surface of a soldered joint as a rejectable condition. In practice, thousands of joints are reworked every day to make them look bright and shiny. There is plenty of evidence that reworking a joint in this way only reduces the reliability and life of the connection, while there is no evidence that a frosty appearance is indicative of poor reliability. Certainly the frosty appearance may indicate the onset of an out-of-control condition that requires attention to the contamination level of the solder pot. It is extremely difficult to write all of this into a specification if it is to be used as a rule book. It is simple to work to such specifications when they are used by inspectors trained in the process and inspecting with intelligence.

SPECIFICATION AND CORRECTIVE ACTIONS

We already know that there will be certain factors in our product we will find difficult to specify—for example, a part that is assembled out of square and therefore contravenes the specification. It may not look perfect, it will not affect either performance or reliability, but do we want to ship the part? If the answer is "No" we have two options.

- Scrap the entire product.
- Rework the assembly and square up the part.

But both of these answers solve only the immediate problem of what to do with the faulty assembly and fail totally to eliminate the problem. Perhaps the specification should say something to the following effect.

> *Squareness of Assembly.* If an assembly is put together out of square and it complies with all other requirements it may be reworked and shipped provided that immediate corrective action is taken to assure that no other parts are made in this way. If two or more parts in any 10,000 are found to have this condition, production shall be stopped until the cause is determined and eliminated.

We need to build into our Specifications and Standards the corrective actions necessary to get rid of our problems once and for all. Of course, it is impossible in a book such as this to do more than define the areas of concern and the action to be taken, because of the many different types of industry with which the readers will be involved.

COST VS. QUALITY

Cost, of course, has to be a major concern, and this is often used as an excuse for accepting lower quality products. There is a widespread but incorrect idea that if the product is low enough in cost it will automatically beat the competition. In general this not true, especially when the customer can select from a large range of products.

If the appearance and performance are as good as or better than the competition, the product will sell initially provided that the price is not more than marginally higher; but it is the quality and reliability found in service that will determine the long-term sales. We have only to look at the automobile industry to understand this.

While the Japanese cars initially took a large slice of the sales in the United States because of their lower costs, they retained their lead by developing innovative designs, providing a high quality of finish, and earning an excellent reputation for reliability. The resurgence of the American automobile manufacturers came from producing quality vehicles at an acceptable price, not by making the cheapest cars on the market. Indeed, the demise of some of the automobiles imported from the old Eastern Block countries showed that customers wanted performance, looks, and overall reliability much more than simply low cost.

Of course price has an effect on the product, but it should not affect the quality as perceived by the customer. No one buying a Rolls Royce expects it to be cheap, but no one buying a Pontiac expects it to be any less reliable. Yet their respective prices are thousands of dollars apart. Cost therefore has to be balanced against the product performance in the design phase. The Pontiac may use plastic instead of leather to cover the seats, but this must not affect the comfort or life of the seating. The RR may be quieter, but the Pontiac has to have an acceptable level of sound insulation.

When perfection is given as the ultimate aim, an attitude often exists which says that this will prove to be too expensive and that "good enough" should be our objective. Yet often, in an attempt to define and work to this mysterious "good enough," we spend more money than if we had gone for the best in the first place.

As an example, on one production line the best tools for the job cost around $150 each, while less suitable tools cost under half that amount. The lower priced ones were bought with the comment that they would be "good enough." Certainly the job was carried out and the product was shipped, but the operation times were excessive, the tools were more difficult to use and broke down more often, and operator defects increased. In the end the better tools had to be purchased to reduce the production costs.

In another case, a piece of machinery was required and capital expenditure approved. The amount of money allowed was insufficient to purchase a machine that met all of the requirements and one of lower capability was acquired. It certainly performed the operation but did not have good repeatability, and process control became extremely difficult. The cost of maintenance was excessive, and eventually the machine had to be scrapped and a new one purchased.

One company purchased fabricated materials from the Far East because they were cheaper than comparable parts made in the United States. In order to save money the entire transaction was carried out by mail, Fax, and through intermediaries, with no direct investigation of the vendor's capabilities. It was only when a full year's supply of materials had been put into stores and began to be used that they were found to be of inadequate quality. Because of the pressure of the schedule the parts were used but only with the expenditure of excessive labor. The result was also a product with a lowered reliability.

None of these problems was basically technical but came from incorrect management decisions made without understanding all of the factors involved.

DESIGN AND QUALITY

If the manufacturing process is truly in control, if all of the variables are eliminated, then each unit of the product will be exactly the same and the product quality and reliability will be determined solely by the design. If the designer has taken into account any possible variations in the materials and parts and in the tools and equipment, controlling the process will not be difficult and minor variations will not affect the product. However, if the design is in any way marginal or if the material specifications are critical, it may become very difficult to set up an adequate process control operation. Ultimately, the product quality should be only a function of the design, but this in turn demands that the designer understands fully the manufacturing process and the limitations that this applies to the design of the product.

In one case, the design of some assembly machines was based on using one component of the product being manufactured to hold an entire assembly during one of the major process steps. Unfortunately, the designer had not understood clearly the various tolerance buildups in the position and size of the part, nor the forces that would be applied to that part during the process. When the machine was finally tested, it consistently broke a small but unacceptable number of the parts during the process step. Several models of the machine had been built and in the end they were all scrapped, as it was quite uneconomical to modify them in any way. This particular design defect was first seen quite early in the manufacture of the machines but was ignored by the designer, who believed that some simple modifications to the completed machines could eliminate the problem. When the mechanical forces were finally investigated, it was found that the stresses on the part were so near its breaking point that nothing could be done. It is disastrous when the realization that a design problem exists comes late in production. These things of course, should have been discovered during the preproduction phase.

Design cannot be separated from production. They are all part of the manufacturing process and must recognize their reliance on each other. Manufacturing must understand the problems of the design team, and design must recognize the limitations of the manufacturing process.

THE PLACE OF QUALITY CONTROL

The term "Quality Control" is, of course, a totally incorrect description of the function of this department. It is impossible for it to control product quality.

"Quality Assurance" is much better but this also does not accurately describe its responsibilities.

If product quality is determined by the design, and if process control maintains that quality level, what is the need for quality control? In theory, we can eliminate this function. We could remove the quality control department entirely and the process should continue with no variations in the product quality, but, as we have already remarked, we live in a less than perfect world, and minor variations will inevitably occur in materials, machines, or operators. Quality control people are certainly an important part of process control, monitoring to identify these changes when they occur and taking the necessary steps to eliminate them. Having developed the process and trained everyone to follow it exactly, we have to be sure that it is always carried out according to the recorded instructions. We have to be sure that the materials are to specification and that the maintenance of the tools and equipments is carried out correctly.

If everyone did his job correctly, including our vendors, then there would be no need for a quality control department. But we are working with people and people invariably make mistakes. Quality control people must monitor every step in the process and immediately report any deficiencies. If this function does not exist, the process will slowly drift and eventually become totally out of control.

The quality control department should not be an inspection function. When inspection is required in any position on the shop floor, it is a manufacturing task. If quality control people are inspecting product, who is there to monitor the work that they are doing? Their prime responsibility is to check the process steps, to know whether the training is correct and whether the tools and machines are in order, to check the calibration on measuring and control systems, and so on.

Quality control people should not be looked upon as policemen waiting to catch the unwary offender, but rather as colleagues ready to assist in maintaining control of the process. Of course, each manufacturing operation is unique, but the overall task of the quality control department remains the same—to control the quality through monitoring the developed process.

SUMMARY

- The only quality objective is perfection.

- If the manufacturing process is totally controlled, the product quality will be determined by the design.

- The product specification must define the limits below which the product will never fall.
- The product specification must define the corrective actions to be taken when the product fails to meet the requirements.
- Specifications cannot cover every possible situation and must be used with intelligence.
- The quality control department must provide the overall monitoring to assure that materials, machines, equipment, and processes, exactly adhere to the developed process.

Chapter 9

ORGANIZATION, RESPONSIBILITY, AND AUTHORITY

It is impossible to split up manufacturing into separate parts each under a different authority. Yet some companies have organizations that are set up in this way, and then they wonder why difficulties occur that cannot be permanently eliminated.

THE ORGANIZATION

A lack of understanding of the importance and the extent of the manufacturing process is usually to blame for poor and ineffective organization, as well as a corporate policy that frequently defines the responsibilities of departments in isolation from the overall process. One example was the company that included material preparation as a function of the purchasing department which reported to a vice president of materials miles from the assembly operation. Inevitably some parts arrived for assembly which had not been correctly prepared. The resulting arguments as to what was the cause, who should pay for the rework, and so on went through the full corporate structure before they could be resolved. Some of the parts had to be precisely formed prior to a complex assembly operation, and the machines for forming the parts and those for assembling them were developed by the materials and assembly departments respectively. Two design teams reported to separate bosses in different locations. What could have been a straightforward engineering task became mired down in corporate politics. The organization had not been set up with any concern for the efficiency of the manufacturing operation; rather it had been laid down to suit corporate policy, which had decided on setting up a central purchasing operation.

It is not possible to split up manufacturing into watertight compartments (Figure 18). Beginning with design and going right through to maintenance of equipment, it is all one process. Of course, it is not possible for any single individual to personally manage all of these different disciplines except in the smallest of operations. But the organization must be set up in such a way as to define clearly each department's responsibility to the manufacturing process, and also to make it absolutely clear that the ultimate objective is to manufacture and ship high-quality products, on schedule, at the lowest cost. Every other aim must take second place.

DEPARTMENTAL RESPONSIBILITIES

There are so many variations in organizations from company to company that it is difficult to describe departmental responsibilities in any form that can be used universally. However, some responsibilities that are common to almost every manufacturing operation can be defined as follows.

Figure 18   It is impossible to split up the organization into watertight compartments. All are part of the manufacturing process.

- It is the responsibility of design to define the materials and the format into which they must be processed, to make a product that will meet the design objectives of quality, reliability, and cost.
- It is the responsibility of manufacturing engineering to develop and define the manufacturing process, including the tools and methods to be used, that will make the product to the specified quality and reliability, on schedule at the agreed cost. In some companies manufacturing engineering also has the responsibility of taking the basic design and reconfiguring it for best manufacturability.
- It is the responsibility of manufacturing to use the defined tools, methods, materials, and people to make the product according to the developed process, on schedule at the agreed cost.
- It is the responsibility of quality control to assure that the developed processes are always used in manufacturing and testing the purchased materials.
- It is the responsibility of receiving inspection to monitor the quality of all incoming materials and assure that they conform to the purchase specifications.
- It is the responsibility of purchasing to acquire materials that meet the specifications, on schedule at a fair price.

Starting with the basic manufacturing objective, we can define exactly how each department must provide the appropriate support for production to achieve this requirement. Once these basic responsibilities to production have been defined, it is possible to begin to lay out an organization plan and get into the secondary objectives in greater detail, until each department has a clear understanding of exactly what it has to do. If this allocation of responsibilities is not carried out carefully and with an understanding of the nature of the manufacturing process, serious problems may arise. There may be disputes as to who should do what, or some tasks may be left undone as no one sees them as their own particular responsibility. In summary, everyone should know who is responsible for each single part of the process.

INDIVIDUAL RESPONSIBILITIES

Once the departmental responsibilities have been allocated, each individual in each department must also agree clearly about his own personal responsibilities. In developing these areas of responsibility the overall process and the way it is to be controlled must be considered. Some typical problems that have been encountered because of errors in setting up such an organization include the following items.

- Manufacturing engineers were not permitted to talk to the operators because any instructions could be given only by the line supervisor. As a consequence, any process problems were a cause of frustration and difficult to resolve.
- Maintenance technicians were not allowed to carry out any work until they had the signed authority of the maintenance manager, and they then could only work on specified machines. This caused such absurdities as a technician who could not oil a squeaking bearing because he did not have the written authority, and one who could not turn off a leaking tap because it was not on his list of machines.
- Receiving inspectors rejected materials because they did not meet the purchasing specification, only to have them signed off as usable by a design engineer. The parts were used and resulted in excessive costs and lowered product reliability. The receiving inspection people were blamed for the problems.
- Machine processing parameters were developed by manufacturing engineering, then changed by the line supervisor. The product quality suffered and unnecessary rework resulted.

What is probably even worse is the case where no one is really sure of who has the responsibility for a particular part of the process. Often, in frustration someone with the least knowledge accepts the challenge with disastrous results. The responsibility for the maintenance of a machine was split between the maintenance department and the operator. Who was to do what was never properly defined. As a consequence, some important items were overlooked, the process slipped out of control, and the machine suffered major damage.

The higher up the organizational ladder this lack of definition is found, the more far reaching are the results, yet it is often in the major items that this lack of clear responsibility occcurs. A manager may have responsibility for working within his budget, but another department may dictate his expenditure. For example, the manufacturing engineering manager in an aerospace plant was responsible for the budget for test equipment, but the design of this was the responsibility of the design department and the throughput was decided by manufacturing. The manufacturing engineering manager had no way of controlling this expenditure, he always exceeded the budget, and his performance as a manager was criticised for his lack of budget control.

RECEIVING INSPECTION

In many plants, while the receiving inspection department is responsible for assuring that materials meet the purchasing specifications, the decision as to whether the parts can be used when rejected lies with other departments. Eventually the receiving inspection department considers itself no more than a rubber stamp and all questionable decisions are passed on to the deciding department. Unofficially the responsibility for material quality has now been transferred.

In some companies, this decision making is placed in the hands of a materials review board, because it is believed that many opinions are better than one. Although this may be true, eventually it is one or two of the more aggressive personalities who will make the decision, not the entire board. In fact, once the board has been operating for a while, it is not unusual to find that it is no longer a group of people and the decisions are made by a single member. If the receiving inspection department is given the responsibility for materials quality, it should be given the whole responsibility. Certainly it should be provided with all the assistance it requires and all the technical skills that are available to assist in making the right decisions, but eventually it must be the sole authority with respect to the quality of purchased materials.

AUTHORITY

If a department or an individual is given a responsibility, the necessary authority to carry out the work also has to be given. It is surprising how often this is not done, or how often only conditional authority is given, such as "Get my permission first." Frequently the reasoning for this is that "I have to know what is going on," or "It's one way for me to keep my finger on things." To the people concerned it says very clearly, "I do not trust you and I intend to have the last word in any decision making."

Any manager has a perfect right to manage in this way if it is appropriate— for example, when training a new employee; but once the responsibility has been planted squarely on the department or individual, he must accept the challenge and the results of poor judgment or actions. However he must also be given the total authority to carry out the task. He must be given the opportunity to make mistakes, for it is through this kind of experience that people grow and improve their performance. The old saying "If you don't make mistakes you will never make anything" is especially true in our management organization.

Deciding exactly what the overall organization should be, will depend so much on the individual company that it is inappropriate to attempt to lay down any rules in this book other than the bare bones ones discussed above. However, some specific approaches are effective.

The first thing to remember is that the people who will compose the organization have a much better idea of the way it should be set up than any corporate officer or consultant. They know intimately the limits of responsibility that they will accept and the authority they will need. Writing these out for any department must be a collaborative effort. The details must be practical items that will provide a measurable performance so that the department can be monitored.

DEPARTMENTAL INTERACTION

Once the individual departments have been defined in this way, the interaction between departments must be checked and the details added to the responsibilities and authorities (Figure 19). Discussing and agreeing on objectives for each department and individual are techniques that work extremely well in developing the organization. They take time, they demand an on-going effort from every manager and supervisor, but they make sure that no small items are missed, that everyone understands his place in the organization, and that the responsibilities and authorities for the job are properly matched.

Setting objectives for a department begins by setting down the overall aim and then refining this into the various details. For example, the responsibility or objective for purchasing is "to acquire the materials that meet the specifications, on schedule at a fair price." But this is nebulous in practical terms and will have to be refined. For example,

- Who will supply the specifications?
- Who will decide the supply schedule?
- How will a fair price be developed for each item?
- How will receiving inspection and purchasing coordinate their respective responsibilities?
- What will happen when materials are rejected at receiving inspection?
- Who will supply technical information and advice when required?
- How will design and purchasing coordinate on the use of specialized components?
- How will manufacturing feed back information on materials problems?
- Who will be responsible for solving materials problems?
- How does purchasing coordinate with the above department or individual?

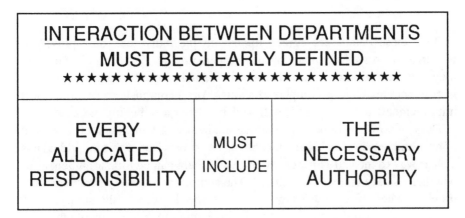

Figure 19   Responsibilities will never be met if the necessary authority is not given.

For all of these questions the responsibility for each particular action must be agreed upon along with the degree of authority necessary to carry out the task. Responsibilities must never be shared or left unclear. Cooperation, discussion, and agreement are part of every task when people are involved, but the ultimate responsibility must be clearly defined.

SETTING OBJECTIVES

In a similar manner, individual responsibilities and authorities must be developed for every employee. This step demands time, for it requires the supervisor to sit with each person on a regular basis and discuss their aims and objectives. Of course, this philosophy has been known for a long time under many different names: "Management by Objectives," "The Managerial Grid," and so on. It is fundamental to good management and understanding people.

The procedure here is similar to that of setting departmental objectives. For instance, consider an inspector who checks mechanical parts. His overall objective may be "to check that all parts meet the drawing." But this can be broken down into small details that are practical, unambiguous, and easily understood by the individual, and also can be measured. Here are three typical items.

- He must be able to read a mechanical drawing.
- He must be able to use a micrometer.
- He has to be able to use a metalurgical microscope and read cross sections.

Once these details are agreed upon with the individual, they provide a powerful incentive for him to improve his performance. For example, one item may say that within six months he will be able to use another measuring instrument, read more complex drawings, or accomplish some other skill improvement, and his rewards will be dependent on achieving these skills.

There is now no doubt whatever that the inspector knows what is expected of him, and he can plan his advancement. The supervisor of this individual has a clear way to measure his performance and there can be little argument as to whether a salary increase is justified. The author once had a typical personnel problem when an operator argued that he should receive the same pay as workers doing similar work in spite of his being much less capable than the other employees. What threatened to become a major labor issue was quickly resolved when the individual was unable to perform the tasks agreed in his last list of objectives.

Thus, from the initial determination of "who is responsible for what," in fairly crude terms it is possible to develop the many areas of responsibility and authority into an overall organization, in which every individual knows exactly what is required of him and the necesary authority is given to enable him to carry out the task.

DEPARTMENTAL INTERELATIONSHIPS AND OLD IDEAS

Without doubt the most difficult phase of setting up the manufacturing organization is the determination of the relationships between departments. It is often difficult to overcome old ideas, when a simpler, more efficient method is so obvious. In one medium-sized company it was necessary to retest certain parts when they had been in stores for six months. The storekeeper carried out the retesting in the stores, which took about four hours once a month. At a similar company the storekeeper had to pull samples of the parts from the bins, package and mark them, and take them to the quality control department. When they completed the testing, the parts were brought back to stores and the storekeeper now had to replace the parts back into their original packages. It took the storekeeper four hours, quality control four hours, and the overall time to carry out the testing was almost two weeks instead of the four hours of the other company. When it was suggested that the simpler, less costly system be used, the suggestion was rejected because, "only quality control people are allowed to do testing."

We have to look at our organization with a very clear eye, unbiased and unaffected by what we have done in the past.

THE UNOFFICIAL ORGANIZATION

Once the organization has been established, we have to monitor the way that it works in the same way that we monitor any other part of the manufacturing process. It is surprising how often the real authority slides away from the individual or department that is supposed to exercise it, for a variety of reasons.

It may be weakness or laziness on the part of an individual; it may be that a more aggressive person takes over the responsibility for a particular part of the organization in order to get something done. More often, it is that the organization has been incorrectly developed in the first place, or that the particular responsibilities and authorities were not carefully defined. If this "unofficial organization" is not corrected or formalized, the entire organization will soon fall into chaos. However, the unofficial version may not only point out the weaknesses of the original system, but suggest the way in which it should be changed to operate more effectively.

In one company it was the responsibility of the quality control department to carry out vendor surveys on behalf of purchasing. Because of the difficulty of obtaining this help when required, one of the buyers trained himself in the skills required to do these surveys and within a few months had enough experience to do the work himself. The quality control manager eventually noticed that his department had not been asked to carry out any surveys for several months for this particular buyer, and found out that the buyer had unofficially taken onto himself the authority for this work. He was initially angry that his authority had been usurped, but found on investigation that the surveys had been accurately carried out.

It was really much more sensible to place the total responsibility for this task with the respective buyer, instead of splitting it between the two departments, and a program was set up to provide the necessary training for all the purchasing staff. The problem here was that the old idea that this was a quality control department responsibility, had been accepted without challenge. In this case the unofficial organization not only had indicated a better way to carry out this work, but also had made the people who were responsible, both formally and informally, ask themselves why the organization had been set up in this way, and why it was not working well. Why not formalize the new organization, which worked so much better than the old?

At another company a quality program involved training the operators in the aspects of maintaining control of the process, reporting any variations, and taking the appropriate corrective actions. They became so good at these aspects of process control that after some time it was obvious that the quality control people were not required on the shop floor, and the responsibility for product quality and process control monitoring was passed to manufacturing. Here the training made the shop floor people more skilled and therefore more useful, until they were duplicating the quality control activities. It does not matter what the group is called; if they can more effectively carry out the responsibilities, we must be prepared to make the necessary changes to the formal organizational structure. As the requirements of the process change we will have to alter the organization to compensate. As with many other factors in manufacturing we can never assume that we have reached a point where we can sit back and relax. We must constantly be aware of changes and be prepared to change the ways that we do things to arrive at the most logical and efficient organization possible.

Chapter 10

MATERIALS, SPECIFICATIONS, AND TESTING

While lecturing at a large electronics company, I was approached by a young man who asked if he could participate in the training program, as he had, only the day before, been appointed to the job of printed wiring board buyer. He was very nervous and explained that he knew nothing whatever about these components, how they were used, or how they were manufactured. Later he mentioned that for the past few years he had been the buyer for fastenings, that is, nuts, bolts, and rivets.

In this particular organization, the task of the purchasing agent was considered to be a specific job skill, and a good buyer was expected to be able to buy anything. This of course is total nonsense, especially where technical materials are being purchased. The young man was responsible for the purchase of over $5M worth of printed wiring boards per year, but had no technical knowledge whatever about the items he was expected to buy; he did not know how they were made or how they were used in the manufacturing process. The impact on cost, schedule, and product quality from any error in judgment on his part could have been enormous, yet there was no attempt whatever to provide any training for this eager but inexperienced young man. He could certainly obtain technical assistance from quality engineering if he believed it was necessary, but he did not even have sufficient experience or knowledge to know when this help was required.

This was another instance in which it was believed that responsibilities could be divided: the quality of the product was determined by the specification to which it was purchased and by a receiving inspection check that the parts met that specification, and quality engineering standing ready to help if things went wrong. The task of the buyer was to acquire the parts at the lowest possible price.

The assumption made here was that the specification would cover every quality problem that could possibly occur with the parts being purchased, and that inspection of the material when received would pick up any possible variations from that specification. This of course will not be the case when the material is anything more than a very simple product.

SPECIFICATIONS

Any specification is rarely more than a guide to the quality required of the product described in that document. Although a great deal of effort is put into attempting to write specifications in such a way that interpretation is not necessary, this objective is rarely achieved. Tolerances of both parts and measuring instruments affect the results, as do the methods used in performing the various tests. For example, in determining the solderability of electronic component leads the specification calls for a minimum of 95% of the lead to be wetted with fresh solder when the lead is dipped into flux and solder under certain conditions. Of course, it is almost impossible to determine the difference between 90% and 96%. The finishes on some metal surfaces must be checked by comparison with test samples, and both of these examples require subjective decisions. Inevitably, subjectivity enters into almost every form of inspection or measurement.

It is amazing how acceptable quality levels can change under the pressure of the schedule, or the nearness to a vacation, or on Friday night a few minutes before finishing time. Materials that would normally be rejected are put into production, not because of any failure on the part of the inspector, not because of any deliberate action to accept inadequate parts, but because the inspector is a human being and his findings can be influenced by many outside circumstances, especially when judgment is called for on his part in the inspection of the materials.

Specifications are useful in determining the quality of materials or product only when they are used as a guide, by honest, knowledgeable people who sincerely desire to produce a product of excellent quality. Unfortunately the specification is usually used to define the lowest level of quality that will be accepted. The quality level then stops at that of the specification with little intention or incentive to do better. Because the parts meet the specification why try to improve their quality?

When a specification attempts to cover every possible variation in the item being defined, it can become so complex that it will be difficult to use and yet will still be open to interpretation. Some of the military specifications are typical examples of this complexity. They are generally looked upon as rules to be applied literally without understanding, they generate excessive costs in the form of inspection and rework, and they produce continuing arguments on the interpretation of the document. Unfortunately they do not guarantee the quality of the product; in fact, the reverse is often the case. All too often meeting the specification is given priority over making a reliable product. As previously mentioned, an official from the Air Force observed publicly that 50% of the cost of Air Force electronics was to pay for the inspection demanded by the specifications and carried out by government inspectors. This sum did not account for the inspection costs spent by the contractor in meeting the same specifications. It is doubtful if military electronics are any more reliable than similar, much less expensive, commercial products made without this level of inspection.

Specifications offer excellent guides to quality when used with intelligence, honesty, and a genuine desire to make a first-class product. For example, in the manufacture of printed wiring boards, many specifications require that test circuitry is included in the border of the boards; this is later cut away and used to carry out accept/reject testing. If the manufacturer uses this feature as a process control tool, it will provide excellent confirmation that the process has been followed correctly. However, it is also easy to place the manufacturing emphasis on making excellent test circuits that may not necessarily be reflected in the product quality. The specification encourages this attitude; the vendor knows his product will be accepted or rejected by the perceived quality of the test circuits, not the ultimate quality of the printed wiring boards, which will not be known until the product has been completed.

ACQUISITION

Before agreeing to purchase materials from any vendor, the buyer therefore has to decide if his supplier will work with him with intelligence, honesty, and a desire to make an excellent product. This is turn requires that the buyer possesses a clear understanding of the materials he is buying, the process for their manufacture, and the way that they will be used in making the final product. This demands training, accessibility to technical knowledge, and time and opportunity to study the subjects. It is a rare company that makes these facilities available to the buyer.

The purchasing agent is often seen as a mixture of paper shuffler and bazaar haggler, with one objective: "To buy at the lowest price." Indeed, as mentioned in Chapter 17, the price paid for the items being purchased is sometimes the only way that the buyer's performance is measured. This is of course a totally incorrect objective; instead, it should be: "To acquire materials that comply with the specification, on schedule at a fair price."

A prime example of the problems that can arise when this objective is not understood took place at a major computer company. The buyer had found a small contractor to supply a complex and important part of the system, and after a few trial purchases had placed a major contract, worth about $150,000 per month, with this company. The contractor responded by producing on schedule, developing the ability to make a high quality product, and generally providing an excellent service. To maintain the throughput he also bought additional equipment and hired more employees.

All went well for almost 10 months, when it became time to negotiate the contract for the coming year. At the buyer's conference the contractor was told that his performance had been excellent, and he could have a second year's contract. He was also told in no uncertain terms that if he wanted more work he would have to cut his price by at least 25%. He protested that he could not stay profitable at such a price, but the buyer knew well that with his new equipment and additional capacity the contractor needed the work. The lower price was finally accepted and the contractor set out to reduce manufacturing costs by cutting corners in his process. The result was a steady drop in quality until the reject rate was totally unacceptable, and in a few months the contractor was bankrupt and his plant closed. The computer company had intended to use this particular material in a new product, but was forced to halt production until it could find another supplier. Eventually it discovered one on the other side of the country, but the loss due to the delay in production was extremely high. When terms were finally agreed upon with the new supplier, the cost of the material was slightly higher than it had been under the original supplier's contract. The buyer could not be faulted in this case; his prime objective, he had been told, was to reduce the purchase price of every item he handled.

It is not usual for the purchasing people to have a close enough link with the shop floor to be able to make a judgment on the ultimate cost of the materials that they buy. It is assumed that the specification is adequate and that if the materials comply with the specification all will be well. Unfortunately this is not always true.

For example, at one company the specification permitted the use of different plastic materials for the housing of a connector block. The buyer was offered at lower cost a part that complied in every respect with the specification. Unfortunately, the plastic from which it was made dissolved in the solvent used in a later cleaning process. This was discovered only when assemblies began arriving at electrical test without the connector. It was initially believed that these parts had never been installed, and correcting the problem caused a considerable delay in production as well as a financial loss. If there had been closer communication between purchasing and manufacturing, this would probably not have occurred. The buyer had no idea of the processes through which these parts passed in the assembly of the product. When the problem was finally resolved, he commented that he would have discussed this with the vendor, but he had only the specification to work with and the parts complied with these requirements. In fact, he had been discouraged from getting out onto the shop floor as this was considered a waste of time and interference in the manufacturing responsibilities.

There are other items to be considered in the acquisition of materials for production. Obviously, the schedule is important, the way materials are shipped and packaged can affect the operation, and the time between the actual manufacture of the materials and their use on the shop floor may be critical. It will be almost impossible to guarantee that all of these various factors are included in any specification, even if they are recognized. A good knowledge of the manufacturing process can assist the purchasing agent in eliminating problems from these and other causes before they arise.

There is no place in the modern manufacturing plant for separation or isolation. We must always remember that almost every department in a manufacturing company is there solely to support manufacturing, and everyone is a part of the manufacturing process. Purchasing, accounting, and administration are only there because there is a product to be made and sold, and making it correctly must be the prime objective of everyone.

MATERIALS TESTING

It is pointless to develop purchasing specifications if the various parameters are not checked in some way to assure compliance. The most common method is to arrange for the materials to be tested, according to the specification, at the receiving inspection station.

This is frequently a site of contention, where different areas of manufacturing pull in different directions. As we have seen, the specifications ultimately have to be interpreted by human beings, each with his particular priorities and objectives that will bias his decisions. The receiving inspection people may believe that the quality of the product is riding on their testing and therefore will apply the specifications strictly and reject materials for the slightest infringement even if in practice it will have little or no effect on product quality. The manufacturing manager, on the other hand, may be more concerned with meeting the schedule and will be prepared to use materials that fail to meet the specification provided that they will enable him to complete production on time. The design team may not object to this latter concept provided that the product meets the technical specification. Thus, if we are not careful we can end up with conflict in the very area where we most need a universal approach to quality.

Here again, the basic cause of any conflict is our inability to write a clear specification that does not require interpretation by the vendor or the inspector. If, for example, we are buying bolts to put together a lawn mower, probably all we need specify is the diameter, the thread, and the head size and shape. Even if there is a variation, say in the thread or the length, it will be easily checked by using a standard nut or a simple jig at inspection. Although the possibility of disagreement is slight, there could be arguments if the bolt is just too short to meet the specification but can in fact hold together the parts of the lawn mower, and if no other bolts are available and the production schedule is in danger of being missed. If dissention can arise over such a simple product as a bolt, imagine how much argument can arise over a more complex item!

Consider a shaft for a machine that has very precisely ground sections to accommodate bearings, and the specification calls for a high finish in these areas. During visual inspection a defect in the finish of one of the bearing areas is found; as it contravenes the specification, the shaft must be rejected. The inspector, however, fits a bearing onto the shaft and finds that the defect will not affect the actual bearing surface. Now he has to make a decision.

- He can reject the shaft because it does not comply with the specified requirements.
- He can accept the shaft because he believes that it will function perfectly well.

If he rejects the shaft he will be following the rules of the specification; his decision cannot be faulted, but it will generate the cost of rejection, obtaining a replacement, rework, schedule delay, and so on.

If he accepts the shaft, he will be open to criticism from any later inspection because he passed material that did not meet the criteria. He may also have made an incorrect judgment and the defect may reduce the life of the bearing and cause a field failure. This type of dilemma is not unusual; if the inspector is not fully attuned to the process and has no formal way of obtaining help, he will almost certainly opt for personal safety and reject the part. If the part is very expensive or if it is urgently required, he may well be pressured to accept it. In other words, it is extremely difficult in the real world to clearly define the accept/reject criteria.

In this particular case it may well be that the specification requires changing. The vendor certainly needs to be approached to develop an action plan to eliminate this problem in future. If the shaft will function correctly, if it will not in any way affect the reliability of the product, it should certainly be used.

This example is not unique. Similar cases occur in almost every manufacturing plant. Specifications will not guarantee material quality unless used with intelligence, by trained personnel who understand the process.

VENDOR/BUYER RELATIONSHIP

A major part of controlling the manufacturing process, as we have seen, consists of controlling the quality of the materials used. In a few manufacturing fields, these consist of such items as ores, oil, wood, or other natural raw materials of which the producer has little or no effect on the quality. In most cases, however, the supplier is processing other materials to produce the parts that he sells to the manufacturer of the final product which will be supplied to the market place. Bearings, sheet or bar stock metals, nails, bolts, and other fasteners are simple examples that are widely used and whose requirements are usually simple enough to be selected from the catalog. Sometimes, however, certain qualities may be very important to the final product: bearing tolerances, metal purity, material strengths, and so on. In these cases the specification is used together with some form of testing as the basis for deciding if the materials are acceptable. We have also seen that neither of these tools is totally effective, and eventually we have to rely on the level of control exercised by the vendor to assure compliance with the specification and consistency in quality. We must always remember the following.

THE VENDORS MANUFACTURING PROCESS IS PART OF OUR OWN MANUFACTURING PROCESS AND MUST BE CONTROLLED IN THE SAME MANNER.

The vendor's plant is an extension of our own factory. It is unlikely that we can directly exercise control in our vendor's plant. However, we have to recognize the importance of excellent process control by the vendor in order to maintain a consistent quality level for the materials that we will buy and eventually incorporate into our own product.

We can apply some simple rules to help us in our day-to-day effort to obtain good materials.

- Carry out careful vendor surveys.
- Develop agreed upon quality and schedule objectives.
- Recognize that this is a partnership between purchaser and vendor, each must do his part.
- Understand that for the partnership to work there has to be personal contact on a regular basis.
- Recognize that the vendor has to make a profit.

These may all seem obvious items, and most people will agree that we have to get away from the old adversarial attitudes between vendor and buyer. Yet purchasing materials of consistently good quality still eludes many companies, although the old idea of "Buy from the lowest bidder" is fast disappearing.

It would be helpful if we could provide a simple list of things to look for and questions to ask when we carry out a vendor survey. But once again we have to remember that we are dealing through people, and this alone makes a simple listing impossible. There are some things to watch for, however.

- The vendor must have a recorded process; if it does not, there can be no control.
- The process has to be a living, used record as indicated by dated changes or similar evidence of current use.
- There has to be a formal method of training the personnel.
- There have to be formal data generated for process control purposes.
- There has to be overall process monitoring.

In other words, we must look at our vendor and expect to see all of the things that we have implemented to control our own manufacturing process. We have to be sure that these things actually exist and are not being supplied merely for window dressing. Such assessments require a good knowledge of the process that the vendor is using and the ability to check for technical accuracy.

For example, the author was carrying out a survey for a client and everything appeared to be well controlled in the vendor's operation. The operator, however, walked over to a plating tank and shook the plating rack. On being questioned, he said that he did so to make sure the contact was good. He could not tell why he selected that particular rack, and the supervisor explained that nothing could go wrong without its being visible on the panel meters. The operator said that although he had seen nothing he thought something might not be quite right. His comments now raised some doubt as to the effectiveness of the control system and the operator was questioned as to what the meters should read. It soon became obvious that the settings depended on the operator carrying out mental arithmetic to multiply the number of panels per rack by the given plating current per panel. Finally it was found that every rack was plated at the same current even though some had fewer panels than others. The currents were monitored and recorded by the computer, in this highly automated plant, but the records were only occasionally reviewed. There was no real time feedback of information; in fact, despite the automation and ready availability of data, there was no process control. This was reflected in the scrap and rework that became obvious when other areas of the plant were investigated.

This particular vendor had been surveyed before, but the survey had been carried out by quality control people who had no clear understanding of the process. The computers, and the automatic systems, were impressive and certainly gave the impression of a well-controlled operation. The quality of the material supplied by this vendor eventually forced a re-evaluation of his process. He was not attempting to confuse the issue, but in fact believed that he had a well-controlled manufacturing process and could not understand why he had such a high scrap rate.

A great deal of work had been put into the relationship with this vendor and several good personal friendships had been made on both sides. The president of the company really wanted to improve his operation both to retain business and to improve profitability. In this case the actions to be taken were obvious. The vendor was guided and helped to install good process control, his people were trained in simple statistical control techniques, the necessary feed back paths were set up, and the quality improved dramatically. These steps of course reinforced the already good relationships and each party saw clearly how they were linked together. Quickly the purchaser became so confident of the reliability of his vendor that all inspection of incoming material ceased, being replaced by random reviews of the process.

This example illustrates the personal side of the equation. A vendor may have none of the technical requirements of process control as listed above, but if there is a genuine desire to work together, if there is a real understanding of each other's problems, and if there is a real intent to produce a quality product, it is possible to arrive at a mutually acceptable and profitable relationship. No amount of automation, control charts, or computers can make up for old-fashioned trust and honesty. These are, and always have been, the keys to the successful acquisition of materials. People require skill, technical experience, and understanding to be able to make this evaluation.

Chapter 11

MANAGING THE BOSS

In almost every manufacturing operation the manager reports to someone with greater authority. It may be a close, informal, friendly relationship, in which the manager is personally responsible for carrying out detailed objectives that his boss routinely agrees with, but he is otherwise free to operate in his own style.

It may, however, be a more formal and impersonal association in which the manager has to work within a strictly defined corporate structure, as part of an organization responsible for achieving his boss's overall objective, which has been developed by an even higher authority. Whatever the relationship may be, it is unlikely that any manager is free to carry out his work without the overall consent and approval of another individual, the boss, who of course is only another manager at a higher level in the chain of authority. The way that the boss and the manager see each other, and their attitudes toward achieving the excellence that is necessary to operate an efficient manufacturing operation, will be critical for the success of the company.

COMMUNICATING WITH THE BOSS

The manager has to keep his boss informed. This may appear to be an obvious part of the manager's job, but it is amazing just how often this is not done. The manager may start out with every intention of keeping open a clear line of communication, but this can quickly deteriorate, especially when the boss is less than sympathetic. There will always be good and bad news to report to the boss, and when the bad news results in anger, temper, or some form of discipline, it is human nature to attempt to avoid this in the future. Bad news will be suppressed or at least delayed until the impact is lessened by time. In turn, even good news may be changed to cover up facts that are not to be disclosed, until eventually—instead of a steady flow of real time information—there will be carefully prepared communiques supplied only when necessary to avoid further inquiries, and real communication will cease entirely. Frequently neither party is aware that this breakdown has occurred until a major problem arises, and by then it is almost too late to recover the rapport necessary for people to work effectively together.

This unhappy result is not usually caused by a lack of skill on either side in the technical areas of management. It is more usually a result of the inability on the part of the boss to understand one of the most fundamental requirements of management, which is so often lacking today: leadership. In every level of supervision, the manager has a responsibility to those whom he manages, other than the technical needs. He has to educate, to train, and to provide support and understanding. A major part of this leadership consists of maintaining an excellent flow of information in both directions between manager and managed. Good news is a time of reward and congratulation; bad news is a time for discussion, training, and help.

COMMUNICATION SKILLS

Unfortunately, the skills of communication do not appear to be taught effectively in our management and technical educational systems. All too often the newly appointed manager does not realize the importance of open communications both up and down the organizational ladder. The young engineer is frequently unable to present information to his boss in a plain unambiguous manner. It is often difficult to arrive at the facts when investigating a manufacturing problem because no one has thought about them clearly and simply, and those who have find it difficult to put them into easily understood speech or writing. Gobble-de-gook and fancy words confuse the issues; jargon and the technical shorthand phrases provide excellent opportunities for misinterpretation. This is a pity; the English language is both expressive and accurate if used correctly. Long words and fashionable slang may initially make the user look clever, but usually they merely hide a mind that is incapable of clear thinking.

The answer is obvious: everyone in the chain of command must be able to communicate easily and unambiguously, in words that are simple and easily understood. Few of us have the time to attempt to interprete the meaning behind a long-winded and muddled memo, which is frequently even more complicated by irrelevant details. These skills can be taught and do not demand a PhD in the English language. Much more important is training that encourages clear thinking and simple unambiguous writing and speaking. For example, lets look at the following quotation from a military specification regarding the illumination required for a magnifier.

> The magnifying device's light source shall provide illumination on the area of interest for at least two directions at least 80 degrees apart so that no shadows fall on the area of interest from objects in the field of view that are not of prime interest.

Would it not suffice to say that "The light source must provide shadow-free illumination"? Yet this type of verbosity fills our documents. It sometimes seems as if we are afraid to say simply and clearly what we mean. The factory environment is a busy place: neither the boss nor the manager has time to sit and wonder what is the real meaning of a report either verbal or written.

THE BOSS AS DICTATOR

All too often, when changes are suggested to make an operation more effective, they are opposed on the grounds that "I don't have the authority to do that," "My boss does not believe in that," or similar excuses. The suggestion that we approach the boss to explain the need for these changes and enlist his help, is likewise rejected, and it becomes apparent that there is little or no communication between these individuals. The boss gives the orders; the manager follows them exactly. The penalty for opposing or questioning these orders in any way, is to be disciplined or perhaps in extreme cases to be demoted or even fired. These extreme responses from the boss are fortunately comparatively rare. However, the attitude behind them is much more common, and the manager has to understand how to attack this problem.

The first step must be to provide the boss with all the information necessary to make a sound judgment. This includes the bad news as well as the good, the disadvantages of a certain method or machine or other approach as well as the advantages. This information must not only be impartial but also appear to be impartial. The boss knows that when you are proposing a particular item that you wish to implement you have a personal desire to gain approval. If you do not demonstrate impartiality he will immediately become suspicious of the honesty of the entire proposal.

The information must be presented simply, you should avoid long words and complex technical terms. The boss is a busy man, he has many problems to consider, and yours is only one of them. If you do not make your ideas clear and straightforward, if they are not presented in a way that will impact his memory, they may be lost in the mass of information that bombards him all day long. This reality was expressed strongly by a manufacturing vice president at a certain factory when he was asked why he had not considered carrying out some actions proposed by his manufacturing manager. "All day long I have people coming to me and suggesting this or that should be done, and I would never have time to consider anything if I did not shut my ears to all the informal comments."

If the response to a particular proposal or request is not the one desired, the manager must express his concern to his boss and there must be some discussion on the differences of opinion. The boss has to be prepared to explain to the manager the reasons for his decision, and the manager must in turn explain to his boss his concerns regarding the effects of his boss's decision. Each side must understand clearly the ideas and reasoning of the other. If a solution that is acceptable to both cannot be reached, the boss will almost certainly have his way.

In this case the manager has to face reality. Either he has to accept the decision and work with it as effectively as if it were his own, or find other work with a different boss. Certainly he can go over his boss's head, but this will never work out in the long run because the confidence and authority of the boss will have been so damaged that there will be little possibility of ever arriving at an effective relationship. The boss as dictator therefore is doomed from the very beginning. Either the manager will merely carry out the boss's instructions without question, or he will give up and move on. In both cases any talents the manager may have will be wasted.

THE "NO DECISION" BOSS

Manufacturing is an ongoing process. We rarely have the option to stop or slow down, and when problems arise prompt action becomes vitally important. The "No Decision" boss usually lacks knowledge of the process and is therefore uncomfortable with his authority and fearful of making an incorrect decision. These failings in turn often lead to suspicion of those who have the necessary skills and knowledge and therefore to ineffective allocation of authority, in which even the smallest decisions have to receive the boss's blessing.

Inevitably this delays decision making, or the responsibility for making any decision is spread over several people and no one has the overall authority. In this way the "No Decision" boss can believe that he is doing something, without committing himself to a single course of action. There is always an opportunity to retract or change course and place the blame on someone else.

If the manufacturing manager has a clear knowledge of the process, is supported by good people, and is prepared to sieze such authority as may come his way, not only can he survive, but he can even thrive in this political environment. If he can demonstrate to the boss that he is willing and able to help him understand the process, support him in the day-to-day operation of the plant, and at least defer in principle, he will probably find that the boss is happy to let him make the decisions. This is not the best situation because in practice the manager is doing the work of the boss without his authority and without any clear backing. However, it is better than letting problems drift on without seizing the opportunity to correct them, for this will inevitably lead to placing blame on the manager.

The danger here, of course, is that the boss is unlikely to back up the manager if he makes a mistake. The boss will see the manager as a scapegoat for any blame that arises. The manager will have to spend time and effort making his position safe; he will have to accumulate evidence to support any of his actions that have not been comfirmed by the boss and will always feel in jeopardy. This is not a situation likely to encourage innovation or change on the part of the manager.

THE AVERAGE BOSS

The boss is human and it is unlikely that he will exhibit any single characteristic or management style. He will probably vary in attitude depending on any particular situation, and the way in which he views his manufacturing manager. In the same way that the manager's approach to his people will affect the way that they work with him, so his approach to his boss will affect their relationship. In both cases it is quite impossible to lay down hard and fast rules as to any particular method or style of management that will be effective. Here, of course, lies the difficulty of management.

We can discuss the various types of boss, but the manager must be able to vary his approach to the boss depending on the specific situation. Understanding some of the boss's problems in the particular environment of your plant can provide a useful guide. After all, the boss's problems will eventually become your problems. It is a simplification to say that the manager's chief job is to keep the boss happy, but ultimately the boss must be happy with your work or it will be impossible to continue the relationship.

One of the best tools is the development of objectives in clear, measurable terms. This provides a base on which to build the relationship without the conflict of personalities. It stimulates discussion, and it provides a clear indication of what the boss wants and expects from the manager. There will undoubtedly be the budget, the schedule, and the value of shipments to provide a measurable base, but these may not be sufficient. In one case a manager clearly had some problem in his dealings with his boss; in fact, their constant state of friction was materially affecting the performance of the department. As the manager was performing extremely well when measured by the budget, schedule, and shipments, there seemed to be nothing for the boss to criticize. The friction was always over very simple things that became blown out of proportion. During discussion it came to light that this boss had a strong feeling about his people staying in the plant after normal hours. He felt that this showed concern for the company's well being, and allowed an opportunity for them and him to chat and discuss the day's work. The manager, on the other hand, prided himself on his ability to schedule both his own and his people's work so that they could get out of the plant at the end of the working day. He believed that they needed to relax so that they could start fresh the next morning. These views were of course diametrically opposed and bound to cause friction. They were resolved when the boss and the manager sat down and prepared detailed objectives. One was that each week time was allocated for the boss and the manager to meet and discuss subjects of common interest. They agreed that the meeting would be after normal working hours.

LIVING WITH THE BOSS

The boss is a part of our working life; we have to make up our minds that we will live with this. If we like our boss, if we can work with him, if he is fair, if his demands are not excessive, if he provides the necessary leadership, we are fortunate and will probably enjoy an excellent relationship.

If there are differences in attitudes or if we believe that he is unfair or unjust, we have two choices. Either we approach the boss, discuss the problem, and arrive at a solution satisfactory to both, or we must move to another job. Temporarily we can do as the boss says even if we feel disgruntled, upset, or put upon, but this is no way to live and it must never be allowed to become the normal way of working together. Unless there is understanding, respect, and honesty in the boss/manager relationship, an efficient operation cannot exist.

Chapter 12

FACTS, STATISTICS, AND CHARTS

The control of any process demands facts—facts regarding the product quality, facts regarding the performance of machines and equipment, facts regarding the materials being used, facts regarding the operator's skills and efficiency. Facts are of no value unless they are presented in such a manner that they can be easily used, either to confirm that the process is performing correctly or to initiate corrective or preventive actions.

Several aspects of the generation of these important data must be considered very carefully.

- The information must be accurate.
- The facts must be current.
- The data must be presented in a manner that is easily understood.

These items may appear at first glance to be obvious, but all too often they are not given the attention that they should have. Let's consider first the question of accurate, factual data. For example, an operator is required once every operating hour to set a control, read the position of a pointer on the dial of a meter, and write up the reading in a logbook that is reviewed weekly by the quality control engineer.

These steps seems straightforward, but we should consider the possible areas of error.

- Can the operator set the control exactly, or is there some unavoidable error in making the adjustment? If it involves moving a pointer or a knob over a dial, there will certainly be some variation. The degree of error must be known. Either it is so small that it can be ignored or it must be considered when the data are used.

- What is the error factor of the meter? There will always be some small error in reading the meter. There will be some small inaccuracy in the actual meter itself. If these errors are not known, the accuracy of all the information will be in doubt.
- Will the operator be able to make the reading exactly on the hour every hour or will there be some variation in the time frame? Is this timing important?
- Finally, will the operator write down the reading correctly every time?

It may well be that none of these small errors will have any affect on the process, but it is just as possible that they may mask a problem because of the inherent inaccuracy of the data. Here is a case in which, what at first appears to be facts may possibly be the operator's interpretation of the facts. If this is a critical area, we can use digital switches and meters to avoid reading errors and an automatic printout to prevent incorrect recording of the data. Thus, the only errors will be those of the system.

If these data are to be reviewed weekly by the quality control engineer, we may well ask why they are being recorded at all. The engineer may use them to find the cause of some past product defect, but they are out of date and unlikely to be of any value in preventing a problem from growing into a full blown disaster. Here is a prime example of the way data should not be used. They are a list of numbers in a logbook. They are not easily used or understood. They are not used by the people carrying out the operation who can affect the outcome of the process.

GENERATING FACTUAL DATA

As we have seen from the example given above, developing accurate data is more exacting than writing down information. Certainly this is a beginning and in many cases may be adequate, but before accepting this form of data acquisition we must ask some questions.

- What inaccuracies will be present in the data?
- Can these be quantified?
- Are they large enough to be important?
- What precautions are necessary to prevent them from varying?

Some typical inaccuracies, as we have seen, may be in the measuring instruments themselves, and in the ability of the operator to read them accurately. The variations may be very small: the instrument, for example, may have an accuracy of 0.1%, and by carrying out some experiments it may be possible to set the maximum operator inaccuracy in reading the instrument to say 0.2%. If this will not have any affect on the outcome of the process—if, for example, we find that any variation of less than 0.8% has no discernable effect—the measuring accuracy is adequate.

In this situation the measuring instruments will have to be regularly checked for accuracy, but it may not be necessary to record the actual readings provided that they stay within certain predetermined figures.

The accuracy of this form of data is not difficult to determine. Some other forms of the data generation are much less easily controlled. A prime example is obtaining information from visual inspection. All too often the ultimate control data for our process come from inspecting the product and reporting any variations from a standard. Unless the inspectors are carefully trained and can inspect with intelligence and understanding, the data may be biased or, in extreme cases, totally incorrect. With this type of inspection there is a natural tendency for the inspectors to report what they believe to be the problem rather than what they actually see. For example, if a fastening is loose, the inspector may report "Fastener not tightened" rather than "Loose fastener." The former report points to a problem in the actual tightening of the fastener, while the latter leaves the cause open for investigation. The former may point in a totally incorrect direction and divert attention from any other possible reason for the problem. It may well be that the fastener itself is out of tolerance—it may have loosened after being correctly tightened. This is an extremely simple example; with more complex systems the difficulties grow. The terms to be used in this form of data generation must be carefully defined so that the information can be used correctly in determining the actions necessary to eliminate the basic cause of the problem.

A prime example is found in the electronics industry, where solder joint inspection is used as a control measure of the machine soldering process. A typical defect terminology that is unfortunately taught in some training programs is "Insufficient solder." While working on improving soldering efficiency in one particular plant, the author had this reported as being the chief problem, amounting to over 75% of the defective solder joints. Because this term is of itself meaningless the inspectors were each asked to show an example of what they considered to be "Insufficient solder." The results were astounding, as no two inspectors indicated the same problem. It required a re-training program for the inspectors before it was possible to obtain data that were accurate enough to show where to eliminate the cause of the defects.

A similar problem can arise in the materials area if the reasons for rejection are not clearly defined and are not agreed upon between vendor and buyer. What may be called acceptable surface variations by the vendor can be defined as unacceptable scratches by the receiving inspector. As we discussed in Chapter 10, these requirements are not always definable, and will inevitably require judgment.

Thus, facts may not always be as factual as we imagine, and when these very facts are to be used in controlling the process, we must always ask ourselves just how much we can trust the facts.

STATISTICS AND STATISTICAL CONTROL

When we operate the manufacturing process, it usually becomes necessary to apply some form of statistical control in order to maintain the quality of our product. If this is to be a level high enough to be acceptable in the market place, it is useless to inspect one or two items and from this attempt to determine the quality of production. Rather we have to inspect many pieces, we have to obtain information regarding field failures, we may have to tear down parts on a routine basis for inspection, we may have to carry out some form of stress testing. We will therefore end up with a great deal of data, of varying accuracy, that we must manipulate to provide us the necessary information to control the process, improve the quality, and reduce the costs. This is the basis of statistical control.

Unfortunately, there is a great deal of misunderstanding regarding the nature of statistics. They are often looked upon and talked about as if they were hard facts. Of course, the truth is that statistics are a form of educated guesswork and always involve an element of uncertainty, which often leads to incorrect conclusions. Statistics are a way of estimating the odds of any particular occurrence.

For example, in checking the quality of in-coming materials we may decide to use some form of sample testing to reduce the amount of work required. We turn to a set of statistical sampling tables telling us that if we can accept no more than 1% defective parts we must test a sample of 350 pieces from a particular lot and there must be no more than one defect in that sample. It is often assumed that if only one defect is found this guarantees that there will be no more than 1% defective parts in the entire lot. But let's consider some of the possibilities. Suppose the manufacturer of the parts has excellent process control in his plant, his parts are all good, but the one part that failed had accidentally fallen on the floor, was damaged, and unfortunately was put back into the main lot of parts. The overall failure rate will then be much lower than 1%, indeed, except for the part that was tested the remainder will be of excellent quality.

On the other hand, suppose that there were many defective parts, but they were all placed at one end of the package and only good parts from the other end of the box were used for the test. No defects were found and the quality was therefore assumed to be excellent with a defect rate of less than 1%. In fact, the defect level was considerably greater than the forecasted level of 1%, with many parts failing in production. This is not to suggest that the use of sampling as a control tool is ineffective. It does point out that whenever we use statistics we must recognize that the figures we derive are not hard and fast facts but educated guesses based on current knowledge and accuracy of the data on which the guesses are made.

In the case mentioned above, if the parts for testing are randomly selected, if they are representative of the entire lot of parts, the sampling tables will provide an excellent guide to the quality that can be expected. But we should note that the tables are not lists of facts that can be guaranteed to apply in every situation. They provide useful information on the probable failure rate based on the mathematical analysis of previous experience.

If we are to obtain the maximum use of statistics, we must start with good data of known accuracy. We must understand the limitations of statistical methods and statistical control and always be aware that we are not dealing with clearly defined facts but with implications based on the factual data. Statistics enable us to imply certain facts about part of, or the total process. It will not tell us what will happen to any single product.

STATISTICAL EXPERIMENTS

When the process contains many variables and it is necessary to refine these variables and arrive at the optimum figure for each, there are several ways of arriving at this ideal.

1. We can "fiddle" with the process, trying this and that until we find something that works. This is rarely successful and usually only engenders the idea that any problem can be eliminated by enough "fiddling."

2. We can set up controlled experiments in which we fix all parameters except one and vary this in a controlled manner, carefully recording the results. The next parameter is then varied in the same way, and so on until each one has been checked. This is the most widely used method and is usually satisfactory if only a few parameters are involved. With many variables, however, this can be a lengthy procedure, and unless the parameters vary smoothly over their entire

range the optimum can still be missed. Suppose, for example, that we have only four parameters in our process, each varying from 1 to 10. In developing the correct settings three are set at 5 while the fourth is swung between 1 and 10. This alone would require 40 measurements. If one parameter is flat over most of its range but suddenly peaks at a setting of 9 when the others are all set at 2, it is unlikely that this form of testing will arrive at the optimum unless a long and complex testing program is instituted (Figure 20). If more parameters have to be checked, this type of testing becomes virtually impossible.

3. We can use statistical experiments. In this case we can use a form of statistical experimentation in which the parameters are varied according to a definite plan based on the so called "Factorial Design" developed by an Englishman, R.A. Fisher, in the 1920s.

Although originally developed for use in the agricultural environment, factorial designed statistical experiments have been applied to many fields of engineering. Correctly used, this technique can materially reduce the time to develop the optimum parameters for a process, or to investigate processing

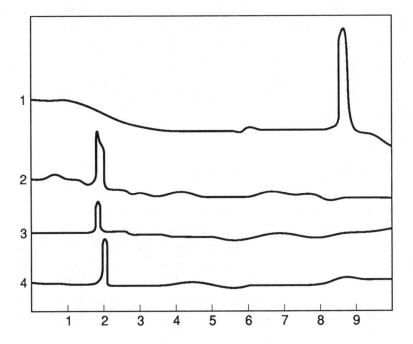

Figure 20   It is unlikely that simple experimentation will find the optimum settings for this four-variable process.

problems. Planning and operating these experiments are not easy; they must be done correctly and with care or the results will be useless. They require carefully developed accurate data and expert interpretation.

RESEARCH

This form of experimentation should not be used indiscriminately or without first fully researching the process being developed. A young engineer presented a paper at a technical conference describing how he had used statistical experiments to develop the operating parameters for a particular process. It had taken him six months, at the end of which, as he proudly explained, he had the process so well developed that his defect rate was no more than 2,000 PPM. If he had only taken the time to research the process a little more closely, he would have found that it was so well documented that his experiments were totally unnecessary and he could have arrived at a much smaller defect rate in a matter of hours, not months.

In a similar vein several philosophies of statistical analysis, methods, and control are publicized in the technical press. They all suggest that they have something new to offer; in fact, some are touted as the answer to all our quality problems. Basically, they all highlight some failure in our management or engineering functions and offer a structured method of improving our operation and eliminating some of our problems. They certainly work under some circumstances, but they are not a universal panacea, nor do they avoid following the standard good practices of engineering and management.

CHARTS AND OTHER VISUAL AIDS

Raw data may not be easy to assimilate and are usually put into some form that is supposed to make them easy to interpret. Unfortunately, they are often put into a form even more difficult to understand than the initial information. Some of the problems arise from the very methods that are taught as part of the more complex forms of statistical control. We can easily fall into the trap of overcomplexity if we use these methods indiscriminately and without thought. We should always keep in mind that information is useless unless it is used and can be used easily.

While troubleshooting a problem at a manufacturing plant, the author asked for any available data regarding the process. It so happened that there was a complete department whose only job was the collection, development, and distribution of process control data. The three people in this department were busy with their computers and printers and produced a variety of charts. The first thing of note was that almost all of the information was at least one week old, because "It takes us a week to put all the data together and produce the charts." The charts were so complex, even for the display of some simple data, that help was required to understand what was being charted. The charts had been designed in this way by the quality control engineers, who had responsibility for this department, because "The quality control manager likes to see them this way." When some of the data were questioned, it quickly became evident that no one really knew if they were accurate or not; indeed, on scrutiny they were found to be quite useless in many areas. The completed charts were sent to the company president and vice presidents, they were used by the marketing department to convince customers that they did indeed have process control, and a set was pinned up on a notice board in each production area.

No one on the shop floor used the information; in fact, the charts were something of a joke among the operators and supervisors, who had developed their own simple but effective method of recording the necessary information to control the process.

Do not fall into this type of trap. Simple data should be presented simply; discuss with the users the best way of providing the information. Often a simple bar chart or graph will be adequate. Given the low cost of computers you might consider using a good data base with terminals for the various people needing the information. Not only can they then view it in almost any format they wish, but they can also manipulate the various sets of data in the manner most useful to them.

There are some simple rules regarding statistical control data.

- The information must be current.
- The accuracy of the data must be known.
- The data must be presented in a format that is easily understood by anyone.
- The data must be used.
- If special charts are needed to keep marketing or the company president happy, preparing them should be a separate function.

There are also some simple rules for using statistical controls to manage the manufacturing process.

- Understand the process in every detail before installing any form of statistical control.
- Decide where any variability may occur, what will cause the variations, and where they will first become evident.

- Set up a procedure to monitor the variation at the point where it will first be discovered.
- Set up a feedback path from the point of discovery to the area where the variation is caused.
- Develop a procedure to take corrective action when any variability is found.
- Set aside the resources to eliminate the causes of variation.
- Train everyone in the operation to recognize the objectives of the control system and understand how they are to be achieved.
- Keep everything as simple as possible. Never complicate what is essentially a simple and obvious method of assuring a high quality product, made on schedule at the lowest overall cost.

Chapter 13

STRIVING FOR EXCELLENCE

When the author wrote an article called "A Pattern for Excellence," which was published in *Printed Circuit Assembly,* there was no thought that it would trigger off this book. However, the enthusiastic response to it suggested that there was indeed a desire by many managers to be able to determine the present status of their operation, and to attempt to see where it would be in the future.

The article simply described the visible and outward signs of the degree of excellence of the manufacturing process as seen by the author in the electronics industry. It is, of course, equally applicable to most other assembly and light manufacturing operations. The article included many of the items already discussed in this book, such as housekeeping, clearly defined process steps, and good training. It suggested that these outward signs could be used by a manager to assess the excellence of his own operation. The following is an extract from the original article.

The Common Pattern for Excellence*

Companies that have attained excellence are easy to identify because they have many of the following factors in common. There is no intent to place these in order of importance but rather in the order by which they are most visible.

1. *Housekeeping Is Excellent.* This does not require expensive factory furniture or fittings, but a consistent effort to see that there is a place for everything and everything is always in it's place. Benches are clean and not littered, materials in the proper containers. No loose parts lying around, machines and tools clean and well maintained.

---

*Printed by permission of *Printed Circuit Assembly* (PMS Industries).

2. *Formal Process Documentation.* Materials, tools and assembly methods are all defined and documented in a formal manner and all personnel work exactly to these instructions.

3. *Engineering Availability.* Manufacturing Engineers are always available on the shop floor. They determine the process steps and produce the process documentation. They are immediately available when a problem arises.

4. *Adequate Formal Training.* All persons are taught how to carry out their work in every detail. They are shown the theory of the task and why things have to be done in a certain way. Training is constantly upgraded and retraining provided at regular intervals.

5. *Management Is Technically Knowledgeable.* All managers have an excellent understanding of the processes, equipments and product under their charge. They are found frequently on the shop floor, listening, observing. They are not isolated by reports and statistics.

6. *A Formal Corrective Action Program.* Defects in the product are seen as an indication of an out of control process which must immediately be corrected. Inspection is seen as a process control tool not as a method of sorting good product from bad.

7. *Continuous Operator Participation.* Shop floor personnel are given every opportunity to present their opinions and ideas in free, open discussion.

8. *Close Design/Assembly Interface.* The design team is well versed in the processes to be used and designs the products accordingly. It is seen that assembly quality and efficiency begins with excellence in design.

9. *Total Cost Considerations.* When parts are specified or purchased the overall assembly cost is calculated, not the individual cost of the part. Purchasing is an accepted part of the assembly team.

10. *"Right First Time" Philosophy.* There is an overall agreement by both management and shop floor that "Doing the job right the first time" is the only acceptable way of working.

The list from the article was a first attempt to qualify excellence from the outward appearance of the factory floor and the organization found there. If we intend to improve the efficiency of our process or even if we merely want to find out where we stand in the manufacturing process ratings, we have to have some way of measuring the current operation.

MEASURING WHERE WE STAND

There are, of course, traditional indicators of productivity, for example, material and labor costs, overhead charges, quality index and so on. Almost every operation has targets of this type which the manufacturing manager has to meet. But these do not appear to be, by themselves, an adequate, overall measure of the health of the operation. Every manager has experienced the almost intuitive feeling that all is not well with the process although all of the indicators described above suggest the reverse. One of the problems is that most of the statistics tell us a lot about what has already happened but can only suggest what will happen in the future. We can at best assume that the same results will continue to be obtained as long as the current production continues.

The budget may show that the figure for direct labor is well under target, that overheads are being controlled, and that material costs have not been exceeded. Everything is apparently going well and according to plan. However, suppose that our process is not well controlled and that sitting in stores is a batch of material that does not meet its specification. Or suppose that a new operator has been hired but has not been properly trained, a machine has been missed from the regular maintenance program and is not performing correctly, or an operator is using an incorrect tool.

Soon production is being held up because the products will not pass the final test. Engineers are troubleshooting to find the cause of the failures, rather than improving the process. A decision has to be made whether to continue manufacturing and attempt to rework the products or to stop work until the problem has been solved. Cost and schedule are impacted and suddenly what had appeared to be a well-ordered and efficient program lies in shambles. Although any lack of process control is not usually as disastrous as this, it is far from rare to see this kind of result. It more often arises as one small problem following another, such that the organization stumbles along rather than operating smoothly, never quite able to get away from the day-to-day difficulties.

We then find ourselves in a "catch 22" situation, where effort is directed toward the "Band-Aid" solution because there is not enough time and effort to be able to get to the root of the problem and eliminate it. This failing of course only generates more problems and demands more effort merely to keep products moving out of the plant. Inevitably, process improvement and planning for the future suffer.

These standard methods of measuring the well-being of the operation will certainly be effective in showing how well we have done, but will not necessarily provide the information needed to forecast how well the production will fare in the future. To do so demands that we consider other functions of the operation which are not so easily measured. It is probably because of the difficulty of assessing future performance in terms of dollars and cents, or of days and hours, that process efficiency is so rarely included in the forecasts of future operations.

Assessing future performance is similar to attempting to forecast the exact time it will take to drive between one city and another. From the performance of our car on past trips we will know that it is capable of an average speed of 50 miles per hour and we know that the distance between the cities is 200 miles.

Thus it is reasonable to estimate that the trip will take four hours, but this will be contingent on several other factors. The car must continue to be capable of the same performance, it must have sufficient gas, it must not break down, the driver must be competent, and the roads must be adequate and the weather good. The past performance is important, but it is only a part of the information necessary to determine the future capability, although the first thing to be decided is whether the car is in fact capable of the speed and duration required to make the trip on schedule if everything else is correct.

In a similar way, the past performance of the manufacturing operation is important as it indicates the capability of that organization. It says that if all else is correct the operation is capable of performing at least no worse than that already recorded. Thus, in order to find out where our particular operation stands, we must first look at its immediate past performance. This provides a basic datum level against which we can monitor progress.

We then have to ask ourselves if our process control is good enough to maintain this level of quality, cost, and schedule. We should review the factors described in the sections on process development and process control.

- Is the process defined in detail?
- Are all of the materials controlled?
- Is the process control effective?
- Are all the operators properly trained?
- Are machines and tools properly maintained?
- Is the control data presented in a simple and timely manner?
- Does it go to the right people?
- Is it used effectively?
- Is there a formal corrective action program?
- Is there effective participation by everyone?

If the responses to the reviews are positive, we should feel reasonably confident that the operation will continue to perform in the same way with the same results. Because we have good process control, we have repeatability and our product quality and costs will be constant. If we can provide the facilities necessary to manufacture the volume of product forecast, we should be able to produce with the same efficiency.

THE SEARCH FOR PERFECTION

The next question to ask is whether this level of efficiency is acceptable. Unless the performance is perfect the answer must always be "NO." Even if the operation is performing in a totally acceptable manner, it is asking for disaster to rest on one's laurels. There must always be a striving for better and better performance.

IF WE AIM FOR PERFECTION WE WILL PROBABLY HAVE A GOOD OPERATION. IF WE AIM FOR LESS WE WILL, AT BEST, ACHIEVE MEDIOCRITY.

"Striving for perfection" is a phrase that is often bandied about in manufacturing and management literature, and we must consider exactly what it means in the context of controlling and improving the manufacturing process. We aim to manufacture a product of the highest quality at the lowest possible cost by operating a completely developed process, using materials that meet the process requirements, and including an effective form of process monitoring and improvement. Thus, striving for perfection means that we must make absolutely sure that the process is followed exactly in every detail. Nothing is ever "Good enough"; either it is right or it is unacceptable.

This philosophy calls for discipline both from management and operators. It calls for monitoring every step of the process in some detail; it demands the generation of data not only to determine if the process is in control but also to make continuous improvements. Only by checking on the presence of these items and assessing how well they perform can we decide if the operation will perform efficiently and with constant improvement in the future.

- Are all levels of management and supervision totally conversant with the process?
- Is the process adequately controlled?
- During the past year has every case of process failure been contained promptly and the cause eliminated in a timely manner?
- Have the control procedures, in every case, been improved to prevent a reoccurrence?
- Does everyone know exactly what to do when the process fails?
- Is the field failure rate of the product measured?
- Is there a formal program to review every failure and eliminate the cause?
- Are the process and the product constantly monitored for possible improvement?
- Have there been steady improvements in productivity during the past year?

These questions must be part of the managers constant concern. By looking for the answers the manager will be forced to dig into his operation. The value of the answers will be determined by the degree of honesty and detail that he puts into finding them. If he can say that all of these responses are positive, the operation will not only be successful it will also continuously improve. This of course is in direct contrast to the more usual procedure for process improvement, of setting cost reduction targets or efficiency objectives and then forcing the operation to meet the targets. This tactic inevitably leads to manipulating the figures, or making reductions that will look good on paper but may not be effective when the overall costs are collected. It may also reduce reliability, or push the cost onto another department.

EXCELLENCE IN PEOPLE

Henry Ford made a statement to the effect that even if his factories, his machines, and his money were all taken away, if his people were left he would be back in business within a year. He recognized very well that people were the real strength of his operation. The same thing applies today: our manufacturing strength lies in our people. Yet all too often we use them inefficiently; we fail to provide an environment in which they can use their talents effectively and in which they can find satisfaction with their work.

Whenever labor problems arise, it is common to blame the workers, or the unions, and they in turn frequently blame unsatisfactory wage scales, medical benefits, or some other part of their compensation. These are, however, excuses. Certainly every worker deserves and wants to be fairly paid and receive fringe benefits that are comparable with others in similar jobs, but this is far from the whole story. It is an oversimplification to say that a company gets the labor relationships that it deserves, but it is certainly not far from the truth.

Most of us spend forty or more hours each week in our work. If this work is not seen as being useful, if the individual does not feel that he is an important part of the production team, the forty hours will seem wasted—only something to get through as quickly as possible and with as little effort as can be spared. This attitude will not produce an efficient workforce or a quality product, and it will have been caused by the way in which we have organized and used our people. This is the responsibility of management.

Most people want to do a good job; they want to be proud of the items that they make and the skills that they possess. The more that we can encourage that pride, the more effective is our workforce.

Excellence in our people therefore has two aspects: first, the skills that our people possess, and second, the way that we use those skills. We can enhance the first by training and by recognizing the need for continuously updating the knowledge of our employees. We can use those skills most efficiently when we arrange for our people to use their brains as well as their hands, when we provide adequate communication channels and then listen to their ideas and act upon them. Nothing is more frustrating to any worker than to feel that he has no possible way of improving the efficiency of his operation, and that he has no way of communicating with those who make the decisions that can affect his future.

Therefore, in attempting to assess our present operation, we have to ask the following questions.

- Do your people readily make suggestions for process or oganizational improvements?
- Do you act promptly on their suggestions?
- Are there free and honest discussions between shop floor people, supervisors, and management?
- Is your operation free from labor problems?
- Do all employees know the objectives of the company for the coming years?
- Do they have an opportunity to suggest changes to these objectives?
- Do you respect your people?
- Do you show your respect and do your people know how you feel about their work?

MANAGING FOR CHANGE

As discussed earlier in this book, the only thing that we can be sure of is change, and in attempting to measure our ability to produce effectively in the future we have to ask if we have planned effectively to manage change. Thus, the manufacturing manager must have a good knowledge of what he will be expected to manufacture. This demands excellent communications with the people who will decide what the future production will be, and the manager then has to dig deeply into his organization and ask more questions.

- Are there regular meetings between design and marketing?
- Are all new designs approved by manufacturing?
- Is the manufacturing engineering department adequately staffed?
- Are engineers kept up to date by attending seminars and exhibitions, and joining technical societies?
- Are employees encouraged to become more highly skilled and knowledgeable?
- Are there excellent communications between departments?
- Is adequate time allocated for development of new product process?

• Are any new techniques or technologies proposed for manufacturing in the future?

These factors will be more important than any figures of estimated labor content relative to a new product. The figures are excellent tools, but the items listed above tell us whether we have the skills ready to use the tools.

SUMMARY

How easy management would be if there were direct rules that could be applied to tell us just how well or badly our operation is functioning. There are many methods of measuring how well we have done in the past, but even these figures frequently tell us only part of the story. For example, at one plant the cost and schedule figures were excellent; indeed, they had exceeded all management targets. Unfortunately, in order to satiate the great god "Schedule," some parts that did not quite meet their specification were used in production. Some hurriedly carried-out testing had showed that they worked, but the first unit failed in the field after a few months in service, followed by a second a few days later. The failure was total—in fact, it was quite dramatic, causing a small fire—and eventually every unit made with parts from that particular batch had to be replaced. The cost ran well over one million dollars and the damage to the company's reputation almost caused a financial disaster. According to the accounting data at the end of the production year, the manufacturing operation had performed superbly. The figures themselves can never be more than a guide to excellence.

If that particular company had been working toward excellence, the faulty parts would not have been used, and the schedule would have been met in some other way. If there were some belief that the parts could be used without causing quality problems, the testing should have been adequate to confirm the decision. The process will not be controlled if we ever accept second best. Excellence must always be the ultimate goal.

In order to look into the future, we have to consider some factors that are even much more difficult to measure. Indeed, in every operation the manufacturing manager will have to look into his own organization and see how well he has planned for the development, the operation, and the control of the process. This assessment regards not only the hardware, but also the availability of skills, people, time, and facilities. It also assumes considering other items that are extremely difficult to assess: the motivation of the people, the team spirit, the attention to detail, the many factors both large and small that can affect the outcome of the operation. They can range from the selection

PLANNING THE FUTURE
BREAK DOWN TASKS
INTO MEASUREABLE SECTIONS
✳✳✳✳✳✳✳✳✳✳✳✳✳✳✳✳✳✳✳✳✳✳✳✳✳✳✳✳✳✳✳✳✳✳✳

OBJECTIVE.
Installation of new Mfg. Eng. Laboratory by Nov. 30th.
Overall responsibility. John Smith, M.E. Mgr.
✳✳✳✳✳✳✳✳✳✳✳✳✳✳✳✳✳✳✳✳✳✳✳✳✳✳✳✳✳✳✳✳✳✳

Layout completed by June 30th. Jack Jones.

Layout agreed with management by July 14th.
John Smith, M.E. Mgr.

Equipment details to Purchasing by July 21st.
Jack Jones.

P.O.s placed by July 25th. T. Hinter.

Water and power installed by July 30th. H. Wouk.

Gas and compressed air installed by
Aug. 7th. H. Wouk.

Flooring completed by Aug. 12th. Jack Jones.

Furniture and fittings installed by Sept. 15th.
Tim Hoh.

Painting completed by Sept. 30th. Jack Jones.

Equipment tested and approved, lab to be
completely ready for operation by Oct. 15th.
John Smith.

Opening ceremony by President Nov. 30th
organized by Charles Wittern.

Figure 21   All tasks must be broken down into simple measureable sections. This step seems so obvious yet is frequently not done, and the result is schedule and cost problems.

and purchase of a new machine to the provision of a notice board on the line, from developing a no smoking policy to fitting better lighting on a work bench. They may include sending an engineer on a course to learn a new technology, or rearranging working hours. It is only when the manager is convinced that all these types of requirements have been reviewed with his people and covered in his plans, that he can feel comfortable and ready for the future.

- There must always be a plan for the future.
- It must be a clearly written plan with everyone's task simply defined.
- Every task must be broken down into measurable items with a scheduled completion date and the name of the responsible individual (Figure 21).
- The plan should be definite for the near future, say the coming three months.
- It will be less and less definitive as the time span increases.
- It should cover three to five years and be updated every month.
- It must be flexible.

From all that has been written in this chapter three simple rules evolve. If these are followed consistently, they not only will help to attain excellence in manufacturing, but also can assist in solving any present problems. Certainly they are an oversimplification of the total task, but they do provide a clear framework on which to base the management of the manufacturing process.

ACCEPT NOTHING BUT EXCELLENCE.
MONITOR THE PAST PERFORMANCE.
CONTINUOUSLY PLAN FOR THE FUTURE.

becomes much more difficult, if not impossible. You should resist the urge to take some actions until you can justify them with hard facts.

At one company a machine was believed to have failed when occasionally parts were incorrectly located during assembly. It was decided to shut down the machine for correction and to carry out the operation by hand to keep production moving and the people busy. The assembly required the accurate placement of parts, which was not easy to do manually. The result was that a large number of assemblies had to be reworked, causing the expenditure of much unnecessary labor and ultimately a complete dislocation of work flow. Unfortunately, all of the faulty assemblies from the machine had also been reworked leaving no evidence for trouble shooting, which as a result took much longer than expected. Analysis also showed that it was much more costly to continue operations, than to shut down the line until the machine had been repaired and use the spare labor to clean and refurbish the work area.

In the manufacturing field there is often a mistaken belief that if everyone has a job and is busy, then through some sort of magic the product will eventually get made and any inefficiencies will automatically sort themselves out. Unfortunately, this is seldom true.

FACT VERSUS FICTION

Writing down all the facts is a difficult rule to follow. First of all, we have to sort out the real facts from the half truths and the assumptions.

This is not to suggest that people deliberately lie about problems when they occur, although undoubtedly this does sometimes occur. Much more prevalent is poor memory regarding events, incorrect observations, and sometimes wishful thinking. For example, the author was involved in finding the cause of a particular problem, which had all the appearances of being caused by faulty material.

The key question was whether the problem had been seen in material from several vendors or only from one. The operator who was the key to this question was adamant that the problem had been seen in material from all the vendors, which would then have eliminated it as the source of the problem. However, an inspector was equally adamant that he had found the defect in material from one vendor only, and as a result of his evidence further testing was carried out. The tests clearly showed that the problem was in fact related to the materials from one vendor only, and the operator was now less sure of what he had seen.

Chapter 14

TROUBLESHOOTING THE PROCESS

No matter how carefully the process is controlled, problems will always occur. The number of problems and the way that we deal with them are major indications of just how good our process control procedures are functioning. At the worst we always have problems: they seem to go on forever, never being totally resolved, the same problems occurring again and again. At best we have a random scattering of problems which are quickly resolved and do not reoccur. In the worst case we spend a great deal of time and effort in problem solving; in the best situation we put more of our attention into preventing the occurrence of problems.

PROCESSING PROBLEMS

When problems arise in the manufacturing process, they invariably fall into three categories.

1. Accidental or deliberate failure to follow the recorded process.
2. An unrecognized variation in the process.
3. A fundamental error in the basic design of the product or process.

Most problems fall into the first category, and we all know of many examples. The operator who uses the wrong parts, the machine that drifts out of tolerance, the missed operation are typical of problems from this source. They all indicate a deficiency in the control of the process and can usually be traced to their source without much trouble, if the control data are adequate and the investigation is carried out in a logical manner.

The second category of problems is more challenging, for unless good data are available it is unlikely that the real cause of the problem will be detected easily. As an example, one problem that took some weeks to find was caused by a machine that had intermittent variations in its performance. These caused a small and random scattering of product failure that nevertheless necessitated 100% inspection and rework. According to the control data the machine was functioning correctly. It was only by chance that one of the investigating team happened to notice what appeared to be a change in the machine's performance. It then took more work to confirm that this was actually causing the problem. The basic cause was the way in which the machine data were collected. It had been assumed that any variations would be slow, gradual, permanent, and long term. Thus, the machine parameters were measured approximately once every half an hour. The variations that were discovered did not last for more than a few seconds and then the machine went back to its original settings.

Problems in the third category are the toughest to solve and indeed may not even be recognized as failures during production. One component of a missile had gone through complete design and development testing and ultimately went into production. The product successfully passed all the functional testing and inspection and was shipped. Several months later during extremely stringent stress testing two units failed, one dramatically, burning up part of the system. An investigation showed that some materials used in the construction were marginal when tested in one parameter, but just complied with the specification and therefore were not rejected. When a detailed analysis was carried out on the design of the unit, it was discovered that the parts could, under some circumstances, be subjected to unexpectedly high mechanical forces. If all the parts were well within the material specification, the assembly could withstand the stresses. If, however, the materials were less than perfect although still within specification, the product would fail under prolonged testing. In other words, the specification had not been completely tested over its entire range.

This conclusion was reached only after weeks of research. During design and prototype testing, parts were used that had fallen well within the specification limits and the problem was never seen. It is unlikely that this deficiency in the design of the product would ever have been discovered if the stress testing had not been carried out, and if it had not, quite accidently, included materials that only barely complied with the specification. If the failure had not been discovered through the stress testing, it might have become another of those mysterious random failures that occasionally make headline news.

FOUR IMPORTANT RULES

Whatever the problem, large or small, continuous or intermittent, it m resolved as quickly as possible. There are some simple but effective ru follow in any troubleshooting situation.

1. Impound all of the defective products, bad parts, damaged con ponents, or whatever physical evidence is available.
2. Go into your office, lock the door, disconnect the phone, and think!
3. Avoid the natural impulse to rush around and do something. It will invariably be the wrong thing to do.
4. Take a sheet of paper and write down all the facts of the situation.

In recording these facts, you should take the greatest care to define exactly what is found to be wrong and be sure you stick with the known facts. Avoid at this time any attempt to define the cause unless it is so obvious that any error is impossible. For example, if a bolt is broken or a component damaged, do not call it "Incorrect assembly." This would immediately suggest a defect in the assembly operation, when in fact the broken bolt may be the result of an incorrect setting of a torque driver and the damage to the component may have been caused by poor handling long after the assembly stage. An incorrect description can misdirect the problem solving.

You should make every effort to find any limitations to the problem. Is it found in every unit? If not, is the problem related to a particular time, to one machine? Is it operator related? When all the details have been recorded, it is time to bring in your people and listen to their proposals for solving the problem.

WE MUST DO SOMETHING!

It is natural, under the pressure of time, schedule, and the possibility that a lot of people are sitting idle waiting for you to make a decision, that you rush into some action. All too often the action is incorrect, but once begun it is difficult if not impossible to stop. It is rather like the story of the squad of soldiers who were marching toward the brink of a cliff, when the officer in charge forgot the command to halt. As they were about to march over the edge one soldier was heard to call out, "For Pete's sake, say something—if only goodbye!" Under pressure there is a tendency to do something, even though on reflection it will be seen to be illogical and useless. In many cases all of the evidence has been destroyed through ill-conceived precipitate actions, and problem solving

Chapter 14

TROUBLESHOOTING THE PROCESS

No matter how carefully the process is controlled, problems will always occur. The number of problems and the way that we deal with them are major indications of just how good our process control procedures are functioning. At the worst we always have problems: they seem to go on forever, never being totally resolved, the same problems occurring again and again. At best we have a random scattering of problems which are quickly resolved and do not reoccur. In the worst case we spend a great deal of time and effort in problem solving; in the best situation we put more of our attention into preventing the occurrence of problems.

PROCESSING PROBLEMS

When problems arise in the manufacturing process, they invariably fall into three categories.

1. Accidental or deliberate failure to follow the recorded process.
2. An unrecognized variation in the process.
3. A fundamental error in the basic design of the product or process.

Most problems fall into the first category, and we all know of many examples. The operator who uses the wrong parts, the machine that drifts out of tolerance, the missed operation are typical of problems from this source. They all indicate a deficiency in the control of the process and can usually be traced to their source without much trouble, if the control data are adequate and the investigation is carried out in a logical manner.

The second category of problems is more challenging, for unless good data are available it is unlikely that the real cause of the problem will be detected easily. As an example, one problem that took some weeks to find was caused by a machine that had intermittent variations in its performance. These caused a small and random scattering of product failure that nevertheless necessitated 100% inspection and rework. According to the control data the machine was functioning correctly. It was only by chance that one of the investigating team happened to notice what appeared to be a change in the machine's performance. It then took more work to confirm that this was actually causing the problem. The basic cause was the way in which the machine data were collected. It had been assumed that any variations would be slow, gradual, permanent, and long term. Thus, the machine parameters were measured approximately once every half an hour. The variations that were discovered did not last for more than a few seconds and then the machine went back to its original settings.

Problems in the third category are the toughest to solve and indeed may not even be recognized as failures during production. One component of a missile had gone through complete design and development testing and ultimately went into production. The product successfully passed all the functional testing and inspection and was shipped. Several months later during extremely stringent stress testing two units failed, one dramatically, burning up part of the system. An investigation showed that some materials used in the construction were marginal when tested in one parameter, but just complied with the specification and therefore were not rejected. When a detailed analysis was carried out on the design of the unit, it was discovered that the parts could, under some circumstances, be subjected to unexpectedly high mechanical forces. If all the parts were well within the material specification, the assembly could withstand the stresses. If, however, the materials were less than perfect although still within specification, the product would fail under prolonged testing. In other words, the specification had not been completely tested over its entire range.

This conclusion was reached only after weeks of research. During design and prototype testing, parts were used that had fallen well within the specification limits and the problem was never seen. It is unlikely that this deficiency in the design of the product would ever have been discovered if the stress testing had not been carried out, and if it had not, quite accidently, included materials that only barely complied with the specification. If the failure had not been discovered through the stress testing, it might have become another of those mysterious random failures that occasionally make headline news.

FOUR IMPORTANT RULES

Whatever the problem, large or small, continuous or intermittent, it must be resolved as quickly as possible. There are some simple but effective rules to follow in any troubleshooting situation.

1. Impound all of the defective products, bad parts, damaged components, or whatever physical evidence is available.
2. Go into your office, lock the door, disconnect the phone, and think!
3. Avoid the natural impulse to rush around and do something. It will invariably be the wrong thing to do.
4. Take a sheet of paper and write down all the facts of the situation.

In recording these facts, you should take the greatest care to define exactly what is found to be wrong and be sure you stick with the known facts. Avoid at this time any attempt to define the cause unless it is so obvious that any error is impossible. For example, if a bolt is broken or a component damaged, do not call it "Incorrect assembly." This would immediately suggest a defect in the assembly operation, when in fact the broken bolt may be the result of an incorrect setting of a torque driver and the damage to the component may have been caused by poor handling long after the assembly stage. An incorrect description can misdirect the problem solving.

You should make every effort to find any limitations to the problem. Is it found in every unit? If not, is the problem related to a particular time, to one machine? Is it operator related? When all the details have been recorded, it is time to bring in your people and listen to their proposals for solving the problem.

WE MUST DO SOMETHING!

It is natural, under the pressure of time, schedule, and the possibility that a lot of people are sitting idle waiting for you to make a decision, that you rush into some action. All too often the action is incorrect, but once begun it is difficult if not impossible to stop. It is rather like the story of the squad of soldiers who were marching toward the brink of a cliff, when the officer in charge forgot the command to halt. As they were about to march over the edge one soldier was heard to call out, "For Pete's sake, say something—if only goodbye!" Under pressure there is a tendency to do something, even though on reflection it will be seen to be illogical and useless. In many cases all of the evidence has been destroyed through ill-conceived precipitate actions, and problem solving becomes much more difficult, if not impossible. You should resist the urge to take some actions until you can justify them with hard facts.

At one company a machine was believed to have failed when occasionally parts were incorrectly located during assembly. It was decided to shut down the machine for correction and to carry out the operation by hand to keep production moving and the people busy. The assembly required the accurate placement of parts, which was not easy to do manually. The result was that a large number of assemblies had to be reworked, causing the expenditure of much unnecessary labor and ultimately a complete dislocation of work flow. Unfortunately, all of the faulty assemblies from the machine had also been reworked leaving no evidence for trouble shooting, which as a result took much longer than expected. Analysis also showed that it was much more costly to continue operations, than to shut down the line until the machine had been repaired and use the spare labor to clean and refurbish the work area.

In the manufacturing field there is often a mistaken belief that if everyone has a job and is busy, then through some sort of magic the product will eventually get made and any inefficiencies will automatically sort themselves out. Unfortunately, this is seldom true.

FACT VERSUS FICTION

Writing down all the facts is a difficult rule to follow. First of all, we have to sort out the real facts from the half truths and the assumptions.

This is not to suggest that people deliberately lie about problems when they occur, although undoubtedly this does sometimes occur. Much more prevalent is poor memory regarding events, incorrect observations, and sometimes wishful thinking. For example, the author was involved in finding the cause of a particular problem, which had all the appearances of being caused by faulty material.

The key question was whether the problem had been seen in material from several vendors or only from one. The operator who was the key to this question was adamant that the problem had been seen in material from all the vendors, which would then have eliminated it as the source of the problem. However, an inspector was equally adamant that he had found the defect in material from one vendor only, and as a result of his evidence further testing was carried out. The tests clearly showed that the problem was in fact related to the materials from one vendor only, and the operator was now less sure of what he had seen.

The operator was not lying; he had genuinely thought that the problem occurred with the material from all of the vendors. But we have to remember that he had not been specifically asked to look for this defect. He was asked to recall what had occurred, and memory can be faulty. In addition, he was of the opinion that his machine was not performing properly, and he wanted it replaced with a new model. If the machine had been the cause of the defect, the problem would have been found with the material from all of the vendors.

Here was a case where a desire to prove his own theory had colored the operator's memory; there was no intent to deceive. The investigator has to expect observations such as this and must be prepared to probe and question and view all comments with a certain amount of disbelief until they can be proved. This, of course, is why it is so important to maintain records of the process making the facts readily available.

CONSIDER THE "GUT FEEL"

Once the facts are listed, other ideas and opinions have to be considered. Just because they cannot be proved at this time is not to suggest that they should be disregarded. However, until they can be proved they remain nothing more than possible solutions to the problem. The amount of credence that can be given to these hypotheses will depend on the individuals concerned, their experience relative to the particular problem, and their past performance in analyzing process failures.

In one plant an operator reported a "gut feel" about a problem that could have been caused by contamination in one of the process steps. The failure rate he reported was in the very low parts per million and was dismissed as imaginary because it seemed impossible for any form of visual inspection to be so accurate. However, the statistical data confirmed the defects and indeed the contamination was found and corrected. Was this a feeling or a subconscious observation of the product? The answer was never found, but in many cases the "gut feel" has been found to be correct. It may well be that the mind collects many tiny bits of information without conscious thought.

The "gut feel" of an experienced individual who has a history of successfully solving production problems should be considered very carefully. List the theories, with some measure of your feeling as to their relevance.

CALL IN THE TROOPS, BUT IT'S YOUR NECK

Now that you have listed all the facts and suggestions, it is time to take the next step, which is to plan the strategy for solving the problem. The manager must take over the leadership of the rescue operation, and remember that he will be working through and with his people. He should sit down with those concerned, discuss carefully and objectively the possible approaches, and listen to all opinions. Then the manager must decide what is to be done. The ultimate responsibility for the output from the factory is his and his alone; he has to make the decisions and be very sure that every individual knows exactly what is expected of him in regard to both the work and the schedule. This is a most critical time and the way that the shop floor backs up the manager will demonstrate, more than any other single item, just how well he has developed the rapport between himself and his people. The discussions must be open and honest, with "no holds barred." Everyone must be able to say exactly what he thinks on the subject. But once the manager has made his decision, he must have total loyalty, no matter what the personal feelings of the individuals are concerning the problem.

Every problem is different from one another in some respects, but the format for resolution almost always contains the following action items.

- Analyze facts and opinions.
- Develop experiments to prove the opinions.
- From the experimental results determine the accuracy of the opinions and theories.
- Using the new information attempt to define the basic cause of the problem.
- Set up the changes to the process, or correct the process deviations.
- Monitor the results closely to confirm that the corrections do in fact eliminate the problem.

It is dangerous to attempt to miss any of these steps. It is natural to want to jump directly to making changes to the process on the basis of the available information, in the hope that this will eliminate the problem and avoid any need for the experimental work. Doing so may well produce a change to the situation, and suddenly the problem disappears. But no one is quite sure why it did, and later the defect returns. The original evidence has by then been lost and problem solving has to begin again from scratch. This scenario occurs all too often, especially when incorrect or defective parts happen to get onto the shop floor. In this case, the evidence is frequently lost when the parts are reworked or scrapped.

REMEMBER SHERLOCK HOLMES

"Elementary, my dear Watson." Most problem solving is simple and easy; we often make it difficult and complicated because of illogical thinking and a strange unwillingness to accept hard facts. In one instance, a batch of bad materials from a particular subcontractor was resulting in defective products. The author carried out some simple tests to show that the materials were in fact faulty, but the production manager just did not want to accept the fact. He urgently needed the materials to meet his production schedule, he had no replacement parts, and he argued for several hours that the materials could not be at fault. The test was wrong, he claimed; if this or that were done, the test would work all right. He was totally unwilling to accept the fact that the materials were useless and that he would have to shut down his production and put effort into obtaining good materials.

A prime case of illogical thinking occurred when one aerospace electronics company had problems in retaining solderability of the printed wiring boards. It was assumed that the cause of the problem was oxidation of the solder coating on the surfaces to be soldered. In an attempt to prevent this oxydation, well over sixty thousand dollars were spent on nitrogen-filled cabinets in which to store the boards to prevent any contact with the oxygen in the atmosphere. However, the boards still exhibited the same soldering problems. Two examples of incorrect thinking are involved here.

- The first example is simple. Does it really matter if the surface of the solder becomes oxidized? The solder is melted when a joint is made and any oxidation is washed away from the base metal, which is where the joint is actually made.
- The second example illustrates the importance of understanding the fundamental nature of any process before attempting to define a solution to a problem. Poor solderability of solder-coated surfaces on printed wiring boards is primarily caused by an intermetallic growth between the base copper and the tin in the solder coating. This growth is not affected by the atmosphere in which the boards are stored.

Some simple rules to follow in setting up experiments to determine the cause of problems.

- Have a clear logical reason for every experiment.
- Write down in detail every experiment carried out.
- Record the results of every experiment in detail.
- Understand the basic theory behind every experiment.
- If the results do not agree with the theory, go back and find the reason.

There are also two fundamental truths that we often find difficult to accept, but which we must believe sincerely if we are to be successful in any trouble shooting.

- There is no magic in manufacturing. If you cannot find a logical reason for some occurrence, it is your reasoning that is at fault, or your lack of knowledge regarding the process.
- If there is a variation in the product, there must have been a variation in the process.

TECHNICAL ANSWERS

In today's hi-tech manufacturing environment many of the problems are not obvious even to the unskilled observer. They may be invisible characteristics such as electrical problems, failures of materials by internal cracking, or a flaw in some component that is so small it is indiscernible to the naked eye. In some cases it is necessary to use highly specialized equipment to carry out any analysis of the defect.

A typical example was the failure of gold wires attached by welding and used to connect a semiconductor to the lead frame that provides the external connections. These particular components had been used for some time with no reported failures. Suddenly all were found faulty when the unit to which they were assembled was tested. When they were cut open, it was discovered that many of the hairlike wires were broken. The troubleshooting began with an attempt to find out why this had occurred. A scanning electron beam microscope was used to photograph the broken leads at very high magnification. A metallurgist examined the photographs of the broken ends of the leads and concluded that they must have been bent back and forth many times before breaking. This finding implied severe vibration of the parts, and the only process step that could have caused it was an ultrasonic cleaning stage. But this stage had been in operation for several years and the problem had appeared only very recently. When a check of the cleaner was made it was found that the transducer frequency had been changed during maintenance the day before the breakages started. Tests proved that this was the cause of the problem and a mathematical analysis of the leads confirmed that their resonant frequency coincided with that of the new transducers that had been fitted into the cleaning machine. It is unlikely that the problem could have been solved so quickly without the use of the scanning electron beam microscope and the expert analysis of the gold wire fractures.

You should get to know what is available in the laboratories around you. Discuss the capabilities of your local university, other companies, and test facilities. Understand just what can be done with the modern technologies, and also understand the limitations of the procedures. For example, although it is possible to analyze the composition of tiny samples of material, the results will be given as a list of elements, not as the composition of the actual compound materials.

If your production includes any small items, buy a good binocular microscope, with excellent illumination of the specimen and the ability to photograph the image. It is probably the single most useful problem-solving tool.

Today it is generally possible to analyze tiny particles of any material: a smear from a finger, the plating on a metal surface no matter how thin. Material can be stripped away molecule by molecule to disclose what lies beneath the surface. However, these expensive services should not be used without expert analysis of the results.

USING THE GURU

Not too many decades ago it was possible for any intelligent individual to understand the technologies of manufacturing, in any particular industry. The knowledge required was a mixture of a good basic understanding of the theory of the process plus a lot of "hands on" experience on the shop floor. Of course, there were always those more highly specialized operations that appeared to be magic, and that generated not only the Guru but also a lot of myths and half-truths. Today we are seeing such an increase in the complexity of our processes that inevitably from time to time we will, if we are honest, just shake our heads and say "I don't know." When this happens we should reach for the phone book and call in the expert. There are still many myths and half-truths in most industries, and there will always be available technical assistance that is thinly disguised, or undisguised salesmanship. The smart manager will sort these sources and develop an "expert base" before any problem arises.

In deciding whom to approach for technical assistance, you can apply a few rules.

- Give your Guru a small task, say for one day, and use the time to observe and get to know the individual. You must each be open and honest with each other or the relationship will not work. You must have complete confidence in the expert.
- Talk with the Guru. Find out his experiences, his practical successes, and failures.
- Try to talk with some of his clients. This is not always easy, as the author is well aware, because many people do not want it known that they have needed these services.

- Agree clearly what the problem is and what you expect from the consultation.
- Unless you require a solution to an academic problem, go to the man with a practical background. Ten years of proved record as a manufacturing engineer or similar practical position is usually more meaningful than an MBA or PhD.
- Make sure that the individual can work well with your people.
- Unless you know the individual very well, view with suspicion any assistance given by an expert who is not completely independent. It is impossible to be a consultant and salesman at the same time.

You must not wait too long to call in the specialist. The moment that the trouble shooting starts to falter, or the path ahead is not clear, call a halt and get some help. All too often, by the time the author is called in to solve a processing problem so much work has already been done that it is difficult to get down to the basic problem. Records are unclear, and no one is really sure of what is fact and what is fiction. Everyone has an opinion and individually a great deal is being done. But all too often the work is uncoordinated and the data are questionable. Not, I would emphasis, because of the failure of any individual, but because there is a failure to coordinate what must be a carefully planned and executed investigation if it is to be successful.

As a consultant does not usually come cheaply, you should make the most of his time by giving him the necessary backup, someone to act as a liaison. After all, you expect him to begin productive work immediately, when he does not even know the position of the nearest water fountain. You also want the work to continue when he leaves and the company liaison should by then have acquired some of the expert's knowledge and be in a perfect position to take over. Remember you are buying experience and knowledge; the consultant has probably seen your problem many times in the past and can therefore provide the information necessary to eliminate it, quickly and easily. This step can save thousands of dollars you would have spent in looking in the wrong direction, or striking out blindly with no real understanding of the solution. When the comment is "I don't know," the response must be "Then find out, and find out quickly."

THE TWO-PRONGED ATTACK

In almost every management decision two types of action must be taken. First is the urgent need to get the line back in operation, the "short-term" solution. This almost inevitably will be the quick and dirty answer to the problem:

inspect the product 100% to find out what is good and what is bad, and rework the bad parts, or strip out the faulty parts and replace them, or use a replacement machine or tools. At this time the last thought in anyone's mind is efficiency or productivity; the only thought is to get production moving again. This is usually done under a lot of pressure, as people work day and night until the product is once more moving onto the shipping dock.

This step is necessary, and the urgency is understandable. It is also very expensive. However, this is only the first part of solving the problem. With production flowing once more, it is necessary to analyze the problem and take every precaution to prevent this from ever occurring again. But suddenly the urgency has gone, for there are many other things to be done. "We can get to that when we have time," we hear, and in all too many cases the entire incident is pushed under a pile of other work and forgotten—forgotten, that is, until the same problem reoccurs and the whole episode starts up again.

Even while the immediate solution is being determined, long-term avoidance actions must be planned. These need not necessarily be done at that moment, but should be planned and scheduled so that the work is not forgotten or pushed to the bottom of the pile. It is obviously important to arrive quickly at a solution, even though it is a temporary answer. It is much more important to develop the actions to prevent the problem from ever coming back again.

SUMMARY

Troubleshooting is rarely difficult if it is carried out in a logical manner.

- Think, before running out and doing anything.
- Separate fact from fiction.
- Listen to all suggestions.
- Decide what has to be done and who is to do it.
- Keep meticulous records.
- Save all the evidence.
- As manager you are totally responsible, therefore you make the decisions.
- First get production rolling; then plan elimination of the basic cause of the problem.
- Eliminate the cause of the problem.

Chapter 15

NOW IT'S ALL UP TO YOU

As a young manufacturing engineer the author remembers clearly his sudden promotion to manufacturing manager. Called back from vacation by a cryptic but urgent phone call, I walked into my boss's office just as he was putting on his coat. "I've been promoted to vice president manufacturing at corporate headquarters," he said. "Here are the keys to the filing cabinets, ask your secretary if you can't find anything, it's all yours now, and it's all up to you."

There was an immediate feeling of pride in the promotion, followed by the excitement of thinking that there were no more petty bosses to consider. As long as the shipments were made on time and the budget was met I was free to rule my little kingdom as I wished. The euphoria soon evaporated when a product manager thrust his head around the office door and wanted to know when I could let him have another manufacturing engineer for a few days, the maintenance manager wanted to know what to do about a boiler that would have to be shut down for repairs, and the cafeteria manager reported a shortage of staff to serve lunch. I suddenly realized that the manufacturing manager does not sit in glory in his office ruminating on how to improve productivity. He lives in a whirlwind of problems, complaints, and suggestions—many frivolous, some with considerable merit, and a few of the utmost urgency.

Of course, as the days passed I began to create some order out of the chaos, but I had learned a hard lesson. It was now all up to me. In the course of working my way up through the manufacturing organization, there had always been a format to work with; objectives had been agreed upon with the boss and formed a framework around which the day-to-day work could be planned. When a problem arrived it was reported to the boss or bosses, and the proposed solution was discussed and given their approval. It was a very comfortable situation, for there was always support and someone to turn to. No matter how difficult the problem there was always the boss to take the final responsibility. Suddenly everything had changed. I realized the truth of the motto on Harry S. Truman's desk: "THE BUCK STOPS HERE."

It was a lonely feeling: my responsibility was no longer only for my own work but for the effort of every one of the people working at that plant. There was no one to blame if things went wrong. I had absolute authority. I also had absolute responsibility.

THERE CAN ONLY BE ONE CAPTAIN ON A SHIP

Throughout this book there has been an emphasis on working with and through people, and today this is obviously the only way that an operation can be successful. The people in our plants are generally intelligent, well educated, and eager to do a good job and be part of a successful team. We have to capture and use this enthusiasm and turn it into the excellence necessary to operate and control our processes correctly each and every day.

However, we must never forget that the manufacturing manager alone has the ultimate responsibility for the operation. We are therefore not running a democratic parliament, but a dictatorship. If the manager is skillful and practiced as a manager he will see to it that his dictatorship permits everyone to have his say without fear, that everyone is listened to with attention and understanding, and that the rules and regulations by which the operation is run are sensible, understood, and accepted.

Manufacturing Is Not a Democracy

It might be ideal if we could operate in a totally democratic manner, perhaps voting on whether this or that should be done. When time permits, the good manager should try to obtain all the ideas on a particular proposed change in the process. However, this is not always possible. When the factory catches fire, there is no time to debate the need to call the fire brigade. It may not be possible to provide the necessary training and understanding on the effects of any proposed changes to all the people concerned, in the time available. There may be personal prejudice, or an unwillingness to accept new ideas.

A new factory was being built and after a lot of thought the manufacturing engineering staff proposed that in the new plant there would be no offices. It would be completely open, but have excellent sound damping, carpeting, and sound screens around office areas, in an all-out effort to make a superb working environment for everyone. As the corporate management was also at that time beginning to train the entire personnel in participative management, and communications, it seemed that all of these things would fit well together. The proposal was initially almost totally rejected, especially by lower and middle management, who had their own offices. Even when some people had been shown similar operations there was considerable opposition. It was at this time that the manufacturing manager, who had overall responsibility for the layout, had to act as dictator. He had heard all the expertise from his manufacturing engineers, had visited similar operations, had hired an architectural expert, and had carefully considered all the options. He called his people into his office. "I have listened to all your opinions," he said. "I have heard the experts, I have visited other plants, and now I have made my decision. We will have an open plan factory, and I do not intend to listen to any more discussion."

The new factory was a total success. Indeed, once it was occupied a stream of requests came from the old section of the plant to convert it also to an open plan layout. Ultimately, two middle managers resigned as they found it beneath their dignity to work on the shop floor without an office around them. Both had already been warned of poor performance and both took early retirement. This is an excellent example in which the manager has to act as the dictator. In his opinion it was best for the company that the open plan be used, everyone had had their say, and it was time for a decision. He made it clearly, honestly, but decisively. If there had been any uncertainty on his part, for months the people in the plant would have spent hours talking about the matter, little factions would have developed, company politics would have boiled up. His decisiveness immediately stifled all of these potential problems.

Many decisions on the shop floor have to be made under emergency conditions in which there is little time for debate. When production is stopped, or the schedule is in jeopardy, the manufacturing manager has to be prepared to make decisions; he cannot pass this task on to anyone else. The moment that he is unwilling to accept the responsibility and the consequences of his actions, it is time for him to step down and find a less demanding job.

FINDING ADVISORS

Almost every manager has to work through a circle of advisors or lieutenants to make things happen. When the manager has listened to all the opinions and discussed all the various ideas, he then decides on the action plan. He has to have the right people, not only to obtain the best information, but also to turn his action plan into practical actions. Any manager can only be as good as the people who report to him, and selecting these people requires great care and skill.

You should not allow personnel into the selection process. With the best will in the world they do not know your needs and they cannot make your selection. First of all, try to find people among those whom you know, someone you may have worked with in the past, someone recommended by a colleague. Next, if you advertise, leave the door open for the experienced man who may well not have a degree. The moment that "must have a degree" is included in your advertising you eliminate many excellent candidates.

Technical Competence

Obviously your technical people must be competent, and it is quite difficult to assess just how good an individual may be at his job. Try to get the applicant to discuss his past work, the particular successes that he is proud of and the failures he has suffered. Often, if you can get an individual to discuss his failures, why and how they occurred, and how he got out of them, you will begin to see the person behind the applicant. Take him out into the plant to see how he handles tools, and how he talks with people.

Look at the applicant's past experience. Look for overall competence rather than expertise in a single area, unless you are looking for someone with a single area of skills and knowledge. If a man has good overall understanding of your industry's technology, he will quickly be able to understand your particular process. If, however, his experience is too narrow, he may find it difficult to expand into another field. Do not place an overemphasis on academic qualifications. If a man has a degree in engineering, it assures you that he has a knowledge of the fundamentals, but it tells you little about the man's capabilities. Often the subjects as taught at many of our colleges are so far removed from the practical day-to-day work that they are almost useless. It is only when a man has taken the information learned at college and translated it into practical terms that he understands what the true nature of the subject contains. The man who left high school and worked for a few years and then returned to college and gained a degree is frequently a much more competent employee than the student who went directly to college without any work experience. Not only will he have the practical experience, but the college courses will have been much more rewarding, as the man was able to relate the theory directly to his practical shop floor work.

You will be relying on this man for technical advice. Do you trust him? Will he be honest when he does not know a particular piece of information and say so, or will he cover up with technical jargon? These are the important things for you to uncover. Do not be in a hurry, for it is important to take time to get to know the individual.

Compatibility

Ask other staff members also to talk to the applicant. As they will have to work with him, they must be comfortable with him. There is no way that you can determine if an applicant is suitable to be part of your organization in a short interview. Set aside a full day to spend with each applicant. Arrange to be completely free for that day—no interruptions, no phone calls. Do not be afraid to ask disturbing questions: "What would you do if my boss came to you on the shop floor and told you to do something completely the opposite to my instructions." Set him some tasks relative to the job and see how he handles them. If he is to work on the shop floor, see how he interfaces with the operators.

It is vitally important to see how he reacts with the others around him. The author once hired a young man with a most impressive work record and also several degrees including a PhD. Technically he was extremely capable and inventive, but within a short time he showed an unfortunate attitude. He could not forget his PhD; he reminded everyone of it constantly and made it quite clear that he considered most people around him to be ignorant. This attitude so irritated his fellow employees that within six months he had to be fired.

When you have decided to hire the applicant you must feel sure of the following.

- He is technically competent in both theory and practice.
- He will be loyal to you in every way.
- He is totally honest.
- He can work well with the other members of your staff.
- He can manage his people in a manner that complements your own management style.
- He can communicate well both verbally and in writing.

Beware The "Yes Man"

There is a strong temptation to hire a man who agrees completely with all of your ideas and theories. It is comfortable to be surrounded by individuals who you know will agree with your slightest whim. But this eventually leads to disaster, as you will be unable to try out your thoughts in the rough and tumble of debate. Beware the man who agrees too much during his interview. Does he have the guts to say bluntly, "I think you are wrong for the following reasons"? He must be able to argue constructively and without rancor.

One very senior manager did not like to be contradicted in any way. As soon as someone raised an opposing viewpoint, he became petulant, his lower lip stuck out, and the unfortunate opponent was made to feel very uncomfortable.

In fact, his responsibilities would be given to someone else, and he would be isolated and made to realize that his job was on the line if he did not agree. The manager had collected around himself a cozy group of "Yes men." Unfortunately, when he began to make some bad blunders, no one contradicted, all commiserated and agreed it was someone else's fault, until eventually his faulty judgment resulted in some enormous financial losses to the company. He was removed, at which time his staff now did an about face and told all who would listen what a terrible manager he had been.

THE NEED FOR HONEST DISAGREEMENT

Every manager needs people who will give honest opinions. He must encourage this honesty by listening to any opposing viewpoint, and not look upon disagreement as a form of disloyalty. The dissident should not be punished or suppressed but instead be encouraged to present his ideas and debate with conviction and honesty.

As Others See Us

The way that others see us will inevitably affect the way that they relate to us. If the manufacturing manager is seen as a self-contained, somewhat aloof individual, it is unlikely that the people on the shop floor will want to talk with him. If he is seen as an aggressive, complaining individual, it is unlikely that he will receive more than formal communication from anyone. We have all worked with people who have by their very attitudes made people avoid them—people who are habitually rude, who like to "put down" and belittle certain groups or classes.

If a manager is to be effective he must be in close contact with all his people; not only must he want to communicate with them he must show them that he is at all times open to their comments, suggestions, and even criticism. He must take time to learn the names of the people on the shop floor as he walks through the plant regularly. He must make the effort to see and be seen.

Ask yourself what your people see when they contact you. Try to put yourself in their shoes and attempt to understand their feelings. As the great Scottish poet Robert Burns wrote,

O wad some Pow'r the giftie gie us
To see oursels as others see us
It wad frae monie a blunder free us
An foolish notion.

If we can in fact see ourselves as others see us, we will be better managers, and indeed better people. This is not to suggest that the manager should put on an act; any insincerity is soon recognized and will have a totally negative affect on the relationship. However, it does suggest that the manager shows his true feelings, makes his pleasure, his annoyance, and his gratitude visible to his people. He needs training to do this in a positive manner, to be able to criticize without seeming to complain, to say, "Thank you" for work well done without any condescention. Certainly there are a few managers who seem to be born with these attributes, we always remember those we have met. But most of us either need formal training in this most important area of management or have to learn it by experience. This can be difficult, time consuming, and involve many mistakes during the learning process.

Company, or Self

Working through people is probably the most important area of management. It is certainly the most complicated area of management, if only because each person is an individual and must be treated as such. This demands that we know the person, understanding his hopes, his wishes, his ambitions, and his fears. Only then can we interact with him effectively and determine the approach that will best communicate with and motivate him. We will be able to do this only when we know and understand ourselves, and what it is we are seeking in our working life. If we are genuinely working for the well-being of our company, we are unlikely to face too many problems in our interpersonal relationships in the work place. If, however, our real objective is personal advancement, we will meet many conflicting demands in our work, and the decisions that we make will eventually make this objective very clear to those around us. Under these conditions it is unlikely that we will be able to develop relationships with our people that will generate excellence in the manufacturing process. In a similar manner, if our boss is more concerned with personal advancement than corporate excellence, our position may be untenable.

Of course, this clash of objectives is the basic cause for all company politics, and it is unlikely that we can ever eliminate it totally. However, once we recognize its fundamental cause we can, with understanding, work towards reducing its effect on our operation.

It would indeed make life so easy if this chapter could end with a list of things to do to make the management function simple and straightforward. Unfortunately, we can only review some of the items that are useful in our developing the necessary interpersonal skills.

- Always remember that every person is an individual. Treat each one as such.
- Never lump people together and assume that they all have the same characteristics.
- Be completely honest in your dealings with your people.
- Listen carefully, hear what is said.
- Anger and criticism achieve little.
- Most people want to do a good job.
- Recognize that personal advancement may sometimes clash with company well being.
- As the manufacturing manager you must supply leadership to the entire manufacturing organization.

Chapter 16

QUALITY, THE ELUSIVE PRIZE

What is this elusive objective called "quality"? Experts have tried to define it in the following terms:

- "Conformance to requirements."
- "Free from deficiencies."
- "Quality isn't specifications, or what advertisers or engineers say it is. It's what the buyer says it is."
- "Fitness for use."

It is extremely difficult to define the exact nature of what we call "quality," especially in a few words. Although we all believe that we know what is meant, when we try to agree on the exact meaning we find a divergence of views. One problem is the many different uses of the word "quality": "This is a very high quality recording" means that it will faithfully reproduce the sounds from which it was made. "Our hamburgers are made from the highest quality beef" can mean anything from advertising hype, to its containing a minimum amount of fat or using USDA choice grade meat. In this sense, Shakespeare said that "The quality of mercy is not strained," that mercy is not limited or conditional. Perhaps this whole issue will make more sense if we consider what we mean in manufacturing when we speak of quality.

QUALITY OF THE PRODUCT

A first attempt to define the quality of the product might be the following phrase.

"The product must meet the performance specification."

This is certainly a good start. Then we have to consider whether the specification can fully define all that the product is expected to do: what if a knob on a radio functions correctly but is stiff to operate; what if the handle on a rake has a rough spot that annoys the user. These are small items that may not contravene the specifications, may not even be consciously noticed by the user, but they are annoying enough to stop a customer from coming back. We have all experienced the automobile which is "nice to drive"; although it may not have the acceleration of a Corvette or the comfort of a Cadillac, we enjoy using it and will probably buy another of the same make. The characteristics that make it an enjoyable car are probably impossible to write into a specification but are vitally important in retaining customers.

Quality and the Competition

What if a competitor's product not only can do all that our product is capable of, but also has additional features and sells for the same price. Can the quality of our product be considered adequate? The marketplace will soon tell us that it is not. We have to take into account not only our own product but also how it compares with similar products at a similar price. We have to consider the life of the product. Should it be expected to last forever, even with minimum maintenance or no maintenance at all? What is the importance of the appearance of our product? We have seen examples of an item that beats its competition because of a better appearance, even though it did not perform as well. It is not sufficient merely to manufacture our product to meet the specification; the design, the finish, even the way it is packaged become important. They are all part of this elusive factor, "quality."

Quality and the Customer

The quality level of our product will ultimately be decided by our customers. If they are satisfied with its performance, reliability, and price and after comparing these items with those of our competitor's come back to buy more from us, we can consider that our product quality is at least satisfactory. Still we cannot rest on our laurels. In this competitive world we must continuously strive for improvement if we are to keep ahead of our competitors. In other words, we must always struggle to improve our quality. Through improved design we must aim to make products that will have more features and will be easier to use; we must look for greater margins of reliability both in manufacture and design. We must always seek out new ways of reducing our costs.

The search for quality is not a simple or a static activity. It is an on-going part of managing the manufacturing process and fits in well with the various aspects of process control already discussed.

- First, we must control the process exactly to maintain the quality, reliability, and cost of the product as presently designed.
- Next, we must constantly review the product, to assure that the process is in control, and then to improve manufacturing methods.
- Finally, through our "Corrective Action" program we must constantly search for ways to reduce cost and improve the reliability and performance of our product.

Perhaps, after this consideration of the nature of quality in our product, we can attempt a better definition.

> Quality is a measure of the performance, reliability, and cost of our product. Our quality is adequate when our customers continue to buy our products.

Quality and the Future

Because it is unlikely that we can ever know what our competitors are planning to do, our struggle for quality can never end. There will never be a clear objective: what will be adequate today will not be competitive tomorrow. Not too many years ago we were quite happy if the tires on our car lasted for 20,000 miles. We would never buy tires from a manufacturer today who could not guarantee a much greater life. Thus, we must recognize that quality is an open-ended objective; as soon as we close in on our target it moves farther away. We must also accept that our striving for quality can never end. Indeed, this constant struggle to improve, to compete successfully, is at the very heart of our society.

We can then add the following reference to the future, to our definition of quality.

> Quality is a measure of the performance, reliability, and cost of our product. Our quality is adequate when our customers continue to buy our products. Our quality is good when we have an increasing number of customers. To stay profitable we must excel in everything we do.

QUALITY AND THE ORGANIZATION

Many companies in the United States are genuinely striving to manufacture products of the highest quality. Some are among the best performers in the world. Unfortunately, the majority fall into two classes.

1. Those who profess to strive for quality but do not translate their words into actions.

2. Those who really do not believe that quality programs work, or if they do, assume that the cost will be prohibitive.

There are many examples of the first classification. In the lobby of one typical company, a large framed document stated the corporate policy on quality. It included all the cliches, "We will always ship the highest quality products to our customers." "Quality is the most important item in our business," and so on. The author had been asked to go to this company to find the cause of certain defects in the product. It was determined that bad materials were the basic problem, and it was suggested that they should be scrapped and replaced as there was no way that they could be used without jeopardizing the product quality. "But we can't do that," was the immediate response. "Look at the cost, and the effect on the schedule." These two items were in fact of much more concern than the quality of the product, and it took a lengthy argument to convince the management that obtaining new materials would eventually prove to be lower in cost and of less jeopardy to the schedule. It is easy to meet the schedule by shipping defective products. It was also difficult for them to recognize that they had to reconsider all of their materials acquisition and inspection procedures, and they had to immediately rescind their instructions to always buy from the lowest bidder.

This attitude is by no means uncommon, and demonstrates clearly that any concern for true quality either is non-existent or has not reached the shop floor. It is easy for senior management to agree that quality will be the watch word, to come up with slogans and posters, to issue instructions accordingly to the lower echelons of management, and then to do nothing more. No budget for quality, no training programs for quality, and no personal involvement. One day it comes as a surprise that sales are falling, costs are rising, and the company reputation is reflected by the falling price of their stock. With the best will in the world, quality will never work upward from the shop floor.

SUCCESSFUL QUALITY PROGRAMS DEPEND ON THE PERSONAL INVOLVEMENT AND LEADERSHIP OF TOP MANAGEMENT.

The second group of companies survives only until the day that competition forces them to take action or when they cease to be profitable. This is frequently too late to do more than file for bancruptcy. Unfortunately, it is often difficult to forecast the cost and schedule improvements that always result from achieving excellence, whether this is called a quality program, or process control, or is recognized for what it really is, good management.

ASKING THE RIGHT QUESTIONS

In addition to the formal implementation of a quality program, which will always be at the heart of good management, we must constantly review all the work that goes on in our operation and ask ourselves if it is being performed as efficiently and as accurately as possible. This questioning has to become as natural as breathing and cannot be limited to manufacturing. As we have discussed, almost every function in the company is there to support the shop floor, and all must be subjected to the same scrutiny. We should ask ourselves a few simple questions.

IS THE JOB NECESSARY?

It is surprising how many tasks can be eliminated: forms that are filled in and never looked at, unnecessary inspection just because someone set things up in this way years ago, computer printouts that are invariably thrown away, end-of-month reports that are filed away and never read. When the day-to-day tasks are scrutinized, it is often surprising how many are totally useless and can be eliminated.

- In one plant all materials were counted twice by two separate departments and then checked by quality control before being sent to the shop floor. A mistake had once been made and this procedure had been installed as an emergency measure. This had been forgotten and the procedure was never removed.
- In some companies a simple action like moving a desk requires filling in a form and obtaining an authorizing signature.

IS THE JOB BEING DONE BY THE RIGHT PEOPLE?

We have to get rid of preconceived ideas—that inspection can only be done by quality control, that letters can only be typed by a secretary, and so on. In these days of computers, for example, information can be manipulated and transmitted in so many ways that we have to reconsider if the right people are using these machines efficiently.

- The maintenance on a production machine was carried out each weekend by the maintenance department. After a short training session and the purchase of a few tools, it was done by the operator during the shutdown time at the end of each day.
- Quality control engineers were responsible for preparing statistical control charts, which were invariably late and not used by the operators. Following a short training course the task was given to the operators, who were able to produce on-time information that they used.

IS THE JOB BEING DONE IN THE BEST WAY?

We become so used to doing things in a particular way that we often overlook some simple improvements in efficiency and quality.

- Would a short meeting between marketing and production each morning be more effective than a weekly written report?
- Can we arrange to eliminate written purchase orders with our major suppliers?
- Can we improve the quality of materials from our vendors and eliminate incoming inspection?
- Can we use bar codes and bar code readers instead of having to input data via a keyboard?
- If our operators are correctly trained, do we need quality control to run a final inspection of the product?
- Would a simple fixture reduce handling of parts in assembly?
- Can we profitably automate any of our processes?

IS THE JOB ADDING VALUE TO THE PRODUCT?

When we look at the process carefully, we will always find items that do not materially add anything of value. All handling is wasted time; moving and storing parts add nothing to their value.

- The first item here is always inspection; remember, it adds nothing to the value or quality of the product.
- Why it is the inspection being done? How can it be eliminated?
- Why are parts packaged and stored?
- If they are not being used, why have they been purchased?

To summarize, whether it is called a "Zero Defect" program, a "Quality" program, or another title, we have to understand that what we are doing is nothing more than good management. It is basically a determination to excel in everything that we do, to accept nothing but excellence in our whole organization. If we get into the habit of questioning every function under our control, we will slowly but surely eliminate many of the areas of waste and inefficiency.

- Quality is nothing but good management.
- Accepting nothing but excellence in everything we do produces products of the highest quality at the lowest cost.
- Quality is a state of mind, not a collection of gimmicks.
- Quality has to be a company-wide attitude, not just one regarding manufacturing activities.
- Quality will never be achieved through inspection.
- Quality requires training for everyone.
- Quality is not the responsibility of the quality control department.
- The achievement of quality demands that we look at our operation with an unbiased eye.

CONVERTING THE NONBELIEVER

The striving for excellence, which is the heart of any quality program, is akin to religion. To the believer all things are possible; to the nonbeliever a quality program appears to be a mixture of magic, nonsense, and hocus pocus. Yet, as we have mentioned above, striving for good quality is nothing more than good management. Excellence in all that we do will eventually result in our making the highest quality product at the lowest cost, and surely that is what managing the manufacturing process is all about. It is not uncommon to come across companies that have almost accidently developed first-class quality programs merely through excellent management of the operations.

It is difficult, if not impossible, to push quality up from the shop floor, but in many cases this is the only route available. Experience shows that all too often it is the people on the shop floor or the manufacturing engineering department who see what has to be done. First they have to convert the manufacturing manager, who is usually close enough to the operation to change attitudes regarding quality. But then the message has to reach the top echelon of management, and this is where the problems arise. The believer knows that any expenditure to improve the process or the degree of control will be paid back in a very short time; the nonbeliever doubts that the promised results will be achieved and therefore sees any expenditure as being money wasted.

Under these conditions it is extremely difficult to preach quality in a convincing manner. The answer has to be one in terms of dollars and cents. Unfortunately, the positive results of a good quality program, which of course is the very same procedure as developing excellent process control, cannot all be directly converted to dollars. Consider the following items:

- A reduction of work in process.
- A reduction of material in stores.
- A lower cost of handling materials.
- Less damage through less handling.
- Less time spent by manufacturing engineering in troubleshooting.
- Improved customer satisfaction.
- Lower costs for warranty repairs.
- Improved accuracy of scheduling.
- Lower inspection costs.
- Shorter in-process time.

Depending on the product and the operation, each company can add other items to this list. However, it is not easy to convert this list to a schedule of cost reductions. Some estimates can certainly be developed, but they become difficult to defend if the basis for them is attacked. A typical argument relates to materials. "If we buy better quality materials, it will add $15.75 to the cost of the product. Now prove that this will result in a cost reduction." Yet almost invariably a well-controlled process will generate savings in these indirect areas which exceed those obvious items of a reduction in inspection and rework.

There is often an attempt to compromise by installing part of a quality program. "We will try it out on one line first and see what happens." This approach ignores the fact that any program of excellence has to include all of the operation if it is to be successful. Starting such a program of excellence is sometimes rationalized by setting up a schedule of cost reduction, but this puts the cart before the horse. For example, an objective might be, "To reduce the cost of repairs under warranty by 25% in the next six months." But who should be responsible for achieving such an objective? Field service has to repair all the defects that come their way. Are they to attempt to do so with fewer people in less time, a step that will surely cause nothing but increased customer dissatisfaction? The objective as set out is ridiculous. The real solution is to manufacture a more reliable product. Should the responsibility then be placed on manufacturing, when perhaps the problem is really tied in with the supply of material? It would be equally stupid to pass on to purchasing the responsibility for achieving this objective. As we can realize, all of these departments have some responsibility for reducing this cost, and the reduction will be achieved only when all of them understand their particular tasks and work together to achieve the common goal.

How then do we convince the nonbeliever? Certainly we should attempt to develop a picture of what our company can achieve and fully discuss this with top management. It will demand some faith in the program on their part, but with the increasing emphasis on quality this is becoming less and less difficult to initiate. Consider all of the possible advantages of developing a program of excellence, aside from the usual direct concerns for cost and quality.

- Increased personnel motivation.
- Reduced scrap.
- Less repair work.
- Increasing innovation in manufacturing.
- Less interdepartmental friction.
- Improved customer confidence.
- Shorter throughput times.
- Fewer problems in direct day-to-day management.
- Greater employee satisfaction.
- Lower employee turnover.

The ramifications are almost endless and from your own knowledge of your operation you will be able to prepare your own list. If this discussion of the advantages of excellence does not have the desired effect, it will be difficult to develop a program. There is some suspicion of quality programs by a considerable number of people in top management positions. Some have heard it all before in one or another of the fads of the day that have come and gone, and with justification believe that the current ideas will also pass. This is one good reason to base any such attempt to move towards excellence on straightforward good management techniques. Process control is basically nothing more than a formal method of initiating good management. It is a simple procedure to understand, it is easy to install, it will produce measurable results in a comparatively short time, and it provides a strong base on which to build any of the more complex quality programs if they are then considered necessary.

QUALITY, EXCELLENCE, AND GOOD MANAGEMENT

Good management will always be the basis for a profitable business. Whether we call our efforts a quality program or good process control we are in fact searching for excellence in everything we do. As we discussed in earlier chapters, what are considered good management techniques today may not be regarded as good management tomorrow. Society changes, our employees change, our products, our methods, and our equipments change. Our management methods have to change to keep in step. Yet some fundamentals never change and excellence is one of them.

The striving for excellence or perfection is open ended and can never stop. When it does our company is doomed to eventual extinction. This objective has to embrace the entire operation, from the very top to the very bottom of the Organization. When this philosophy has been developed, and the personnel have been trained to understand, agree, and accept it, exciting things will happen.

In this book we have discussed the various effects of many of the actions that relate to excellence, from developing the process correctly to demanding excellence from our vendors. Yet the fundamental striving for excellence has little to do with the many practical actions discussed in prior chapters. We are really looking at an overall attitude to work that is extremely difficult to define precisely. It is an urgent need to accept nothing but perfection, not only in our own actions but also in the actions of those who work for and with us. Not only the operators carrying out the work described in our process, but the storekeeper handling the materials, the janitor who keeps the place clean, the secretary at the word processor, the telephone operator; that is, the entire organization. The action items such as developing the process, setting up controls, and so on, are tools for us to use in our striving for quality. If, however, the basic desire for excellence is not there we will only be going through the motions and it is unlikely that we will be successful. When the driving force throughout the organization is to achieve excellence in every part of the operation no matter how small, success is guaranteed.

ACHIEVING EXCELLENCE

Excellence is attained through four main stages (Figure 22).

1. A total acceptance by upper management of the idea that only through striving for excellence can a company remain profitable. It must recognize that quality is not some remote philosophical dream but the

---

FOUR STAGES TO EXCELLENCE

(1) ACCEPTANCE BY MANAGEMENT

(2) TRAIN AND SET UP THE PROCESS

(3) DEVELOP IMPLEMENTATION PLAN

(4) MONITOR, REVISE, AND MEASURE

Figure 22 Achieving excellence is not difficult and produces the highest quality product at the lowest cost. It requires total acceptance and understanding from top management if it is to succeed.

heart of good management, which translates into practical dollars and cents.

2. Development of a plan for explaining this philosophy in practical terms to everyone in the organization, and providing the training in the techniques to be used. In manufacturing these steps involve setting up the process, as we have already discussed.

3. A detailed implementation program, that makes each step simple, but with a scheduled completion date and one individual responsible for that program step.

4. Daily monitoring of the overall program as to performance to the plan, and revisions of the program as they are found necessary. As part of this monitoring, the resulting improvements in the overall performance of the operation must be measured against that forecast.

Installing a program of excellence such as this is not something that will happen overnight. In a small well-organized operation it may be achieved in less than a year; with a larger company and its accompanying bureaucracy it may take two, three, or more years. Results do not come quickly or easily.

Indeed, at first it may seem that the program has generated nothing but costs and chaos. For this reason it is essential to plan carefully and measure the performance frequently against the plan. Otherwise, it is all too easy to give up in disgust. Finally, we must remember that once embarked on the search for excellence we cannot go back. We will never achieve our objective but in the searching we will constantly find unexpected riches.

Chapter 17

COST, BUDGETS, AND FORECASTS

Our search for excellence will inevitably demand that we set up total process control. Before this can be planned and installed, the question of cost will always be raised. It is often assumed that making a quality product, or buying excellent parts, or obtaining the best machines will inevitably increase the cost of the product. The reasoning behind this is simple: suppose that we can buy for $5.00 a part that generally meets the specification, but we find an occasional piece that is defective, say an average of 1 in 200. However, the so-called "good" parts are also frequently found to be barely within the specification limits and cause some minor problems during assembly; for example, they may be slightly difficult to load into an assembly fixture. Another vendor can supply parts that meet the requirements fully and consistently, without the minor loading problem, but the price is now $6.00 each.

Any suggestion to use the more expensive parts will almost certainly be objected to on the grounds that this will raise the cost of the product. The only counter to this argument is to demonstrate that using the better parts will save labor in assembly and thus compensate for the additional cost. The argument can then be expanded as follows. If only one part in 200 is found to be faulty, we will be paying an additional $200 to eliminate that one faulty part. Why not just inspect the parts and throw away the bad ones?

We then enter into an area that is difficult to quantify.

- What is the cost of inspecting the parts?
- What is the cost of the additional handling?
- What is the impact on the schedule when 0.5% of the parts have to be thrown away?

• How accurate will the inspection be?

• What will be the impact on cost, of the few faulty parts that get through the screening?

• If defective parts get into a product, can they affect reliability?

• What will be the cost impact of this?

• How do the difficulties of assembly affect cost?

PRODUCT COST, NOT MATERIAL PRICES

The arguments can go on forever about a list such as this. Depending on the attitudes of the participants, the final total costs can be made to support both arguments—that is, to use the old or the new parts. However, it does not take much knowledge of the operation to see that the effects of using the bad parts are much more widespread than is obvious, and determining the cost is not a simple equation. Out of this discussion, however, one factor becomes obvious: we must never consider the price paid for any item in the total equation, but the cost impact on the total product. Many cases abound where paying a higher price for materials will reduce the cost of the product, yet all too often purchasing and design work totally independently of manufacturing and cannot see the whole picture.

Similar arguments can be raised when it is suggested that a new machine would perform more consistently, or that some other aspect of the process should be improved. It is difficult for many people to accept change, and cost is all too often used as a way of objecting to change without appearing to present a negative attitude.

Eliminate Emotional Arguments

The only solution to arguments regarding cost is to present facts. The facts may not be too accurate, they will certainly contain some "best estimates," but they will be much more accurate than the guesswork that is inevitably used in these cases as the basis for emotional argument. The difficulty is to foresee the extent of the effects of quite simple actions. Invariably, the end result of improving the quality of either the materials or the process will be to reduce the product cost, even when this may not be immediately apparent.

This effect is well illustrated by the results of one company that had for several years been struggling to implement a "just in time" program. Somehow they could never quite achieve their goal, partly because they could not forecast with accuracy the length of time that parts would be in final assembly and test. Eventually they tackled this area of manufacturing, which involved buying more costly parts and some additional equipment. Suddenly they found that the process flow was smoothed and that they could begin to work truly on a "just in time" basis. The cost savings and quality improvement of implementing the "just in time" program paid for the expenditure many times over and on a continuing basis. Yet the savings had not been forecast, as it was not easily apparent that the improvement in the control of the assembly process would remove the last obstacles to achieving the "just in time" system. The process improvement had in fact been undertaken as part of a program to achieve excellence and the expenditure had been partly an act of faith in that program.

Consider Overall Cost

Cost then has to be considered over the entire use of the parts or the machine and the overall affect on the price of the product must be calculated as accurately as possible. If the cost argument can be overcome even temporarily, the measured effect once the changes are in operation will prove the accuracy of the estimate. In a similar vein, expenditure on training is frequently seen as a loss, with the return as a vague series of events that may happen sometime in the future. It is strange that when business starts to fall off the first thing to be cut is the training budget. Surely when business is slow this is an excellent time to improve the skills and knowledge of the staff and use that training to improve the efficiency and productivity of the company and restore the competitive edge.

BUDGETS

Any business, no matter what size, has to develop some form of budget to be able to plan for the future; yet all too often this is done without any attention to the manufacturing operation, and without an understanding of the processes involved. This is unfortunate, as the budget can be a useful tool in developing the excellence that is our objective. One large corporation had a corporate policy that budgets had to reflect the yearly profit. When profits stayed the same, budgets were subjected to a small cut, in order to make the managers think about cost reduction. When profits fell by 10% there was an across-the-board cut of 12% in the budgets. This had ridiculous effects.

On one occasion the past year had resulted in a reduction of profits, the manufacturing budget had been cut. But the budgeted year contained the introduction of several new products plus an increase in the volume of some of the other work. The result was a major increase in shipments for the budgeted year but with a reduced expenditure. People had to be laid off, tools could not be purchased, and the entire future of the corporation was jeopard-ized. Corporate accounting was adamant; they had merely stuck to rules that could not be changed. Eventually the manufacturing manager formally reported that he would overspend his budget by a considerable amount. Each month he received a strongly worded letter from accounting advising him of his excessive expenditure, and at the end of the year he had in fact overspent almost exactly according to his forecast. Nothing more was said, for he achieved his production figures. In this case the budget was a total farce; it was completely useless and all the time and effort spent in producing it was completely wasted.

Budget with Honesty

In all too many companies the budget that is submitted is always subjected to a cut. This practice of course becomes well known, and the budget that is sent to the boss is always padded by a certain percentage to assure that the money required is forthcoming. Once again the practice is the height of stupidity. If it is accurately developed, the budget can provide an excellent guide to our future activities, and we can use the weekly or monthly report of expenditures as a simple and accurate tool for measuring just how well we are achieving our objectives.

We have to remember that the budget is a series of figures printed on a piece of paper, not some unchangeable truth carved in stone. As circumstances change, the budget must change; it is useful only when it reflects the actual operations from which it was planned.

The example once again illustrates how impossible it is to separate depart-ments in our manufacturing organization. Accounting must understand what goes on in the manufacturing process; they must recognize that the figures in their budgets and financial reports are translated on the shop floor into people making products. The way that they develop and lay out these documents can assist or hinder the manufacturing process. The production of a sound budget requires the cooperation of both accounting and manufacturing. Obviously if the money is not available it cannot be spent, but working together these departments can arrive at the best way to use the company's resources. The budget must be based on facts as far as possible, and the best forecasts available. It must also be flexible. If the production rate is increased, the budgeted expenditure must be increased to reflect the additional materials and labor required, and any new machines or other equipment necessary to meet the new demand. Similarly, if production has to be cut, the budget must reflect the new circumstances. It is not a fixed legal document, but a living, changing tool to assist in controlling the manufacturing process and monitoring the overall performance.

FORECASTS

If you set sail on the ocean, first of all you must know your starting point and where you are heading. Then you will need a compass and a chart to know which way to steer to arrive at your destination. In manufacturing it is usually top management who decrees the general direction in which we are to travel, and marketing decrees the exact destination. How to get there is usually laid out in some form of production forecast that acts as our chart and compass.

Some managers have said that they cannot forecast their production because it is too complex, it changes too often, or other similar excuses. The fact is of course that they do forecast, even if only in the very short term. They must know today what they intend to make tomorrow, even if only in general terms; they are constantly mulling things over and developing plans for the next day's work. What they really mean is that they do not know how to go about forecasting their production in any formal manner. As a consequence, they make life extremely difficult for themselves and those who work for them. Everything is operated on a hand-to-mouth basis, which can never be very efficient.

The Impossible Forecast

If their production is truly so impossible to forecast, it becomes essential that these managers plan their manufacturing facility to be able to respond to the ever changing demands of the marketplace and to do it better than anyone else, not sit back and say that they cannot forecast their future production. One company found that their products although basically similar varied considerably depending on the need of each customer. They set out therefore to develop a manufacturing process to take care of these requirements. Initially it took several weeks to produce each unit from initial order through design to shipping, but with refinement they were able to reduce the time to three days. In developing the process they improved the quality, reduced the cost, and this operation is now one of the most efficient and profitable in the United States, if not in the world.

Marketing Forecasts

Very few companies have a demand for their products as variable as this. Good forecasting begins with understanding the demand for our products and involves the marketing department. It is amazing how often marketing people will claim that they cannot forecast what their sales will be. Again in most cases this is not true. Once people can be persuaded to sit down and begin to put down their best information on paper, it is surprising how accurate forecasting can be. After all, if no one attempts to make a forecast, there is nothing to work with. Any forecast is more useful than this, and with experience it is surprising just how accurate the forecasting can become.

The author was once involved with an operation that made many different products, and it was becoming extremely difficult to plan production. At first the department believed that any attempt to forecast production was doomed to failure. But in order to make anything we were already informally planning two weeks ahead; thus, together with marketing we attempted first to plan four weeks ahead in detail. This proved to be quite accurate, much more so than we had anticipated. We then estimated the production for each month for six months ahead, and made our best judgments for each month for the remainder of a total of twelve months. Finally we made a best estimate for the next year and frankly some rather wild guesses for the following three years. Each week we met for a few minutes to update the monthly forecast, and once a month we discussed the longer range plans for the full five years. Of course mistakes abounded, but with time and experience the forecasting for the first six months became quite accurate, and week by week it was only necessary to make minor adjustments to the plans. While the forecasts for the later periods were obviously not so accurate, it was surprising how good they turned out to be. The experience had an important effect in forcing us to consider and plan for the future instead of merely accepting surprises when they happened.

COOPERATION IN FORECASTING

The manufacturing forecast is essential if the process is to be planned efficiently, and like all the other aspects of the process it cannot be developed in isolation. The future manufacturing schedule is an important tool for the entire operation. Because it is impossible to suddenly crank up production or change the product mix, it is necessary for all concerned to have a plan to work to. Marketing must take the lead in developing the forecast, but it is equally important to purchasing, to personnel, to training and all of the other areas of the operation. It is the foundation for all planning.

Chapter 18

THE NEW TECHNOLOGIES

As we discussed in the first chapter of this book, in the early part of this century the manufacturing manager worked with comparatively simple machines and technologies that could be easily understood. As an improved machine or process was developed, it was not difficult to decide if it would be a profitable addition to the plant. As technologies developed, machines became more complex and the whole rate of change accelerated, until today it sometimes seems as if a new process is being touted in the marketplace before the last one has been fully proved.

The manufacturing manager today has to walk a very fine line between falling behind in regard to the ever changing technologies and falling for the frequently unfounded claims of some of the new processes and equipments. The technical magazines view any hint of a new technology as a gift from heaven—something to fill the columns and increase the advertising revenues. The new technologies are also the basis for most of the papers presented at the trade seminars. The seminars and magazines are prime sources of information for the manufacturing manager to keep up to date on advances in manufacturing technology.

These new ideas, however, then appear to be much more pervasive than is often the case. Nowhere is this more apparent than in the electronics industry. For example, any reader of the popular trade journals could well believe that his operation will be left far behind if it does not immediately convert to surface mounted technology, and that he will soon be working with even smaller devices. Of course, nothing could be further from the truth. Many companies are using the technologies of the 1960s and 1970s in making their electronic products and there is really no reason for them to change. From a very rough and ready but personal assessment of the industry as a whole, it appears to me that about 10% are working at the "cutting edge" of technology and are the subject of most of the publicity. They are almost invariably aerospace and military vendors. Another 25 to 30% are working with newer packaging and manufacturing technologies, while the remainder are working in almost the same way as they have been for the past 20 years. They will certainly change eventually, as it appears profitable for them to do so, and of course this is the sensible way to determine the value of any new technology.

The Japanese are often used as examples of the advantages of using the latest technologies, but the author well remembers being invited a few years ago to see some new products under development at the labs of a very well-known Japanese electronics company. On commenting that the design used an old assembly method of attaching components to the printed wiring board, the design engineer explained that "This is the technology we understand." In other words, until the new technologies had been proved, until the company had gained experience and understanding of them, they intended to use the methods and components that were familiar and proved.

This is a very sensible philosophy, and if it is applied to any new machine or method it will avoid major mistakes. If the process is not clearly understood, or if the machines are totally new, you should proceed with caution. Try to find someone who has experience with them; go to the vendor and ask to operate the machines under the conditions you will use, and ask to see the process in operation under the same or similar conditions as you will be using it in your plant.

IS THIS PROCESS FOR ME?

It is all too easy to become seduced into implementing a new process. Often the reasons for deciding to use it are obscure and not clearly thought out. At one company the decision was ultimately traced to the vice president of engineering, who after attending a seminar on a new manufacturing method had become so enamored with the technology that he proposed to his senior engineer that it be implemented immediately. When the system was reviewed in detail it was discovered to be unsuitable for this particular company. This finding placed the engineer in an untenable situation, as his boss had been so enthusiastic about the whole idea he had boosted it at some length with the company president. Ultimately the company brought in an outside consultant who was able to show that improving their present process was more effective than making the proposed changes. As an outsider he was able to do this without damaging any egos.

There are many factors to consider before deciding that a new process is the right one for any particular manufacturing operation. It is all too easy to see a new process in operation, to believe it perfect for your particular company, and then find that it does not work as originally conceived. No two companies are the same; the product mix, the product volume, even the situation and layout of the plant can affect the outcome. It is almost impossible to transplant a process directly from one operation to another unless all other factors are the same.

As an example, a brand new process was installed at considerable cost but was found to be totally unpredictable. Sometimes the product was of excellent quality, but at other times much of it had to be scrapped. For over a year the engineers struggled to bring the system under control, but finally they had to accept that as installed it was not a profitable project. It had worked beautifully under laboratory conditions and as a pilot plant, but would not function in full production. It was ultimately discovered that some stages of the process had to be so tightly controlled that any manual controls were ineffective. The final solution was to automate the entire process, which then dramatically exceeded the planned cost.

Provide the Facilities

Before considering changes to the process, or changing over to a new process, we must very carefuly consider all of the many factors that may affect the new operation. This step has to be carried out in detail by people who are skilled and knowledgeable in the proposed process. It is often advisable to operate a pilot line in order to become experienced, to "get the hands dirty"—in other words, to gain experience about the minute details of any process which are difficult if not impossible to record fully, but which can have a major impact on the ultimate results. This all requires time, patience, and knowledgeable people. They need facilities to carry out a full investigation. They may need to travel to other companies or countries to view the proposed process. They may need to carry out experiments, to buy materials, to investigate possible subcontractors. They may need to consult specialists in particular fields. They must be given the opportunity to do this work correctly, and this means adequate people, time, and funds.

SHOULD WE BUY THAT NEW MACHINE?

Promotions for the new automobiles all promise a better performance, a quieter ride, and more comfort—much superior to the one you are driving today. Yet you know that in many cases under the new sheet metal they are the same cars as those sold last year. But the glitter and the gimmicks are attractive, and many cars are sold solely because of the appearance of the new models. As experienced managers and engineers we are not likely to be influenced by such things, or are we?

Of course we are, for we are human beings with human traits. Unless we look objectively at any new equipment, we can fall into the same trap as anyone else. It is interesting to see the number of machines purchased with computer control, or computer monitoring, as an optional feature. When management is asked why the computer is necessary, in many cases their reply is vague, or they suggest it might be useful in the future, or some similar reason. Yet there is undoubtedly some pleasure of ownership in punching up instructions on the keyboard, and watching the screen, in being able to say that the plant is equipped with the latest and best, and this accounts for some of the popularity of the systems.

The author was once given a pocket computer to use as a data collection system, to keep telephone numbers, record appointments, and make notes. It also had a clock and an alarm built into it. It was an amazing device that gave him much pleasure while he waited in airports, as he attempted to find out how it worked. It was never used otherwise, as a pencil and a scrap of paper were much faster and easier to use. In a similar manner some of the exotic equipments that promise much in the way of efficiency improvements in industry have unexpected problems that are not discovered until they are put to use, at which time it is too late to turn to another system.

At one company an entire manufacturing operation had been automated, with the parts moving from station to station by means of conveyors that gripped the product on opposing sides. One step in the process required that the product be absolutely flat, and it was found that it was not rigid enough to pass through this stage without producing a considerable number of defects. Unfortunately this was not discovered until the entire automated assembly line had been installed. The problem could only be corrected at this time by changing the design of the product to make it thicker and more rigid, a change that then increased the product cost beyond the planned figure.

Before considering the purchase of any new equipment, you should write down the reason for the purchase and develop a specification that lists in detail the performance that you expect. Then comes the time to ask some questions.

- Is the reason for purchase justified by cost reduction, quality improvement, increased capability, or what?
- Are these figures substantiated by facts or are they estimates? Can they be believed?

- Will the performance of the proposed machine meet the requirements of the specification in all details?
- Is the machine a stable, proved design?
- How many are in use?
- Is it possible to see one in operation under conditions similar to your own?

The Hidden Problems

You should look for the hidden problems that may not be evident until you have some practical experience with the equipment. For example, a machine was purchased that performed according to expectations until the product mix changed, when it was found that the setup time became the limiting factor and the planned throughput could not be reached. During machine selection it had been assumed that the setup times would improve with experience; they did not.

If a machine is new and there are few in use, you must recognize that you will be taking some chances. It may not work as planned, it may have reliability problems, and it will certainly demand a long introductory period. This is not to suggest that it is not worthwhile to take a chance, but you should do so with your eyes open and plan for the worst.

Consider maintenance if the machine is at all complex. It may be better to purchase a machine with a less efficient performance if you can be assured of excellent service when breakdowns occur. In this respect it is often unwise to purchase foreign machines unless the company has a local maintenance network.

Watching the machine in use is probably the best possible test, but here again be cautious. If you are seeing it at the vendor's premises, make sure that it is set up and operated in exactly the same mode that you will be using. Look for repeatability in operation; do not let the operator fiddle with the controls. If you are reviewing it at another user's plant try to talk with the operator, find out the maintenance record. All of these points may seem obvious and perhaps out of place in a book on management, yet these are the very mistakes that are seen every day.

Plan the Installation

In planning the introduction of the new machine, you should allow plenty of time for installation, in order to make sure the site is correct. The author has not infrequently found a machine so poorly placed that the doors could not be opened for maintenance. Consider all of the ancillary requirements—water, compressed air, power supply, venting, and so on. It is much more costly to have to go back and refit them.

In one plant a machine had been placed in an non-airconditioned area, on the grounds that it generated too much heat. Unfortunately it was sensitive to high humidity and when the summer came around and the humidity went over 75% the system would not function. It had to be moved into an airconditioned area. The additional cost and loss of production could have been avoided if more thought had been given to the requirements of the process.

Make arrangements for benches, shelves, and storage cabinets. Lay in a stock of spare parts and consumable components. Do not stint on these items. Arrange for personnel to be trained in the operation of the new machine, and do not forget manufacturing engineering, who will have to develop operating parameters, and the maintenance people who will have to keep the machine operating consistently. If all of these items are taken care of by a logical plan there will be few surprises and the machine will operate without many of the problems that arise when these are handled in an unorganized manner.

Of course, acquiring a single machine is a much smaller task than adding several machines or a complete manufacturing system. The same concerns arise, but in addition there will be the problems of compatibility. Machines must be capable of being operated together; throughputs must match. The difficulties of moving parts from one machine to another must be overcome. One system was being installed when it was discovered that the heights of two of the conveyors differed by almost 12 inches. An interface then had to be designed and built, which in turn required the layout of the machines to be changed, pushed the installation cost over budget, and delayed the startup by several weeks. The height variation had been noticed during the initial planning but had been considered a minor problem that could be taken care of during installation.

Software

In today's world of computers we have also to consider the cost and the compatibility of software, and the need for computers to be able to work together. These concerns can frequently prove to be more difficult than the acquisition and installation of the hardware, and in many ways this aspect of compatibility is the most important of all. Standardization of software is growing but it is still all too easy to find that machines cannot talk to each other or require complex translation systems to be able to communicate freely.

When the system is to be incorporated into an overall computer-controlled manufacturing operation, the software packages are of the utmost importance. The cost of acquiring, installing, and debugging software may well exceed the cost of the hardware and should be carefully estimated.

TOTAL AUTOMATION AND ROBOTICS

The idea that we can install a totally automated production line is certainly an attractive concept. The potential exists for minimizing labor costs, process repeatability can be improved, and many of the day-to-day scheduling and quality problems can be more easily brought under control. Of course, the facts are not quite so positive and simple. In the first place we have to decide what degree of automation is applicable to our particular operation. This will vary for many reasons, but primarily because of product volume and mix.

High Volume–Low Mix

Automation is usually considered the obvious manufacturing method when considering high-volume production. But in order to make total automation a practical possibility we need to consider three factors regarding the product volume and mix.

1. The volume of product to be made.
2. The stability of the volume of the product required from manufacturing.
3. The stability of the product design, and the number of different designs to be made.

1. It would obviously be ridiculous to invest much money in automatic equipment if the intent is only to manufacture a few items each day. Yet this statement could be challenged on the grounds that the value of the product must be taken into account. For example, an automated plant designed to produce aircraft might well only manufacture one or two airplanes each week yet still justify the cost of the automation. However, this sort of argument will always be with us simply because the variations in manufacturing are so enormous that no matter what rules we try to apply there will always be some particular operation that will be the exception to the rule.

In general then we first of all need to have a high volume of product. The volume needs to be such that the cost of the equipment for automation is repaid within a reasonable time, but there are other factors to be considered in this equation regarding payback.

• Will the life of the product comfortably exceed the estimated payback time?

For example, if we are making sausages, it would be reasonable to assume that they will be manufactured for the foreseeable future, and if the cost of automating the process will not be paid back for five years this would not be of major concern. However, if we are automating a plant that will be manufacturing, say video tapes, we would certainly need to know that the cost will be paid back in a much shorter time as the technology could change and eliminate the need for the product. We have many examples of such technology changes. The calculator eliminated the slide rule; compact discs and tapes have virtually wiped out the vinyl disc as a recording medium. The computer and the word processor have totally replaced the mechanical typewriter.

• If the product demand is reduced can the plant be used for another product?

Generally the answer is NO unless the plant is deliberately designed for this purpose. Of course, you could probably make pork sausages in a plant designed to make beef sausages, but even here some variations in the properties of the respective meats may make this impractical if not impossible. Generally, when a plant is designed to make one product, it can be designed to do so very efficiently, but making it possible to change to another even similar product will increase the cost and complexity of the process.

A fine example is a well-known computer manufacturer who developed a highly automated plant that proved to be extremely efficient. However, it was made clear during the development of the automation that when the product came to the end of its life the plant was to be scrapped. The added complexity of making the plant capable of manufacturing more than one range of products would have proved totally uneconomical in this particular case.

This is not to say that such a plant is either impossible to develop or uneconomical to operate. Another well-known manufacturer has in fact developed such an installation, which is capable of making several different types of computer on the same line. Every situation is different and the possibilities must be considered carefully before any decisions are made with respect to automation.

2. The stability of the product demand is vitally important in deciding the limit of automation. For example, if an automated plant is set up to manufacture 5,000 items per day, and if the design and development of the plant and the process are sound, the cost per unit will be at or near the minimum possible, say $250 per unit. If the demand for the product falls and the production rate is cut to 3,000 per day, the cost per unit is bound to rise. The manufacturing costs will stay the same, the cost of the equipment remains constant, and with automation there is little possibility of reducing overheads by laying off people. In other words, the payback period increases. The answer may be to design the plant to manufacture less than the maximum demand for the

product, and to hold product in store to cover the periods of low demand. However, now we have to consider the costs of storage and the possibility that from time to time we will be unable to fill the demands for the product.

3. Design stability is of vital importance if an automated manufacturing facility is to operate successfully. Too often design changes are added to the product when manufacturing has begun. This of course shows a significant deficiency in product development and has at times caused the failure of the entire project. In one company with an automated assembly line there were so many design changes to the product after the line had been installed that there were more people modifying the product after it had been made than were engaged in the actual production. The subsequent changes that had to be made to the production equipment put back the manufacturing schedule by several months and almost shut down the company. What may appear to be a very simple design change can have major ramifications when the product is being made on an automated assembly line. Design stability must be assured before the line design is completed and the designer must understand the requirements of the intended automation.

The ultimate simplicity in automation is a plant developed to manufacture one product in high volumes, at a steady rate, with an expected product life of several years. The equipment designer is not hampered by multiple requirements; although the design of the machinery may be anything but simple, he can tailor it specifically for the single task and for the ultimate in efficiency and quality. The moment that the product design varies—for example, when the plant has to make several different versions of the same product—even if the variations are small, the complexity of the automation increases. When the designs of the products change widely, the complexity of automation reaches the extreme.

Low Volume–High Mix

At the opposite end of the manufacturing spectrum we find automation that is developed for making many different products, each in small or medium quantities and with widely varying demands. This type of production goes under several different terms, but "Flexible Manufacturing" is one of the current fashionable phrases. The concept here is quite different from that of the High Volume–Low Mix, as the emphasis is on flexibility.

Inevitably the cost of equipment for this type of manufacturing is high. The overall efficiency will probably be much lower than that in the plant designed to make one product only. We have to consider the different manufacturing methods available to us, and here the electronics industry can provide the perfect example.

Consider the manufacturing operation that has to assemble, solder, clean, and test many different printed wiring boards (PWBs). It is not at all unusual to find companies who have 2 to 300 different board types running through their assembly lines at any one time. Each board may be different in size and shape, use different components, and have widely varying packaging densities. The alternative assembly methods are few.

1. Assemble all components to the boards by hand, solder on a manually loaded and operated wave solder machine, clean, and finally test on an automated test system, with the boards being manually moved from operation to operation.

2. Assemble the parts to the boards automatically by machine, and then continue as described in item 1 above.

3. Assemble the parts to the boards automatically, with mechanized transfer to an automated solder machine, with the remainder of the process as described in item 1 above.

4. Automate every step of the entire process, with automatic transfer of the boards through all of the process steps.

Method 1 is of course the simplest and the most flexible, and is the normal operating method in many plants.

Method 2 improves the quality of assembly as it reduces the "people factor" and eliminates some of the problems of incorrect parts being assembled in the wrong places. It may well reduce the labor content slightly, but now certain other factors become of importance: for example, the accuracy of tooling or locating holes in the boards, machine and process limitations that may require the boards to be redesigned and may limit the ability to change at will between component manufacturers. In other words, the improvements in quality and efficiency come at the cost of reduced flexibility in the working of the shop floor and in other ancillary areas of production. The cost of the equipment may be high and the design of the product must take into account the limitations of the machines. They will also require more highly trained operators and maintenance and setup people than those used in hand assembly. This is the most widely used level of automation, offering the highest productivity and largest number of quality improvements without causing too great a limitation on manufacturing flexibility.

Method 3. The next stage becomes more difficult. It is quite possible to buy computer-controlled soldering machines that will automatically set up the correct soldering parameters, change the conveyor width to suit the board size, and so on; it can usually determine these by reading a bar code placed on each board. But this form of automation can limit throughput and/or manufacturing flexibility. Every time the solder machine conveyor width changes, the machine has to hold back any new product until the machine is empty; it then resets the soldering parameters, the conveyor width, and once more accepts product. Either the throughput is dramatically reduced because of all the waiting time or the products have to be batched into lots with the same characteristics, a step that reduces the line flexibility.

Method 4. The final stage of total automation is seldom if ever implemented, as the ramifications are just too widespread and the costs too expensive. The line may have almost total flexibility to assemble any type of PWB, but the cost can become prohibitive, the complexity too difficult to handle, and the throughput slower than that of the manually assembled line. Indeed, some companies have found that the opposite method of setting up the operation is more profitable, with simple automation on several lines each dedicated to assemble boards of similar design.

Flexible manufacturing, or the automation of High Mix–Low Volume production, is an attractive concept, but is seldom realized. What is frequently achieved is the so-called "Islands of Automation" philosophy in which individual operations are automated one at a time, according to the ease with which this can be accomplished and the quality and cost payback that can be achieved. When the limit is reached on the individual operations, an attempt can be made to link the operations together with some form of automated material transfer system. Here again it is not unusual to find that some operations cannot be successfully automated and remain as manual functions in an otherwise automated line.

It makes sense to automate wherever possible, but there are no clearly defined rules for deciding when and what to automate. Much depends on the particular circumstances of each manufacturing operation. We rarely have the opportunity to start from scratch with a new product, a bare shop floor, and unlimited funds. In most cases we have an on-going production line, we are told to improve the efficiency and product quality, we have to keep production moving, and therefore we have to automate a step at a time.

Under these circumstances, similar criteria apply as with developing the process. Plan, review all of the options, look at cost and payback, and above all consider the implications of linking together the various steps toward the optimum level of automation. The concern for process control must be continually in the forefront of these activities, together with the collection of processing data and the transfer of this information to the process steps that can use it effectively.

Robotics

A few years ago, while the author was visiting Japan, and he attended a lecture extolling the high degree of automation of Japanese industry. As an example the speaker pointed out how many more robots were in use in Japan compared with the United States. A film that was shown described many robotic systems that were nothing more than simple pick and place machines. On being asked what was the accepted definition of a robot, the speaker smiled and agreed that the figures would be very different if the United States counted robots in the same way. So that we do not fall into that trap, we should define a robot as a handling device or other similar form of automation that is programmable through software and external or internal sensors. We have all seen the weaving arms of the welding robots on automobile assembly lines, and other similar examples, although of course there is no need for a robot to be designed in this particular style.

Some years ago there was a tremendous amount of publicity on the future capabilities of robots; although their use is growing the expected rush to put them into the workplace has not occurred. Certainly they have replaced the human worker in many of the jobs that have to be done in bad environments, but even here their use is by no means universal.

There is nothing fundamentally wrong with the robot—it is an extremely useful tool—but it is often an expensive and unnecessarily complex tool for the particular task for which it is intended. As the Japanese showed in their film, a pick and place machine or other simple form of automation can frequently perform the same task as a robot. The difference is that when the job is finished the robot can usually be transferred to another task by means of a simple software change, without the need for a highly skilled operator. The simple automation machine will probably need the services of a skilled tool designer and a machine shop to be modified for the next task.

Because of its inherent flexibility the robot may be considerably slower than simple automation designed specifically for one task. The pick and place machine is a fine example: when one part has to be picked up from one designated spot and placed consistently in another, the simple machine will usually run rings around the robot as far as speed is concerned. However, if the parts are of differing shape or if they have to be precisely oriented or very accurately placed, then this becomes a suitable task for the robot. If any decision has to be made as to which part has to be placed in a particular spot, because of the ability to program the robot by making comparatively simple changes to the software it becomes an obvious choice. For example, a robot was used to place parts very accurately onto an assembly. It was found that some of the parts, which were quite fragile, were deformed and would then not function correctly. It was not difficult to install a television camera to view the parts and program the robot to place those that were deformed into a special die set to be corrected before being assembled.

Of course, installing a robot is not quite as simple as the popular press would have us believe. The cost of the ancillary equipment that is necessary can easily exceed the cost of the robot. Such items may include special containers for the parts so that the robot can pick up each piece successfully each time, and equipment to move the filled containers to the robot and remove the empty ones, and to bring the part to which the piece is to be assembled exactly to the correct spot for assembly. If precise placement is necessary for assembly, the equipment may include television cameras to act as "eyes" for the robot and sensors in the gripping mechanism. If a television camera is used to assure placement accuracy, the necessary "targets" have to be accurately placed on both the parts to be joined, and the tooling accuracy of the auxiliary transfer equipment becomes vitally important. These and similar ancilliary requirements have in many cases amounted to a cost of from one to one and a half times that of the basic robot.

In spite of the ability of the robot to handle almost any object, some items will inevitably be difficult for it to handle successfully. In one assembly operation every attempt was made to arrive at total automation, and several robots were in fact installed on the assembly line. However, there were also six operators who were employed to place the few components that could not be handled in any other way. The parts were standard purchased components and the shapes were either inconsistent in size or were such that the robot could not easily hold the part during the transfer and assembly. In almost every case, if the design of the parts could have been changed, then the robot could have been used successfully, but this alternative was far too costly.

DESIGN AND AUTOMATION

In a simple manual manufacturing operation the design of the product will have minimal affect on the efficiency of the operation. The human being is the most flexible piece of equipment that exists. The moment that we begin to use tools of any kind we begin to restrict the designer. As the complexity of the tooling increases, the limitations on the product design also increases. If the designer is not part of the automation decision team, it is possible to arrive at some ridiculous situations. The author was once asked to review some manufacturing problems and found that the designers had used materials in the design that would not withstand the temperatures necessary for the manufacturing process. This fact may seem ridiculous, but the designers concerned had never seen the product manufactured and had no idea of the implications of the process on the materials being specified.

The designer and the manufacturing people are part of the same team and must work together at all times. This comment has been made many times in this book, but nowhere is it of more importance than when we are attempting to automate the manufacturing process.

STATISTICS, REPEATABILITY, AND THE COMPUTER

As we have discussed elsewhere in this book, in our search for excellence we will have to use statistics to control the process. We also mentioned the problems of obtaining data that are accurate and timely. One of the main advantages of using computer-controlled machines and processes is the ease with which accurate data can be generated in real time. It can be stored in almost any form, from paper printout to recordings on magnetic tape or floppy and hard disks. In the latter format it is possible to manipulate the information in almost any way that we please. As an added advantage we can easily transmit such data to other areas of the plant or even offices in other countries.

This ability to generate, store, and manipulate data may well be one of the best reasons to install computer-controlled machines and systems. Manually generated information is rarely totally accurate, for the human being is not very good at carrying out a mindless activity like writing down numbers all day long. The computer, however, thrives on this task. To set up such an operation, especially in a complex system, requires a great deal of detailed planning by individuals with highly specialized skills and knowledge. It will only be done correctly if all concerned sit together and consider every requirement.

- What is the basic objective for the system?
- What data is required to provide the necessary control?
- What data will have to be collected, and from where?
- How often, in real time?
- What is to be done to the raw data?
- What information is expected from the final data?
- Will it be used directly or via human intervention?

To answer these questions the team must include software, computer, and systems experts, manufacturing engineering personnel, quality control people, and management. The manufacturing manager must lead this team; their work is too critical to the overall efficiency of the operation to leave it in any other hands. It may be necessary to keep the team's feet firmly on the ground. Always remember that data themselves are useless; it is only when the data can be used to control the process or generate corrective actions that they are of value.

SUMMARY

- Never move into a new technology because it is fashionable.
- If it can be justified, move cautiously and to a well thought-out plan.
- Try out equipment under the same conditions that you will use it.
- Beware of hidden snags. They are always there.
- Plan the supply of ancillary services.
- Set up a formal training program on any new equipment.
- Do not be seduced by the "bells & whistles."
- Understand just what the computer can and cannot do for your process.
- Recognize the cost and the importance of excellent software installation.

Chapter 19

COMPUTERS AND MANUFACTURING

The development of the computer at first had little effect on the actual manufacturing operation. The large main frame systems were primarily used for accounting, for maintaining stock and purchasing information, and for similar data base generation. Some attempts were also made to use these systems for design purposes and the author well remembers the problems that were encountered in installing an early CAD system using an IBM 360 mainframe. It was primarily the introduction of the personal computer that made this a cost-effective tool in the manufacturing field.

COMPUTER-CONTROLLED MACHINES

It has become common to find machines that are "computer controlled" and this term is widely although sometimes incorrectly used. In some cases the computer is a monitoring tool only and has little or no effect on the actual operation of the equipment. However, as has been mentioned in an earlier chapter, this can be a most useful function with the computer providing valuable data for process control. For simplicity, in this section we are primarily considering the computer as a machine control tool or a method of generating data to assist in controlling the process.

Used as the controlling system for a machine, the computer can provide repeatability and a reduction in the manual labor necessary to carry out the operation. For example, consider a simple machine tool such as a metalworking lathe. Once the necessary information has been entered into the computer's memory, it can install the correct tool and set the appropriate rotational speed of the workpiece. It can monitor that the cooling fluid flow is within the specified limits and that the tool is fed into the workpiece at the right rate. It can check the final size and shape of the workpiece, and it can carry out these tasks faster and to tighter limits than can the human operator.

The computer-controlled machine does not generally have the flexibility of the human operator. This limitation emphasizes the importance of many other facets of the operation, which are often forgotten or taken for granted and may now have to be tightly controlled. The human operator can stop the machine at the first sign of the tool not cutting correctly; the computer, however, will allow the machine to continue to function until one or more of the preset limits are exceeded. As a result tool wear has to be checked regularly, and tools with a long life between replacement or sharpening will be required. The computer is unlikely to be able to check the hardness and similar properties of the materials being turned and these factors may have to be controlled more closely. In other words, many of the things that are instinctively compensated for by the operator now have to be controlled.

It is theoretically possible for the computer to monitor every possible step of the process. For example, the torque required to drive the workpiece in the lathe could possibly be used to monitor the material hardness, and we are seeing an increasing use of such sensing devices that make the computer-controlled machines draw nearer and nearer to the capability and flexibility of the operator without the problems of fatigue and variability that the human being brings to the process. Of course, these make the system more and more complex and expensive, and it seems that there are also always some aspects of the human ability that the computer can never quite duplicate.

While the computer can certainly improve the performance of the simple machines, it really comes into its own when it is is used with machines that are designed to make use of the tremendous capability, in terms of memory and its computational speed, of the modern computer. One excellent example is the machining center, where the workpiece can be drilled, turned, milled, and so on all within one complex metal removal system. The computer can store all the information necessary to carry out the complex movements of many different workpieces; it can also program to change tools, set up speeds and feeds, and transform a piece of raw metal into a finished item in one set of operations.

In a similar way, although the computer can be extremely useful at controlling one machine or process step, its full potential will be realized only when it controls a complete line or process. For example, it is capable of monitoring the position of every workpiece; it can control the movement of parts into and out of the various process steps, as well as control the individual operations. This degree of complexity now makes it possible to automate the process in ways that would have been unthinkable before the advent of the computer.

Of course, as the computer-controlled system becomes more and more automated the cost increases, and a balance has to be struck somewhere between the cost of automation and the advantages to be gained. The expense of the actual equipment is frequently the least costly part of the entire venture. Installation costs, debugging the system, and of course the cost of software are too frequently underestimated. In addition, as the complexity of the system grows, the need for first-class maintenance also grows, as well as its cost. It matters little if one simple mechanical lathe breaks down, for almost any proficient technician can make the necessary repairs. If a machining center stops for any reason it may well mean that the entire shop floor is halted and some very experienced and well-trained people will be required to bring it back on line quickly.

THE COMPUTER AND INFORMATION FLOW

The computer can be used in many other ways to improve the manufacturing operation, and one of the primary uses is in the transfer and manipulation of data. Of course, it is not necessary to use a computer to transfer information. It can be done by word of mouth, by writing, by telephone, or even by beating on a drum. However, the computer has several advantages over all of these systems.

1. The information can be transferred in real time. That is, the data shown on one screen is available on all screens at the same time.
2. The information can be manipulated to suit a particular requirement. Nowhere is this capability used more than in the electronics industry. For example, the circuit designer can simulate the operation of the circuit on the computer, and the board designer can use this information to lay out the PWB (Printed Wiring Board) with a suitable CAD (Computer Aided Design) program. From this layout the board fabricator can produce the drill tapes for the PWB as well as the programs for routing the board from the base material. The equipment designer can use the same data to make the test fixture and develop the programs for the automatic component insertion machines. The purchasing agent can interpret this information in terms of the amount of board material that has to be purchased for any particular manufacturing lot size, receiving inspection can use the data to produce inspection fixtures, and so on.
3. The information can be transmitted and received at extremely high speeds, over almost any distance and to practically any spot in the

world. For example, one U.S. company has plants in Puerto Rico, Mexico, and Europe. All are linked together through satellite technology and all use the same data base.

This flow of information itself has many obvious advantages. No longer does any department have to wait for the "end-of-the-month" report, which was in any case often out of date by the time it was received; it can now see the facts in real time during the manufacturing operation. Drawings, parts lists, and other technical data are immediately available, and can be controlled and updated much more easily than when in the form of documents. When all departments are working to the same information base the chances of error and misunderstanding are minimized if not eliminated. In addition, the fast and in many cases very personal transfer of information between departments forces the realization that it is no longer possible for any part of the operation to function in isolation and encourages the close cooperation that must be achieved if we are to operate efficiently. If we now add to the basic data base the information available from the computers that are actually controlling an automated production line, we can see that it is now possible to develop a totally integrated computer-controlled operation. This is often called CIM, or Computer Integrated Manufacturing, and offers the possibility of the ultimate in manufacturing process control.

COMPUTER-INTEGRATED MANUFACTURING

Consider some of the possibilities that are now available, for example, to a company making bicycles. Let us assume for simplicity that its product line consists of three basic designs: a street bicycle, an off road version, and a racing bike. Each design is offered in four sizes and four colors. In addition, there is an array of optional extras that the customer can order.

At one extreme of manufacturing complexity each order could be given to one assembler who would go to stores, pull all the necessary components, and then make bicycle according to the order. This would offer tremendous flexibility, but high labor cost, long delivery times, and the possibility of quality problems due to the varying skills of the operators. At the other extreme, it would be possible to set up four automated assembly lines, one for each model, but the automation would be complex as it would have to take into account the different sizes and color ranges of each model. In addition, if one model became less popular, that manufacturing line would have to be shut down or it would operate in a very inefficient manner. The optional extras could possibly be taken care of in a final assembly area, as a manual function.

A computer-integrated manufacturing operation would have many advantages over this method of operating, provided that the production volume could support the capital expenditure. The system would have to be flexible enough to handle each model, color, and size of bicycle, and the computer would automatically set each machine according to the product requirement. As the customer's order is entered into the system it would trigger off the manufacturing cycle: the computer would pull the correct parts from an automated controlled storage area and move them in the right sequence to the various areas of the assembly line. As each bicycle moves along the line, the computer would set the appropriate machines to perform the necessary assembly tasks, finally checking the completed bicycle and adding the optional extras. In addition, the system would automatically and continuously display the position and status of each assembly, and the stocks of components. It would automatically place orders for materials with the vendor as required, and print out the invoices and the labels for the packaging area.

In addition, the many ancillary operations that would automatically be carried out could markedly reduce costs and errors in the overall operation. Not the least would be the elimination of the many traditional pieces of paper such as work orders, job travelers, stock transfers, and so on. There would be no need to hold completed bicycles in stock as the manufacturing cycle time would be very small. If one model dropped in popularity, it would have little effect on the operation as the machines would merely increase their output of other models. Coupled with the virtual elimination of assembly labor this could indeed prove to be an extremely efficient and competitive operation.

On the other hand, the operation would, as has been discussed earlier, need first-class maintenance, for any breakdown would bring the entire system to a halt. Changes to the design of the bicycles would probably be difficult and costly to integrate into the system as the machines and software would almost certainly have to be modified. The repeatability of the materials would have to be assured and monitored closely. The advantages of CIM are extremely attractive; the requirements are very demanding.

Once again the role of the software must not be underestimated, for it is the most vital key to the success of the entire operation. Remember that many different people will be using the system and they will need the data base information to be easily available in an appropriate form if they are to use it effectively.

Chapter 20

ROAD BLOCKS

From time to time in this book we have considered the problems of working with and through people, because of the enormous diversity of attitudes, behavior, and ability among our employees. In spite of this, nothing that we have discussed is impossible to implement, much is not even difficult, and most is plain commonsense. Yet there are many operations that do not even attempt to work toward excellence, high quality, or whatever phrase you like to use to describe good management of the manufacturing process. If we consider some of the reasons for this, we may make our own implementation of a program for excellence much easier.

THE POWER AT THE TOP

In Chapter 11, we saw that without the full backing of top management it is difficult if not impossible to develop a plan for excellence. Yet excellence as an objective will eventually produce the highest quality products at the lowest possible cost. This has has been mentioned repeatedly in previous chapters of this book, and must surely be the ultimate aim of every manager no matter what his position in the company. Managers are not stupid people—they would not retain their positions if they were, so why is there this lack of support for something that seems so desirable?

The Cost of Excellence

Excellence is not something that appears overnight. It requires the many actions described in earlier chapters, and most of these activities cost money in one way or another. Developing the process needs engineering time; and setting up the controls is also dependent on having adequate engineering skills. Buying excellent quality parts may well raise the initial cost of materials; better maintenance may strain the facilities department, who will then need additional people. Shutting down the line when a manufacturing problem arises and putting all the effort into eliminating the defect, instead of adding more rework and inspection, sound admirable in theory, but what effect will these steps have on the schedule? The list goes on and on. Top management therefore is confronted with finding facilities and money, often at a time of financial constraints when temporary reductions in shipments and schedule disruptions are occurring. In return, they are offered a promise—a promise that in time everything will be wonderful, defects will virtually disappear, inspection and rework will be eliminated, quality will improve, and the manufacturing cost will be reduced.

Excellence in Dollars and Cents

Any senior manager will demand to have these promises defined in terms of dollars and cents, before he makes any expenditures, but any attempt to quantify these savings asks the manager to believe that mistakes can be eliminated. This may well be difficult to accept when he has been used to working with defect rates of 1 or 2% as the normal, acceptable quality level. Indeed, for years he has been presented with these figures as proof of the efficiency and productivity of the manufacturing area. Now he is asked to accept as fact that this small number is excessive and can be totally eliminated.

First of all, our top managers need to be trained. Not only do they need to understand the changed philosophy of good manufacturing management, they also need to recognize that improvements in technologies make these changes to the philosophy esssential if an operation is to remain competitive. They also need to understand the practical issues that will show them that such a program of excellence is neither difficult nor expensive to achieve. They must recognize that the whole manufacturing process is changing: people are changing, machines and methods are changing. Although the basic principles of good management remain constant, the details and the tools of management are in a constant state of flux and we have to be flexible to keep up with the changes.

Changes with Technology

As an example, in the early days of electronics a simple device such as a radio probably had about 200 soldered joints in it. If the defect rate in making the joints was 0.1%, one in five radios would be faulty and require a joint to be reworked, which was simple both to find and to fix. A typical television receiver today, or a personal computer, may have well over a thousand joints. If the defect rate is no better than 0.1%, nothing will ever work until the defects have been found and reworked, and these will be much more difficult and time consuming to fix, because of the increased complexity of the products. One large computer had almost 100,000 joints on each of many printed wiring boards. Nothing less than perfection was acceptable if the product was to work at all. The concepts of quality of a few years ago are no longer acceptable today, and our customers are no longer prepared to accept products with the quality and reliability levels common at that time.

One fine example is the common television receiver. Not too long ago we purchased a set from our local television dealer, who set up the receiver in our home and was on hand to make the service calls that seemed inevitable and were accepted as part of ownership of a television set. Today we expect to buy a receiver at any store, take it home, and plug it in with immediate and excellent results. We do not expect it to break down or require constant adjustment and service, and a receiver with such a low level of reliability would not be salable in today's market place.

We have become used to the highest reliability in most products that we use; in fact, we probably do not recognize the high levels of reliability that have been achieved in many of the items that we use every day. For example, one writer calculated that if airplanes were only 99.9% reliable, we would have 16 crashes each day in the United States. Any airline passenger therefore has a very good reason to demand excellence and reject "Good Enough . . . "

THE GREAT GOD SCHEDULE

Of course, the schedule is important, but when a problem arises the most important action is to eliminate the cause of the problem, not to meet the schedule. This may sound like heresy to some managers, but consider an example and it may not then sound so ridiculuous.

Suppose that we are making painted metal patio tables on a continuous automated line, and suddenly through the normal process control inspection tables are discovered that have been unevenly painted. Production is temporarily halted, and it is found that an automatic paint spraying machine is defective. The maintenance people immediately begin to effect repairs, but to keep production moving in an attempt to meet the schedule, an operator is told to handspray the tables.

We then find that the operator could not spray as evenly as the machine, and some tables have to be stripped and repainted. The operator could paint only 20 tables an hour in comparison with the machine's 50. If it takes two hours to fix the machine, even with the hand operation the schedule will be 60 tables behind, rather than 100 if the line had been shut down completely. But let's consider some of the other ramifications. There are the tables to be stripped and repainted, and piles of tables waiting to be painted, while the line downstream from the painting station will be out of work anyway.

If all these factors are analyzed, in almost every case such as this the cost of getting back on stream will be higher than that if the line had been completely shut down and the people had been used to clean up their area and do all the little housekeeping tasks that they put off for a lack of time. Not only are the direct costs important but the excellence of the product will have to be considered. The hand-sprayed parts will all have to be inspected; some tables may be damaged by being piled up prior to painting. The process will have been changed during the hand painting, and product quality changes will be inevitable.

The pressure to use parts that do not meet the specification in order to keep to the production schedule has been discussed in several previous chapters. It seems ridiculuous when put into writing, yet it still remains one of the prime causes of poor quality in the manufacturing industry.

The attitudes toward the schedule are changing. Slowly, management is recognizing that meeting the schedule can best be achieved by seeing that every aspect of the process is properly controlled and that putting the effort into this is much more effective than trying to find ways around the problems when they occur. Meeting the schedule is important, but how we meet it is even more important.

IT'S MY JOB YOU'RE TALKING ABOUT

When the old system of inspection and rework is operating in a company, it is inevitable that a hierarchy develops with quality control people at the top of the ladder. After all, these are the people who will inspect each and every product and decide if it is fit to be shipped. They literally hold the schedule and costs hostage in their hands, and we have just discussed the old ideas regarding the schedule. They become very important people in the pecking order of the operation.

Suddenly we are proposing that their authority will be eliminated. No longer will production have to ask if the product is good enough to ship, no longer will they be an elitist part of the organization who can just say "Reject" and walk away from the problem. They will become an integral part of manufacturing. When defective products are found, or when the process begins to slide out of control, they will be as responsible for causing the problem and finding the solution as the rest of the manufacturing team.

Opposition will be inevitable if the quality control people are not brought into the program at the earliest possible moment and the entire philosophy explained to them carefully and in detail. They must understand that we do not intend to eliminate them, but are setting out to use their skills in a much more effective manner for the good of the entire company. Similar fears are frequently expressed by rework and repair operators. One sat silently through the opening remarks of a zero defect program. Finally when the objective of eliminating defects and rework was discussed he could not hold in his fears any longer and blurted out, "But you are trying to get rid of my job." When it was then explained that waiting for him was a choice of many more interesting jobs than repairing defective products, his fears were at least reduced.

RUNNING OUT OF STEAM

The implementation of any program of excellence will inevitably take time. A lot of training will have to be done, attitudes and organizations changed, and equipment improved. It is unlikely that any immediate effects will be seen in the overall operation. Indeed, the rate of improvement will initially be slow and then accelerate as the program takes hold. There is a strong danger that individuals may become disenchanted with the whole thing when the additional work does not seem to be having any affect on the operation. In fact, it may sometimes appear that the performance of the plant has gotten worse, parts are rejected that would have been used previously, the schedule is not being met, and yet almost everyone has more work to do. During these early days it is all too easy for top management to look at the statistics of shipments, efficiency, and similar data and call off the entire program.

It is not difficult to prevent this from happening. What is required is a carefully planned introduction. Take the program a step at a time and allow a pause before taking the next step. Only so many new ideas and changed ways of doing things can be absorbed by the human mind. Allow time for each stage of the new program to sink in before adding to the burden with something else new.

In the planning stages, do not be afraid to define the negative things that may happen. At one plant, when the materials in stock were tested for compliance with the specifications, over $1,000,000 worth were found to be defective and had to be scrapped. This loss had been suspected, management had been informed of the possibility, and the reasons for scrapping and the cost and quality implications were carefully explained. These factors were then included in the plan and did not surprise management. At another company a newly purchased machine was found to be unsuitable for the proposed process and had to be replaced at a cost of several thousands of dollars. Again this problem had been forecast as part of the implementation program.

Recognize that the new and the old systems may have to operate side by side for a while and this dual operation will impose a strain on everyone.

When defining the schedule of implementation, list all the small but positive things that will happen; make sure they are measureable. Keep the schedule in detail, and publish the results regularly to show that the program is going ahead according to plan, even if initially the progress is slow. In other words, make sure that everyone understands exactly what is planned to happen, both good and bad. Show that the bad things are only necessary steps in the overall implementation, and that with patience and adherence to the plan the desired objectives will be achieved. Once the improvements begin to occur, on schedule and according to the program, much of any possible opposition will disappear.

SHORT-TERM PLANNING

After the attitudes of top management, one of the most difficult negative pressures to overcome is the prevailing short-term planning in many companies. This concern for immediate profits is of course one of the reasons for top management to operate in the way that they do. We all know the importance of the "bottom line." Most managers are measured on the yearly figures of profit/loss, productivity, and expenditure. Yet we are considering here a program that may well take a year or more to implement. How long will depend on the size of the operation, the layers of management involved, and many other factors.

One of the main areas of concern will be the present efficiency of the operation, and of course the more severe the problems the longer it will take to change and the greater will be the cost. Now we arrive at a "Catch 22" situation. If the manufacturing is inefficient and the quality poor, there will be a greater need for change, but almost certainly the poor performance will have produced a tightening of the belt and a search for a quick improvement in profitability.

The idea of spending more money, of possibly seeing a reduction in output for several months or more, is difficult to sell. In fact, these circumstances frequently trigger the search for a "quick fix" such as buying cheaper materials, turning a blind eye to quality problems, cutting back on process controls, and similar attempts to save a few dollars here and there. The result is invariably disaster.

If the company looks instead at the longer view, it makes so much sense to accept the immediate problems of implementing a program of excellence, as a step to the profits that will accrue and will continue to accrue in the foreseeable future. In addition, the savings from the intangible advantages may more than outweigh those from the improvements in efficiency: the ability of the operation to thrive on change, the flexibility of the organization, the improved personnel relationships, the reputation for quality in the marketplace. It is impossible to place a cash value on these.

A certain company had for many years attempted to become a supplier to one of the top ten corporations in the United States. Every time a survey of their facility had been made they had been rejected until they were no longer able to even bid for the corporation's work; in addition, their reputation in their industry was not good and their sales were falling. Their top management accepted the need for a long-term plan and instituted a zero defect program. Management put every effort into making this program successful, including providing the necessary resources, and in just over one year they achieved their initial objectives. Quality improved dramatically, sales grew, and three years after the program was completed the corporation they had previously courted so unsuccessfully approached them with a request that they become a sub-contractor because of their reputation in the industry. None of this would have occured if the top management had not accepted the need to look at their operation with a longer view than their normal year-by-year profitability.

CORPORATE INERTIA

Invariably the time it takes to implement any program of excellence is dependent on the size of the organization as well as the number of management levels. For example, a company of around 300 people, with an owner and president who directly ran the operation and only two levels of management, successfully implemented a Zero Defect program in six months. A slightly larger sized division of a major corporation made two attempts to do the same thing and failed. Only on the third try and after eighteen months of effort was the implementation successful.

In this latter case there were several levels of management, the plant manager changed twice during the implementation period, and the organization was fragmented, with several independent engineering specialist groups each struggling for power. There was active hostility to the program because it would change the organization, integrate the specialist groups into production, which was considered a form of demotion, and reduce the number of management levels. There is some inertia in every organization and it appears to be related to the size of the operation and the number of management levels. However, the attitude and leadership of top management are the all important factors, and must never be underestimated. In this case the message from the top was unclear, with no firm direction and little if any involvement of any senior personnel.

SUMMARY

It is inevitable that road blocks will appear in our journey toward achieving excellence in controlling the manufacturing process. By recognizing that these blocks are inevitable we can watch out for them, we can take the necessary advance actions to eliminate them, or at least we can find a way around them. By far the best overall preventive action is to communicate to everyone the ultimate objectives, to show that in the end this will only make their job more interesting, provide greater job security, and develop an organization that will be responsive to their ideas as well as producing the best products.

Chapter 21

MANUFACTURING & INDUSTRIAL ENGINEERING, TOOLS & FIXTURES

Although these functions exist in most companies, they have many different titles: "Manufacturing Services," "Production Engineering," and so on. First lets review some brief definitions of their primary responsibilities (Figure 23).

- Manufacturing engineering has the responsibility for developing and defining the process, for specifying and procuring the tools, and for coordinating training. It participates in specifying and acquiring materials, defining storage and handling, and approving product design.
- Industrial engineering has the responsibility of measuring and predicting the labor content of the various process steps, in cooperation with manufacturing engineering, and setting up the data recording and distribution necessary for process control.

Of course, these responsibilities vary somewhat from industry to industry, but they provide a base for the discussion of these tasks in this chapter. They also indicate just how closely these activities are linked together, and why they are usually under the control of the same manager or in smaller organizations are combined.

MANUFACTURING ENGINEERING

In the smallest operation the line supervisor may well carry out the manufacturing engineering function; in a large organization the manufacturing en-

188

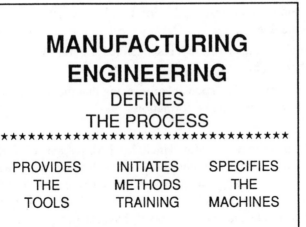

MANUFACTURING ENGINEERING
DEFINES
THE PROCESS
★★★★★★★★★★★★★★★★★★★★★★★★★★★★★★★★★★

PROVIDES	INITIATES	SPECIFIES
THE	METHODS	THE
TOOLS	TRAINING	MACHINES

Figure 23 Manufacturing engineering is a key department in developing and installing the manufacturing process.

gineering department may contain quite a large number of individuals, including experts in every phase of the process. No matter how large or small, the
manufacturing engineering capability is vital in the search for excellence and
the control of the process. Someone has to constantly review the manufacturing
operation and ask if it can be made more efficient in any way, if the quality of
the product can be improved, or if labor or material use can be reduced. This
work is so closely tied into the actual production that the manufacturing
engineers must be closely integrated with the people on the shop floor. Where
applicable it is a good idea to make the performance of the line a joint
responsibility of the supervisor and the engineer. While the engineer will
obviously need a desk and possibly some laboratory facilities to carry out his
work, the real activities will always be on the shop floor, and his services must
always be on call if he is not actually situated on the line.

MANUFACTURING ENGINEERING ON THE SHOP FLOOR

Of course, the engineer and the line supervisor must work together as a team;
they must trust each other in every technical aspect of production. If this close
relationship is to develop and flourish, some fundamental authorities have to
be established and agreed upon. The following represent the bare minimum of
guideline to avoid conflict and disagreement.

- The line supervisor is responsible for the allocation, use, and control of all labor on the line.
- The manufacturing engineer is responsible for defining the process, tools, and methods to be used.
- The line supervisor is responsible for seeing that the process is carried out according to the recorded information.

Other items that should be defined include who is responsible for any routine maintenance, who initiates troubleshooting on the line, who decides if and when training or retraining is necessary, who takes care of materials problems, and who has the authority to shut down the line. Of course, every manufacturing facility is different and will undoubtably have its own requirements. If these fundamental authorities are not defined and agreed upon, all kinds of misunderstandings arise and can damage the excellent relationship that is required if we are to achieve excellence in the process.

One of the most common areas of dispute occurs when the operator is told by the supervisor to carry out the process in some way other than that which is recorded in the process. The manufacturing engineer or process inspector, seeing this, reprimands the operator, who says that this is the way he has been told to do it, and an immediate confrontation takes place between the supervisor and engineer. In some plants this problem is avoided by not permitting the manufacturing engineers to go onto the line, or not allowing them to talk with the operators. This of course is nonsense and eventually causes only more problems. The supervisor has to recognize that the recorded process is not to be changed. The manufacturing engineer also has to understand that any request from the floor has to be given priority and the process formally changed if problems arise and suggested improvements are found to be applicable.

THE MANUFACTURING ENGINEER AND PROCESS DEVELOPMENT

The manufacturing engineer of course has to provide the leadership in the development of the manufacturing process, and works with both design and the shop floor to see that every possible variation is eliminated in all aspects of production. This cooperation is of the greatest importance. Note that the word leadership is used here. Obviously the engineer will provide the main inputs, but he cannot carry out the development in isolation. The designer will have to supply information and make design changes as may be necessary, and obviously the people on the shop floor will be able to provide important information on the practicality of the process. If this team approach is used, later problems can be minimized and faster product implementation will result.

The team approach does not however release the manufacturing engineer from the responsibility of providing the ideas, the creativity, and the "knowhow." Moreover, it does not remove his authority to make the final decisions regarding the process, and his ultimate responsibility for its excellence.

The manufacturing engineer has to be both a specialist in the particular process that he is working on, and a generalist in the use of engineering skills. For example, if he includes a stenciling step in his process, he will have to understand the chemistry of the materials being screened; the physical attributes such as viscosity which can affect the results; and the mechanical requirements of the screening machine, such as blade hardness, flexibility, shape, movement tolerances, parts positioning, and so on. He will have to learn how to set up the particular machine correctly and how to monitor its performance. Finally he will have to instruct the operator in the use of the machine. There may well be many dissimilar machines in the process and he will have to understand the functions of each of them in detail.

FINDING NEW ENGINEERS

Skilled and experienced manufacturing engineering people are the manufacturing industry's most precious resource. Unfortunately, there are not enough of them; the salary scales and the lack of prestige and respect for the professionalism required to carry out this important work do not encourage the best people to take up this demanding profession. Our educational system is lacking in providing replacements for those who are leaving industry. The now forgotten apprenticeship system was an excellent way of bringing the smartest people, who had limited opportunities to gain formal educational skills, into manufacturing engineering.

Many of the best manufacturing engineers still come up through the ranks from the shop floor and this source of expertise should be encouraged. Few colleges have the facilities and teaching skills to be able to produce manufacturing engineers who can do the job without considerable time spent learning on the job and acquiring practical experience. They certainly provide the basic theoretical understanding, but this is a long way from the practical engineering expertise required from an efficient manufacturing engineer. Industry may have to take on the demanding task of training the engineers who are so badly needed, through a rebirth of the apprenticeship system or some similar practical, "hands on" educational program.

INDUSTRIAL ENGINEERING

Industrial engineering is of course another highly specialized part of manufacturing engineering, but in many companies it is organized as a separate department. However, both manufacturing engineering and industrial engineering are so linked together that it is sensible for them to be under the same department head. Manufacturing engineering will always be in need of the industrial engineering function. When developing a process step, or designing a new tool, or laying out a bench set up, the manufacturing engineer needs to know which is the most efficient system, which requires the least labor, which method of performing an operation takes the least time or needs the least skill, and here the industrial engineer can supply the answer. There is really no way that these functions can be separated.

Once the process is set up and ready to put into operation, it is necessary to have some basic measurements of the labor content, to know just how long a particular process step takes to complete. These figures are necessary not only in order to monitor the line efficiency, but also to calculate the labor required for future manufacturing and to predict the throughput of a process or machine, to know how many of a particular tool are to be made, and so on. These are fundamental figures; it is possible simply to measure them with a stop watch, and this is probably accurate enough for many purposes.

Efficiency Improvement

An experienced industrial engineer, however, can do much more than the few responsibilities listed above. By observing the operation, he can find the wasted movements and the incorrect placement of materials or tools and provide important information regarding possible improvements to the process. On one line there was a problem from incorrectly placed parts. As there seemed no logical reason why this should happen, the industrial engineer was called in to observe the line. He soon showed that the materials were packaged in trays that were too large and that were placed too far from the operators. These factors were corrected and the problem disappeared. There was an additional advantage as the time to assemble each unit was slightly reduced; because this was a high-volume line the overall effect was a cost reduction as well as a quality improvement.

In another example, the industrial engineer was able to work with the manufacturing engineer in the development of a machine and advise on the best placement of the operator's controls, parts storage, and so on. With this information on the ergonomics of the system, the cycle time was considerably reduced from that of the original design. Most of the data required to carry out this work are today provided by statistically developed tables of such items as hand motions, weights to be picked up, distances to be reached, and so on (Figure 24). An experienced industrial engineer who has been trained in these techniques can develop extremely accurate data in this way, but eventually they will have to be verified by actual timing of the operation on the shop floor.

TYPICAL TIME DATA DEVELOPED FROM STANDARD TABLES

★★★★★★★★★★★★★★★★★★★★★★★★★★★★★★

Assemble front panel
Part No 18357B

Action	Minutes
Mount fuse holder with 1 screw, nut, and washer.	0.77
Fit terminal with 1 washer, 2 nuts, and solder tag.	1.06
Mount handle with 2 screws.	0.88
Mount clip with 1 screw.	0.55
Mount name plate with SH89 adhesive.	2.83
Mount to unit with 8 screws, wipe off finger marks.	3.98
Total labor in minutes	10.07
Plus 15% allowance	1.50
Work standard	11.57

All work carried out according to process document S245, using methods and tools as defined.

Figure 24   A typical work study sheet. This is often derived from standard data which consider such things as reach, weight to be lifted, number of operations, and so on. It is usually confirmed by direct measurement.

Time Studies

Although an experienced industrial engineer can eliminate from any time study many of the variances introduced by the operator, if there is no cooperation between the operator and the engineer during the actual timing of the operation the operator will always be able to swing the results in the way he wishes. Of course, this variance can be discovered if enough people performing the same operation are timed, but this step may not always be possible. Here again we come face to face with the people problem of management. In this case we have to recognize the importance of the feelings of the individual.

The author was the manufacturing engineer involved in a case in which one operator made all of the cable harnesses for a particular line. This operation had been timed on many occasions and showed that 12 harnesses per day was the maximum output. However, on odd occasions when there was a real need for more cables, the manufacturing manager would personally and informally ask the operator for an extra effort and he would produce 20 or more harnesses in a single day. The operator explained that he believed 12 per day to be a fair number for the pay he received; he did not want to work faster, although his wages were based on his output. This operation had been studied many times, but there was no way that any industrial engineer was able to show that a greater number of cable harnesses could be produced in the working day. As other operators were tried in this position and found it difficult to maintain the 12 per day output, the operator was probably quite correct in his assessment of a fair day's work.

The industrial engineering function is vital to the efficient operation of the process, and coupled with inventiveness and curiosity can make a major contribution to the continuous improvement of the operation. The industrial engineer must always be asking "Why." Why is a process step performed in a particular way? Why is this or that necessary? Why cannot an operation be eliminated? He must never be constrained by past practices. Working together with the manufacturing engineer they can make a formidable team in the drive toward excellence.

In too many companies these two engineering functions are not given the respect that they deserve; they are classed as "overheads" and not seen as contributing to the actual manufacture of the product. Certainly they do not directly affect the daily production figures, but without their contribution the efficiency of the process will deteriorate as small problems arise that if not promptly attacked turn into larger problems. Far too often when business falls off they are the first to be laid off. This of course is the most ridiculous decision any manager can make. This is the very time that their expertise is necessary to improve efficiency and quality, develop new production methods, and prepare production for the eventual return to profitability and growth. When their experience is lost, it will take a long time for someone new to the process to pick up the pieces again. A good manufacturing engineer will be able to generate yearly cost savings that well exceed his salary.

TOOLS AND FIXTURES

The tool and fixtures field is a wide one, and these terms can encompass everything from a major computer-controlled assembly station to a simple cardboard box. The major skill required to develop effective tooling is inventiveness. Many real labor-saving tools have been made with pieces of wire and clothes pegs, wood, and paper clips. Of course, most tools have to be machined and fabricated from metals or plastic, but the inventiveness of the designer or manufacturing engineer is the chief ingredient for successful tooling.

The Tool Designer

The tool designer must have a detailed understanding of the way that a tool is to be used. It always pays to discuss the tool with the people who will be using it, and simplicity must always be one of the major objectives. On one line the operators had been provided with some rather complicated fixtures to hold the parts as they were being assembled. However, the fixtures required several adjustments when there was a change of product and were quite difficult to load. One by one they disappeared from the line to be replaced by cardboard boxes with suitably sized holes cut in the top to retain the parts. The manufacturing engineer was smart enough to recognize that the fixtures he had supplied were not as efficient as the cardboard boxes; using the operator's idea, he made fixtures in the same manner but of more durable materials.

The tool designer should also work closely with the industrial engineer to minimize the labor content of the operation or to improve the product quality. In one instance, a complex cable harness was made on a tooling board; when completed it was electrically tested for accuracy of placement of the wires. Inevitably one or two were found to be incorrect and had to be replaced. The industrial engineer asked why the electrical testing was not carried out as the wires were put in place. This had never even been considered, because a separate expensive automatic fixture had been built to carry out the testing. The idea made sense, and the clips holding the ends of the wires were connected into a computer that not only carried out the testing but also indicated clearly the site of the next wire to be placed. Not only was the incorrect wire placement eliminated but the labor content was reduced because the operator no longer had to decide where to place the wires.

Tooling and Automation

Given the tremendous developments in automation, many companies will be looking at some very complex tooling and automation including the implementation of computer control. As mentioned in Chapter 19, the key issue in any form of computer-controlled automation is software, and understanding the nature and use of this is another skill that the manufacturing and industrial engineers must acquire. The hardware is too often developed and designed before the software is considered, and this is the wrong way round. We should start with the software and then make sure that the hardware is compatible. This of course is vitally important when a manufacturing tool has to mate into a total computer control system. Often when these forms of overall automation are installed, linking the various computer systems together causes the major problems, and not infrequently the highest cost. We should never underestimate the compatability requirement.

Robots

In a similar way, putting robots into a production line is frequently not as simple or as cost effective as has been suggested in the past. Some years ago the number of robots being used in any country was being touted as a measure of their advancement in automation, and the United States was shown as being far behind much of the world. The figures were generally wrong, being based on an incorrect definition of the word "robot." Moreover, the fascination with robots has largely died as we have come to recognize that they are only one form of the larger overall automated systems. Parts placement, design and tolerances, and the way that the components have to be presented to the robot can complicate its use, and as with software and the computer these aspects of an installation can frequently exceed the cost of the actual robot. In one system, a simple robot system was installed to form some purchased parts and had more than enough throughput to keep up with production. Once in operation, however, occasionally parts were found that had minor deformation due to some very thin metal sections that became bent in the packaging and handling from the vendor. A computer-controlled vision system was therefore installed to check the accuracy of the incoming parts, and those that were bent were passed to a station for straightening prior to forming. Although this system worked very well, now the throughput was limited and two stations had to be provided to keep up with the rest of the line. The robotic systems had become complex machines that required the services of a full-time engineer to set up and maintain. What had started out as a simple, straightforward project, using a standard robotic system, suddenly became a very expensive development project.

Simplicity in Tooling

The message with respect to tooling is clear. As with the development of the process, you should examine every aspect of any proposed tooling in absolute detail. Do not assume that anything will work in such and such a way unless you have absolute proof. "If in doubt, try it out" is an excellent motto. Simplicity is preferable to complexity, and always be prepared for unexpected problems with any untried tooling or machine system. There is no intention here to suggest that new, untried systems or tools should not be used, for it is from new ideas that some of our best manufacturing systems have been developed. They should be approached with caution and a very clear understanding of the jeopardies that exist. With any new idea comes a tremendous initial euphoria suggesting that this is the answer to all our problems, that any minor deficiencies can be ignored or will take care of themselves. If for any new system we define the problems as accurately as the advantages, we will almost certainly be able to find a way to eliminate them. If we ignore them, they may eventually cause the new idea to be rejected simply because it fails to meet the initial overenthusiastic expectations.

Chapter 22

A FEW PERSONAL WORDS TO TOP MANAGEMENT

The responsibility for the day-to-day operation of a company does not leave much time to read books on management. Obviously you would not be in the position that you presently hold if you were not experienced in management skills. Yet I would ask that you spare a few moments to read this chapter. I believe you will find it interesting, you may find it relevant to some of the problems that beset your own and many other companies. You may even be tempted to read the entire book. In the following pages I am not suggesting for one moment that any manager deliberately operates in an inefficient manner, but I do suggest that it is too easy to miss the implications of the changes in technology, complexity, and industrial relationships that are affecting our industries today. Without really noticing the fact, we may well be using manufacturing management philosophies of the 1950s to run the factories of the 1990s.

I am writing this the day after leaving one of my clients, a major electronics company that is very well known in the industry. They have been experiencing defects in their products which are costing a lot of time and money to inspect and rectify. During my investigation of this problem I talked with many inspectors, operators, and manufacturing engineers. Although they understood the nature of their problems and it was not difficult to arrive at the basic causes, their elimination involved changes in corporate policy. Two phrases cropped up continuously.

"How can we get management to understand this?"

"But what can we do, that's a management decision?"

This is not an unusual situation. The technical problems were easy to solve, but communications and understanding between the shop floor, and the people who had the authority to initiate the corrective actions, were completely missing. Ask yourself if you have a simple assured method for your people on the shop floor to pass on their problems, ideas, and suggestions to you.

The Japanese Miracle?

The driving force behind this book has been my concern for the quality and efficiency of our manufacturing operations. Here in the United States we have the best people in the world, the most motivated, highly skilled, and inventive work force. When lecturing in Tokyo a few years ago, a senior manager from one of their top electronics companies genuinely could not understand why the United States was doing so badly in the international market. He explained that in North America there are the best technically trained people in the world, people who can use initiative and who are inventive. In Japan, on the other hand, people do not like to stand out from everyone else, and are not very inventive. Therefore he felt we should be the leaders in manufacturing efficiency and product quality.

The fact that this is not so cannot be blamed on the people on the shop floor. It is a lack of excellence in management that is at the bottom of our failure to compete in the world markets. Unfortunately, in too many companies those who make the corporate policy do not appreciate the ways in which those decisions affect the manufacturing process.

If you have any doubt about the truth of this statement, look at the companies in this country that have been taken over by Japanese management. Without changing the people, without expending large sums of money, and without changing the design of the products to any great extent, we have seen cases where product quality has gone from terrible to excellent in a matter of months, and as a consequence the bottom line has changed from red to black in a similar time. I am not suggesting that the Japanese have any magic in this field of management. Most of what they know and practice comes from this country and from the people who have been preaching good management for many years. There are many excellent companies in the United States, but the majority did not want to listen; they were out for the "fast buck"—the yearly profit—with little concern for long-term growth. The Japanese listened and acted on what they heard. Now that the pressure is on industry in our country, management is beginning to listen. Please take the time to read this chapter and then listen to the people who know much more than I do about management philosophy. Especially listen to your own people out on the shop floor. They have a better understanding of your company's problems and their cures than all the outside experts put together.

THE STATUS OF MANUFACTURING

Manufacturing is all too often the "Poor Relation" in the organization, subordinate to design, marketing, purchasing, and all of the other fringe departments. Yet, if the purpose of our company is to produce items for sale, manufacturing is the sole reason for the company's existence, and every other department is there only to provide support and assistance for this operation.

One of the technical magazines was bemoaning the fact that it is difficult to persuade young people leaving college to go into manufacturing. They prefer marketing, office work—anything but the shop floor. Engineers have the feeling that working in manufacturing is a second class job; they would prefer design or sales. Yet manufacturing is the very area that needs the best people. Our limitations in producing new products almost always lie in manufacturing, which demands the highest levels of knowledge and skill if we are to be profitable. Unfortunately, our attitudes to manufacturing and the prestige that goes with the job, as well as our salary scales frequently back up the engineers' desire to work anywhere but the shop floor.

Of course, all of the other departments are important. If marketing cannot decide what the customer wants, and if the product is not designed to meet these requirements, anything that production does will be pointless. Yet these two departments cannot work in isolation. All too often manufacturing problems extend back to the design of the product, or even to the basic marketing concept, yet the production department is blamed for the deficiencies and is expected to find the cure. Similarly, quality control is often used as a kind of policeman to discipline the manufacturing department rather than cooperating with the operation to produce a quality product. We find rejected materials being forced onto production in order to "meet the schedule."

The examples are as many and as diverse as the types of products and processes involved. The relationships between departments, their lack of cooperation, and the way that authorities and responsibilities are allocated can all have a major effect on the efficiency of manufacturing and the quality of the product. They all derive from the decisions that we make, which not only affect these items directly but also determine the overall attitudes found on the shop floor. If we are going to attract the brightest and most innovative people into manufacturing, we have to begin with corporate policies and wage scales that clearly tell the world the importance we place on this operation.

COST VS. PRICE AND BUDGETS

Budgets are obviously extremely important tools in the control of any company; however, they are frequently misused and misunderstood. The very word "Budget" implies a planning tool, and as such it should be revised as circumstances change. Unfortunately, budgets are too often seen as allocations of resources that once set are never to be altered. The manufacturing area is frequently hamstrung by budgets set in isolation by top management, with little thought of the practical consequences.

When business is slack, it is easy to solve the liquidity problem by making a 15% budget cut across the board. In the case of manufacturing this often involves losing skilled people who may be hard to replace. Machines, equipments, and their maintenance cost the same whether they are used 50% or 80% of the time. It may take several months to bring production back to its original level and this then requires additional resources. The budgets set today will probably have a major effect on the efficiency of next year's production. When times are hard, all parts of the company have to make sacrifices. But you should discuss the problem with manufacturing, ask them to propose savings, and listen to their arguments. You should certainly probe and press for reductions in expenditure, but if you understand the long-term implications you may well find that what appears to be a reduction today will involve a greater expenditure tomorrow.

Cost Reduction

Even when business is good you should demand a continuous program of cost reduction from the manufacturing area, but do not be too insistent on making the "fast buck." Recognize the long-term implications of any proposed cost reduction and be prepared to provide the up front resources that may be necessary. With the complexity of many of today's processes, money spent on training, new equipment, and similar items can produce a marked improvement in efficiency and product quality. Do not be too emphatic in demanding a certain payback time. It is all too easy to approve a new machine when it can be shown to pay back the cost in 12 months; indeed, many companies refuse to allocate money unless the payback is shown to be an extremely short time span, such as 18 months. This is a pity, and many excellent ideas are eliminated by such a policy.

Often the hidden effects on quality, schedule, materials cost, and so on will produce savings that are many times greater than the direct figures that are usually used to justify an expenditure. But these items are suspect because they cannot be clearly and easily defined in a formal report, and the manufacturing process is not clearly understood by those who have the authority to allocate the resources. Money spent on training is all too often looked upon as wasted because it is impossible to show the payback in the usual terms. Yet money spent on training our people is probably the best used resource in our entire operation. The value of any company lies in the skills of the employees, but it is often impossible to obtain a few hundred dollars for a specialist to obtain training in the latest techniques of his particular field. We are willing to spend several thousands of dollars on a new machine and then we refuse the cost of properly training the operator.

In times of financial shortage it is always the training budget that is the first item to go, followed by cuts in manufacturing engineering personnel. They are considered "overheads"; they are seen as not contributing to the shipment of product. Of course, this is ridiculous, for the use of the term "overheads" is only an accounting ploy to make their calculations simpler. As any manufacturing engineer will save his salary and more, this should be the last area to be cut. When I was running manufacturing engineering I asked of every man in the department to show yearly cost savings of at least twice his salary. Most showed savings considerably higher than this figure.

Budget Games

In some companies any budgets that are submitted are invariably cut. This then becomes a little game, in which the departments send in budget proposals that they deliberately have made 15% too high because they know that these will be cut by about that percentage. Although this practice sounds ridiculous when written down on paper, like children playing a stupid game, unfortunately it still occurs in too many cases to be a laughable matter. You must demand honesty in the preparation of budget proposals and genuine discussions in arriving at the final budget figures. Be prepared to change them as conditions change, and make it clear that budgets are tools to be used, not legal documents cast in stone.

Cost vs. Price

I have already spent some time discussing the cost of materials. However, I will mention it again, because it is an important factor in controlling the process, and problems with materials too often derive from a top management directive such as "Purchasing is to cut the cost of materials by 20%." Not infrequently the performance of the purchasing agent is measured by the amount of the savings. This sort of edict once again shows a lack of understanding of the process and assumes that every detail regarding the materials can be defined by the designer and the specifications. It would be much more sensible if the edict from on high said: "Working together, design, purchasing, and manufacturing will seek to reduce the cost of the product by at least 20%." Purchasing cannot work in isolation, but I see this being attempted every day. In 1988 I saw a store area filled with materials bought in Taiwan because they could be obtained for 20% less than in the United States. They were useless— they did not even meet the specification, but because they comprised one year's supply, on instructions from management they had to be used because it was impossible to get new materials in time to meet the schedule. In any case, they had been paid for and could not be returned. The ultimate cost in production time and product quality could not be calculated. This is not an isolated case, as I see similar examples every week.

Cost is, of course, a most important factor in any operation, but one department cannot succeed in cutting cost on its own. It demands cooperation, it demands an excellent knowledge of the process by all concerned including the senior managers who have to initiate and overview the cost reduction programs. You should never consider the price of materials in isolation; instead, ask about the cost effect on the product.

THE OVERALL PLAN

As the ultimate seat of authority you must develop the overall philosophy for your operation, and then you must assure that it is in fact followed in the day-to-day manufacturing process. You have to provide a leadership that is real and visible. It is useless to issue a corporate policy declaring your full support for "Total Quality" and then make decisions that ultimately involve accepting second best. You may well reply that any decision you make is not intended to have this result, but all too often this is in fact what happens.

Planning and Manufacturing

Not only does the manufacturing operation need a philosophy of industrial relationships, production, and quality, it needs a plan to work with to achieve these objectives. This must define both the immediate aims and also the long-term directions that the company expects to take. Changes in products— in the design, the mix, and the volume to be produced—take time to implement. They may require retraining, they certainly need an adequate manufacturing engineering capability, and they may involve developing new processes and procuring new machines. Yet all too often inadequate time is allowed for these items, and manufacturing is expected to respond immediately. While many other areas of the company are usually part of the planning function, manufacturing is frequently not called in to participate until the major decisions have been made and is then presented with the plan and told to "make it happen." You should bring manufacturing into any long- or short-term planning at the very beginning and listen to their comments. If they say that such and such a part of a plan cannot be accomplished in the time available or with the allocated budget, listen to them, certainly work together to find a way out, but do not assume that they can work miracles.

I well remember being told at a corporate meeting some years ago that a certain product was to begin production a certain date. After I explained in considerable detail that with the people and facilities available this was not possible, I presented a modified program. I was told in no uncertain terms that any changes were unacceptable, no more facilities were available, and it was my job to find a way to get the product out on time. As there was no possible way that this could be done, the original schedule was not met. The cost to the company was considerable. My department was blamed for the delay.

Long-Term Planning

Planning must include the long-term objectives. The yearly plan may be a useful accounting tool, but it must not be allowed to impact the manufacturing program. It is frequently impossible to work to such a short-time scale; as our products and therefore our production process becomes more and more complex and automated, we have to incorporate the long-term objectives into our day-to-day planning. Five years is not too far ahead to consider in many manufacturing operations today.

A sound, practical plan that is agreed upon by all, is essential. It is the groundwork on which everything else depends. Too often the response from areas outside manufacturing is that an accurate production plan cannot be made. This is usually nonsense and indicates a lack of understanding of the planning function. It may also arise through previous cases where the forecast did not work out as developed and the instigator was disciplined. Because it is after all a best guess as to what will happen, any plan may ultimately turn out to have been incorrect and have to be changed. This is then a time to discuss, regroup, and go forward to correct the situation as well as possible, not a cause for discipline.

If you have one of the few situations where future sales and therefore future production genuinely cannot be forecast, it will be necessary to develop a strategy to provide total flexibility of manufacturing and in consequence a close relationship between design and the production capability. In turn, this will involve a similar flexibility in the acquisition of materials. Here again everything will have to revolve around the needs of the manufacturing process.

UNDERSTANDING THE PROCESS

The many day-to-day decisions that you make can often affect areas that you may not even consider to be involved. You may give a department head additional responsibilities, or change the authority for a particular function, and in no case does it appear that these changes can affect manufacturing. Weeks or even months later it is found that some area of manufacturing is not functioning as required because of the changes that you made.

One case that comes to mind was the introduction of a plant facilities department in which the manager reported to the engineering vice president. Up to this time manufacturing had carried out its own equipment servicing, using the maintenance mechanics only for major repairs and overhauls, and the machine operators to carry out basic cleaning and simple repairs. The new manager was given the responsibility for all machine maintenance and was instructed to place it on a more formal footing. The operators were now permitted only to superficially clean the machines, a step that placed a larger load on the maintenance personnel. Eventually minor repairs were often not carried out until several days after they were needed. Variations inevitably occurred in the process, and after some time the product quality as well as the schedule suffered.

These problems would not have occurred if the senior manager who set up the new facilities department had understood more clearly the process requirements and the advantages of the informal but effective maintenance program that had been developed over time in the manufacturing area.

No matter how senior the manager, if he is making decisions that can affect manufacturing he must understand the manufacturing process that he is controlling. Even though you may feel that your decisions are not directly implemented on the shop floor, you should either understand the process in detail yourself, or listen carefully to the advice of those reporting to you who are skilled in the process and then act on their advice. Make it a regular routine to visit the shop floor, see the process in operation, and talk to the people. Show that you want to hear their opinions, and you will be surprised what you can learn about your company. Today there are not many manufacturing processes that can be efficiently controlled from the executive office, at least not without a clear knowledge of the intricacies of the manufacturing operation.

ORGANIZATION AND COOPERATION

The days have long gone by when it was possible to split up a company into discrete functions. Of course, the basic responsibilities must be clearly defined and allocated, but possibly of even more importance is the need for departments to cooperate with each other. This does not mean lip service to cooperation, but demands that departments work together each and every day. The attitudes of senior management, and the way that the organization is defined, will have a major effect on the degree of cooperation that exists in any company. If you demand discussion and concurrence before any major decision is made, if you see that information is circulated to all departments, even those that may not appear to be directly involved, this will become the normal way that the organization operates.

If, however, you make decisions independently when they affect others, if you permit department heads to function in an autonomous manner without question, cooperation will soon cease to exist except when it is formally demanded, and the value of such cooperation will be severely limited.

It is always surprising to find the scant degree of cooperation between departments in some companies. I have been in many plants where the product designers have never been on the shop floor and have little understanding of the methods and machines used to make the products they are designing. In one factory I was asked by a purchasing agent what exactly was the product made in the plant, and what did it do. He had worked there for over five years. I made a short survey in that plant and found that over 50% of the employees outside the shop floor had never seen the product in operation. Yet these were the people who were providing the necessary support functions for manufacturing.

Cooperation does not happen automatically: it requires training, it requires promotion, and it requires example. All of these will happen only when they are made a formal part of the company culture emanating from top management.

The way that responsibilities and authorities are allocated determine the organization of the company. Look carefully at the way that these are decided. All too often we attempt to follow a certain pattern that has worked in the past. For example, in most companies we tend to make receiving inspection a part of quality control. But is this logical? Perhaps it would be better placed under the control of purchasing, or even stores. If each department is responsible for the quality of its work, do we even need a quality control organization? We should determine the organization according to the needs and efficiency of the operation, not to suit some preconceived ideas or some personnel pattern already in existence.

SUMMARY

As I have reiterated throughout this book, it is impossible to list the rules for managing an operation that includes manufacturing as if this were an engineering manual. Everything that we do is achieved through people and every person is an individual with his own ideas, ideals, and objectives. Every manufacturing operation varies in some aspect from every other. However, there are a few universal truths.

- Manufacturing is the most important department in your operation.
- The skills and knowledge of your people are the most valuable assets of your company.
- Understand and know your people. Let them see you as an individual.
- Understand the manufacturing process in detail.
- Trust your experts, and listen to their advice. If you do not trust them get some that you can.
- Develop honest budgets that all departments can work with.
- Develop an organization that supports manufacturing.
- Demand cooperation between all departments.
- Leave your office door open to everyone and listen to their comments and advice.
- When you have heard all the opinions and ideas, make a clear decision, and remember that you have the final authority and the overall responsibility.
- Provide the leadership and example for your operation.
- Manage for the long-term profitability of your company, not one year at a time.
- Success or failure is your responsibility alone.

Chapter 23

STARTUP, GROWTH, AND THE ENTREPRENEUR

Many new companies have a short life, and most that fail do so in the first few years of business. Of course, many were doomed from the very beginning because the whole idea on which the business was based was unsound. Yet a surprising number falter and fail when to all outward appearances everything is going well. Frequently, the excuses given for failure are: "under capitalized," "bad debts," and similar general comments. In truth, the failure of most manufacturing operations is simply a lack of control of the manufacturing process.

STARTUP

Startup is without doubt a difficult, but exciting period in any organization, and rarely does failure strike at this time. There is an invigorating air of success, a certainty of a great future for all, and everyone pitches in to make success a certainty. The company is usually small and there are frequent personal contacts between all of the personnel.

There seems little point in spending time and money, both of which are usually in short supply, in setting up any kind of formal organization, or defining who is responsible for what. These steps can come later when the business has become established. Yet this attitude is often the tiny crack in the operation which later grows and ultimately causes the company to fail. Similarly, under pressure to ship products and earn money, often the product is not fully designed and the manufacturing process is undeveloped. These items have already been discussed in connection with a functioning operation. We will now see just how much more important they are to the growing company.

In one case a young inventor had a brilliant idea for a new product. He was funded by a well-established corporation and set up as operations vice president in a small independent plant. The man was technically extremely clever but had had no management training. His main objective was to get the product out as quickly as possible, and the first few units were handbuilt with his personal assistance in the laboratory. They were finally put into production with a constant stream of design changes. As there was no time to fully develop the design, almost every unit shipped was different in some way from every other. Of course, the costs were well above the sale price, and many of the units were returned because they failed to meet their specified accuracy. The vice president decided that he had to take more personal control because he believed that all the problems were due to a failure of the manufacturing operation. After all, if he could make the units work one at a time in the laboratory, there was no reason for the manufacturing people to have so many problems.

Because the materials had never been properly specified, purchasing was having difficulties in obtaining the right components on schedule. Thus the vice president also decided he would have to take over this department. Finally, he was personally running every department in the plant. In the meantime, the real problems of product design and manufacturing process development were not being attacked, as he believed them to be unnecessary and assumed that manufacturing could "fiddle" the product through just as he had done in the laboratory. After several unsuccessful attempts to change this pattern of management, the parent corporation took over and fired the vice president; shortly afterward the operation was permanantly closed.

This is obviously an extreme case in which the problems were directly attributable to the lack of management skills of the vice president. However, a similar but less extreme pattern of behavior is frequently found in many firms during their startup phase.

The newcomer to manufacturing management can learn three main lessons from this sad tale.

1. No matter how brilliant the individual, no man can run an operation by himself.

2. What can be done one unit at a time by a skilled engineer in the laboratory cannot necessarily be reproduced in volume on the shop floor. The shop floor is not a large laboratory.

3. No matter how technically brilliant the individual, he must learn the skills of management before he takes charge of any operation. It is

too often assumed that they can be picked up or absorbed by some form of osmosis once the individual has been promoted to a management job. We would never dream of putting a man into a technical position if he had not received some training in the technology and proved his understanding and ability.

None of these lessons is a new concept. We have already discussed all of them many times in various forms in the preceeding chapters. Their effects, however, are much more disastrous at this time in the life of a company, and it is easy to fall into this pattern of operation during the early days. It seems so much faster for the boss to do the job himself than to waste time teaching someone else how to do it correctly. It is so much simpler for everyone to pitch in and do whatever is necessary rather than spend time deciding exactly what each person's responsibilities should be.

We can also learn some other lessons that are not so immediately obvious. The vice president in the above example could not understand the manufacturing and procurement problems caused by the constant design changes. He understood and enjoyed the technical challenge of continuously improving the performance of the product, but he genuinely could not recognize that the changes would cause so many difficulties in production, and that design stability was urgently required.

The vice president believed that everyone should pitch in and do any job that came along. No one in the operation knew what was expected of them, and managers were frequently criticized for not carrying out some task that they did not believe was part of their responsibility.

What eventually happened could have been forecast by any skilled manager. As the vice president took over more and more of the responsibility and authority of the various managers, and became more and more critical of their efforts, they in turn did less and less in order to avoid criticism. They made no comments when they saw things that were obviously wrong, as the vice president did not accept criticism lightly. By the time the parent company took over the operation, it was in a state of anarchy.

In an established organization the vice president would probably have managed to struggle through; tradition and experience would have been adequate to keep things moving if only in a very inefficient manner. In this case, however, he could fall back on none of these things. Most of the managers had resigned, and a large number of the shop floor personnel had left the company when the ax finally fell.

Because the startup period is such a critical time, it must be properly planned if it is to be profitable and the base for continued growth. It is a time to plan and plan and plan. This takes a certain amount of determination, for when there are so many things to be done, so many obvious tasks to be completed, sitting down quietly and thinking and planning seem to be the height of folly and a waste of time.

At this time we must develop the organization that will see the company through at least the first year of business. It is also a time to lay the foundations for the future. The type of management structure and the amount of involvement of the shop floor people are extremely important, as they become difficult to change when the operation grows larger. As we have discussed in previous chapters, bringing the employees into the management decisions and making sure that good communications exist at and between all levels are vitally important to the efficient operation of the manufacturing process. This is the time to lay the foundations for all of these activities. For example, if good housekeeping habits are established when there are only a few employees, it is not difficult to expand these into the normal practice for the shop floor. It will be extremely difficult to persuade people that good housekeeping is a necessity if it has not been enforced during the first year of operation.

Growth

This is often the most important and dangerous period in the life of a company. We all know of new companies that grew quickly and just as suddenly disappeared from the manufacturing scene. The reasons are not difficult to find.

The startup period of any company demands a great deal of enthusiasm, drive, and dedication from the entrepreneurs that initiate the operation. They are frequently the type of individuals who will tackle any task with all of the energy that they posses. Intolerent of delays and excuses, and willing to crush any opposition, they are the very people who are needed to get the company off the ground. When the organisation is small, it is not difficult to work in this way, to understand in detail every facet of the operation. As the company grows, it becomes necessary to pass on some of these duties to others, and with them must go the authority to carry out the work.

All too often, in the growing company, the boss is reluctant to let go of the reins; he believes that if he does he will eventually lose control of the company. As a consequence he hires managers, and then expects them to work for him as personal assistants. The author was once working in a new plant of a multimillion dollar company that had experienced one of the fastest growths seen in that industry. A problem had arisen with the operators: they were cluttering up their benches with personal items, and they were asked to keep them in their lockers. They explained that although new lockers had been placed in this beautiful manufacturing plant they could not use them because they had not yet been painted. When asked why they could not be painted it was explained that only the president could decide on the color of the paint and he had not found time for this detail. One could only wonder who was making the important decisions in the company. In fact, it almost foundered a short time later and was saved only by a change of leadership.

Although this example may sound ridiculous, in many growing companies this level of decision making is not uncommon. Often the first sign of a problem in a growing company is the inability of the lower managers to make any decision without the personal approval of the boss.

When a company grows very quickly, it is not unusual for the people who start the business to lack the knowledge and ability to manage a large operation. The wise entrepreneur willingly seeks people with proved ability to take over the top management and provide the expertise that the company needs for continued growth. All too often a business falters and suffers until the original top management team is forced out by unhappy creditors or shareholders.

Developing the Organization

Even if the growing company consists of only a few individuals, it is crucial that each person clearly knows his responsibilities. This is important in a developed organization; it is life or death in a growing company. The boss has to recognize that he does not have the time to do everything himself and that his time is spent much more effectively in training his people to carry out the work.

It is equally important that each individual is truly given the authority to carry out this work and make the necessary decisions. If the boss believes that the wrong decisions are being made, it becomes a time for discussion, possibly more training. Eventually, if a common understanding cannot be reached, then a parting of the ways is obviously the only solution.

All of these management duties take time, a lot of time, and it is too easy to put them off when a shipping schedule has to be met. It is now that the manager has to look clearly at his own responsibilities and understand that his prime task is to achieve his schedule by working with and through his people. It may take longer, but he is at the same time providing the necessary training so that the schedule will be met the next time and every other time without his direct intervention.

If the company growth continues, the management skills necessary to run it correctly will become more complex. Not infrequently, as we have already mentioned, the managers who started the operation do not have the skills to carry it through this stage of growth. The wise entrepreneur will recognize these limitations and hire skilled and experienced people to run the operation and provide training for himself and his original crew.

This is a time where many tasks change in the growing company. For example, initially one individual will be able to take care of purchasing all materials and will need the abilities of a buyer. As the department grows, he will need to learn the skills of a manager and become less and less involved in the day-to-day buying function. He will have to lay down purchasing policies, hire new staff, and monitor performance. Similar changes will occur in almost every department. Thus, with growth, many of the original members of the company will either have to increase their abilities and become skilled in supervising others, or be passed by in the promotion race.

This is not an easy fact to accept, either by the employee or the boss. In the initial enthusiasm of starting a new business, it is easy to hold out the carrot of advancement. How many times have we heard the promise "You will grow with the company"? At the time it is meant sincerely. However, when growth occurs and the individual cannot perform in a supervisory role and eventually has to be replaced, the damage to company morale has already been done. In this case the policy should have been decided during the startup phase and every employee should have been given the facts. There are really only two options.

1. As the company grows the old employee will be provided with an opportunity to learn the management skills required for the job, and to be promoted provided his ability meets the job requirement.

2. New skilled, experienced employees will be hired as management positions need to be filled.

Product Design

In previous chapters the importance of good product design has been mentioned several times, but nowhere is this so important as with the growing company. Yet this aspect of manufacturing is often glossed over just because this is a new operation: there is the belief that the design can be improved later, that with experience we will be able to do the job better, and that there is simply a lack of understanding about the manufacturing process. But when there is such a need to meet a schedule, keep down costs, and grow a satisfied clientele, a sound product design is critical to the entire operation.

At one growing company a small design error was found that was not corrected because doing so would delay an important delivery date. The designers understood that it could possibly cause product failure, but they believed that this was not likely to occur, and took no further actions. The product was in the field for several months when the first failure occurred, followed shortly afterward by a second. Eventually all the units made from that design had to be called back to the plant. The cost was several millions of dollars and the effect on the company's reputation almost ruined the business. Startup and growth are not periods when a company should take chances. In the same way that the seedling of an oak tree can be easily broken by a careless footstep, whereas a full grown tree cannot be easily damaged, a growing company can be destroyed by many small factors that would easily be overcome in an established operation.

A growing company provides an excellent time to get the designers onto the shop floor to assist in the development of the manufacturing process. It educates them in the manufacturing techniques and at the same time brings together the design and manufacturing people as a basis for permanent cooperation.

Constant design changes, no matter how small, can play havoc to manufacturing, and will adversly affect quality, cost, and schedule. Any additional delay or cost generated by finalizing the product design is more than compensated for in the actual manufacturing cycle.

Process Development

There are always plenty of reasons to delay developing a sound manufacturing process. "The operators know what they have to do," "It will all change when we get the new machines," and so on. In all too many cases this means that the process is never fully developed, it is never recorded, and therefore no one really knows if it is working correctly or not. In too many cases the operators manage to get the product out using their own techniques, little tricks that they find it difficult to describe. Of course, rejects have to be reworked, but with a lot of hard work the shipments are made.

The production volume starts to increase, automation is being introduced, and suddenly the defect rate and the cost of inspection and rework becomes unacceptable. Just when a firm, defined manufacturing process becomes important, there is nothing on which to base the production growth. In all too many cases the operators find it difficult even to describe exactly how they are putting the product together.

From the beginning there have to be some recorded instructions defining how to make the product. If nothing more, you should ask the operators to write down exactly what they do and check the accuracy of their instructions. From the beginning demand that data are generated and maintained on the defects found relative to the various steps in the manufacturing process. If these simple functions become recognized as standard procedure, it will not be difficult to install statistical control at a later date. Remember always the utter simplicity of defining the process and controlling it through simple statistics. Simply taught, in plain easily understood terms, everyone will become used to the philosophy. If it becomes necessary to use any of the more complex aspects of statistical control they will be readily accepted and easily implemented.

People, Once Again People

The excitement and novelty of starting a new company will keep people working at the peak of their ability. The promise of the future is a wonderful morale builder. This is the time when 18-hour days are not unusual, and weekends are just more days to get out the product. Then the letdown begins; it becomes difficult to persuade people to work late or to come in on weekends, no matter how pressing the need. Before the enthusiasm fades, it is a good policy to sit down with all the people and frankly discuss their future. Not in general "aim-to-please" terms, but in solid factual discussions regarding the financial terms of their future employment, together with health, pension, and similar benefits, all clearly defined. If you are the boss, it is fine for you to work every hour that you have available, for when the company does grow you know that you will almost certainly reap the financial rewards. But why should the operator or supervisor give the same intensity to his task when he knows that he can very well be terminated at some future date? Remember at this stage the company has no personnel reputation to hold up in front of the employees.

The author is a firm believer in the advantages of some form of co-partnership in which the employee knows that he will gain in direct proportion to the profits made by the company and also lose if the company fails to meet the profit objectives. When these simple facts are presented to the employees in a clear, legally acceptable manner, everyone has the same incentive to put their total effort into the work.

Of course, all the things already discussed with respect to people and the manufacturing process still apply; indeed, in this stage of a company's growth they are vitally important. Train to make sure that everyone understands exactly what is expected of them, and clearly define paths of communication through all levels of the operation.

SUMMARY

There is much repetition in this book and the author makes no apology for that. Basically, managing the manufacturing process is a very simple task, and no matter what the management task only a few rules apply. They have been covered so many times in previous chapters that there is no need to repeat them here.

When we consider a new or growing company, these rules apply with brutal consequences if they are not applied. As a manager of a business in these stages of growth, perhaps you should apply one more rule. PLAN, PLAN, AND PLAN. Consider what might happen, and make contingency plans for every possibility. Remember that your prime task is to plan for the future, and to lay the foundations for the developing organization. Never forget that your employees are your strength and your weakness, depending on your skills in managing them and providing the leadership in the growing company.

Chapter 24

PUTTING IT ALL TOGETHER

We have looked at managing the manufacturing process from many angles. The task would be very simple if each view showed us the same thing. Unfortunately, we often see conflicting requirements that call for compromise, and making decisions that cannot always satisfy all our objectives. We have repeatedly mentioned the balance that must be maintained between quality, cost, and schedule; there is also the psychological conflict involved in asking our people to conform consistently to the process and yet use their inventiveness and intelligence. There is the need to have an excellent understanding of the technology that is being managed and also the ability to work with and motivate the people who operate the machines and provide the skills that make the process function.

Inevitably we have encountered a lot of repetition, in some instances one could almost say contradiction, as we have viewed a task or objective from different perspectives. For example, we have seen the need for discussion when a processing problem arises, and an overall agreement is to be determined on the corrective action to be followed. But we have also mentioned the definitive, firm decisions that have to be made by the manager when total concurrence cannot be achieved. Although attempting to provide a clear pattern of excellence therefore is not a simple matter, this chapter should provide a lasting mental picture that will stay in our minds as a useful ruler against which we can measure our actions when problems arise or the day-to-day activities seem to overwhelm us.

A BASIC SIMPLICITY

Like many other tasks that face us in life, managing the manufacturing process is basically simple, but we often make it appear complicated in our minds, by becoming so immersed in the details that we forget our simple main objective.

"To make the highest quality product at the lowest cost, by striving for excellence in all that we do."

We cannot compromise on achieving this objective, and if we balance any decisions against that simple need to achieve excellence we will never stray far from the right path. But the question arises as to what is meant by excellence, and the simple answer is as follows.

"To do everything as well as humanly possible with the people and facilities available."

This is certainly an oversimplification of the day-to-day tasks that are involved in managing any process; in many cases when a decision has to be made, the correct response may be unclear because of a lack of information, contradictory data, or some other confusing situation. At this time it is extremely useful to have a focus, a standard rule against which to measure the various options open to us. The very simplicity of this objective of excellence may make it appear to be nothing more than a slogan to be pinned on the wall and then forgotten, but it is a much more potent tool if it is constantly in the forefront of all our decisions.

If we begin to do EVERYTHING as well as we possibly can and demand the same level of quality from our people, it soon becomes the standard way of doing things in our operation. Whether it is cleaning the windows, writing a memo, quoting a million dollar contract, or merely going through the day-to-day operation of the manufacturing process they must all be done as well as we possibly can. "Good enough" is never good enough; only excellence is acceptable. Roger Milliken, the chairman of Milliken & Co, which received the 1989 Malcolm Baldridge National Quality Award, is quoted as saying, "Good is the enemy of best. And best is the enemy of better."

EXCELLENCE AND THE PROCESS

We can apply the same simple philosophy to the process that we are managing. If the product has been properly designed, if the process has been correctly developed—that is, if we have achieved excellence in every step, if we have excellence in our materials specifications and assure that they are always met—the process will always repeat, perfectly. Our product will always be of consistent quality, determined only by the excellence of the design.

Any variation from excellence will indicate that we failed to meet this objective in the process development or in some other associated area. Either we have deliberately accepted "good enough" or we have missed some aspect of the process which has affected the repeatability.

Accepting "good enough" is so easy to do, especially under pressure of the schedule or the budget. For example, a machine is selected because it meets the budget limit, although it is not the most suitable for the task, because accepting the limitation is easier than fighting for a larger budget. The installation and setup of a process are incomplete because the schedule demands it be on line by a particular date and insufficient time was allowed in the schedule to do the job correctly. Here again it is easier to get the process running, no matter how poorly, rather than attempt to change the schedule. We have all experienced these things; we have all seen the ultimate effect on the product cost and the schedule. Although the budget and the schedule are not violated at the time the decision is made to attempt to meet them, the cumulative costs are frequently excessive. That they are sometimes not directly identified is too often simply because our accounting system does not show them as single items but collects them together in some such category as "overheads." This is surely a sign of a lack of excellence in the accounting department.

The lack of excellence in developing the process can be equally devastating. It is easy to miss a small factor that can have a major impact on the product quality; it may be something that has been genuinely overlooked but more often it is something that has been brushed aside as unimportant, a case of "good enough." A typical example was the failure of soldered joints in a military radar system, which was eventually found to be caused by tiny variations in the length of time that the operators held the joint during solder solidification. During development, this part of the process had not been considered important enough to automate, as it was believed that the operators' skills were "good enough." A simple timer on the machine cured the problem, but the cost of finding the basic cause and reworking the product was extremely high. The effect on the company reputation could not be measured.

EXCELLENCE AND PROCESSING PROBLEMS

Almost invariably when problems arise with the process, the cause is a lack of excellence in some operation. We should never lose sight of a simple rule.

Any change in the product quality indicates a change in the process.

The change may be in the materials, in the machines, or in the methods being used by the people concerned. Find it and you will have found the problem. Do not let complicated ideas and suggestions obscure this simple fact. All too often problem solving gets bogged down in the details of the process and the obvious variation is missed. As manager, one of the chief things that you can do when a problem arises is to keep the problem solving on the right lines and demand that the simple facts are reviewed first.

In one instance a complex program of experiments had been implemented to find the cause of a product failure. It was not producing results. The production line was meanwhile at a standstill. It was easy to find the day that the defect was first seen and then to ask what had changed at that time, no matter how remotely it could be related to the process. It was found that a drum truck had been introduced into the stores on that day to protect some newly installed floors. The chemicals for the particular process step where the problem arose had been wheeled onto the shop floor for the first time, instead of being rolled down the aisle as had been done for years past. The chemicals, which frequently stood for several months in storage, had unknowingly been mixed by the rolling. This factor had been completely missed during the process development; in other words, excellence was lacking in developing the process.

Another example will demonstrate how striving for excellence can provide a practical guide. Some materials fail to meet their specification. Do we reject them and miss the production schedule, or do we use them and jeopardize the product quality? Excellence demands that any possible jeopardy to the product quality is not acceptable. If we find that we can use the materials without jeopardy to the product, the specification must be incorrect. In other words,, we must now ask for a change to the document and demand excellence in preparing the specification. If the materials cannot be used, we must go back to our vendor and in turn demand excellence from him and his operation, to prevent the problem from reoccuring.

What of the schedule? We will achieve excellence in meeting the schedule only when we have excellence in the specification and in the parts that we receive from our vendors.

The quest for excellence therefore shows that there are not many options open to us, and points clearly to the correct decisions. Of course, we always have to consider the question of cost, but invariably the decision that will guarantee excellence in product quality will coincide with the decision that will provide the ultimate lowest cost. Perhaps not the immediately obvious lowest cost . . . The effects of rework, repair, and customer satisfaction on company profitability cannot be easily calculated, except to indicate that they are critical to the success of the operation.

PEOPLE, PEOPLE, AND MORE PEOPLE

The manufacturing manager has to be totally knowledgeable about the process; he must have an excellent understanding of the technologies involved. He may have achieved excellence in many fields, yet still finds that managing is a difficult and sometimes disturbing way of making a livelihood. We have all encountered the brilliant engineer who is promoted and turns out to be the world's worst manager. On the other hand, most of us have known the individual who is almost ignorant in the technical area of the business yet turns out to be a first-class manager who achieves excellence in his operation.

The answer of course lies in the ability of the latter individual to work with people, and not only demand excellence from them but to so stimulate them in their work that they too demand excellence of themselves and of those around them. Inversely, the lack of this skill in the more technically oriented manager allows the operation to descend into mediocrity. Yet even in this most complex area of any manager's working life there is the same simple objective of excellence to provide a guide. However, we are now working with people, not things, and we have to remember that here lies the greatest variability that will exist in the entire manufacturing management process.

We want excellence from our people, and thus in turn we have to offer excellence to our people. This does not necessarily mean the highest wages, the most comprehensive medical insurance, or the longest vacations. Of course, all of these things are important and everyone deserves his fair share of whatever the business can afford. Yet all too often improving these items is looked upon as the solution to any form of labor discontent. Certainly these benefits can silence the outward signs of people problems, but they rarely eliminate the inner felings that trigger off the problems. We are all human and we all have some very human needs in our daily life. We need to feel wanted, in our work as well as in our personal life. We need to feel an important part of the operation, not a number in the employee files. We need to know that our ideas, our wishes, and our concerns may not only be expressed freely and without the fear of recrimination, but that they are heard, discussed, and acted upon according to their merit. We need to know that we can influence the future of our company or at least the process for which we are responsible. In other words, we need to have the opportunity to participate fully in reaching for excellence.

When this opportunity is denied, increasing the wages and benefits can certainly keep people from leaving their jobs, but too often they then carry out their work solely from the fear of losing these practical advantages. Unfortunately, the result is always a long way from excellence. It creates an atmosphere of fear, where the individual does the minimum amount of work to satisfy his boss and avoids any form of controversy. Safety becomes the watchword, and creativity and excellence disappear.

It is not unusual, especially in the larger companies that provide superior wages and benefits, to have people comment that they hate their job, but they have become so used to the standard of life it provides that they will put up with anything to keep it. This results in mediocrity, not excellence or creativity.

If we intend to control the manufacturing process, if we aim to operate with excellence in all that we do, we have to avoid this attitude at all costs. The intelligence and the inventiveness of our people are two of the greatest advantages that we posses; we have to encourage them in every way, and this is nothing more than excellence in management. Once again, it is not a difficult concept: we have to demand that the process is followed precisely, that any changes to it are formally tested and entered into the documented process before being implemented. But we also have to provide clear, responsive channels of communication for our people to input their ideas. This is the way that the process is improved. Our people are then part of the process. It is their process, and they want to do everything to make it operate with excellence. They are not mere robots doing exactly what they are told.

EXCELLENCE FOR PEOPLE

We cannot guarantee happiness or wealth for our people but we can aim to provide excellence in their working conditions, not only by providing for their physical needs but also by involving them in every facet of the process, from its development to the day-to-day operation. It implies an on-going training program to improve the knowledge and skills of each individual, and an open policy regarding information about the organization, the performance, and the future plans of the company. It is surprising what positive effects such a working arrangement can generate.

The author well remembers working in an company that functioned in this way. It was an exciting experience, and it was an extremely efficient manufacturing operation. The atmosphere that developed was summed up by an operator who exclaimed one day, "I just love coming to work." It was exemplified by the operators who, although paid according to output, would come and explain that their job had been incorrectly studied and the standard time should be reduced. Their work had become much more than a way of earning money, it had become a society in which they participated fully and in which they could exert a measure of control. They also wanted to be proud of their work; they wanted it to be the best operation of its kind, and they wanted it to grow and be profitable. They too were striving for excellence.

To confound the issue, every person is an individual and wants to be treated as such. Surely we all possess certain basic feelings and attitudes, but even stronger may sometimes be the particular quirks of personality that make each of us different. One supervisor proved to be reluctant to accept any instruction without a great deal of argument. No matter what he was told to do he always wanted to do it in a different way, a different time. He simply did not like to take orders. It was quickly found, however, that if he were given instructions in the form of asking for his help in solving a problem or in achieving some objective, he would willingly accept orders if they were in the form of suggestions. He had been moved several times by managers who claimed that he was an uncooperative individual, when in reality he was an excellent employee. If we aim for excellence in management, we have to know the people whom we personally manage as individuals and adjust our way of working with them to take into account their idiosyncrasies. Even here we can still aim for excellence, this time in our understanding of our people. We have to look at each individual and ask ourselves if we really and truly understand him. Knowing someone, of course, can only occur through communication, through talking together, and excellence in communication is one of the most important management skills.

ALL THE OTHER THINGS

There are not too many managers who only have the responsibility for the manufacturing process, there are usually many other tasks that have to be included, from running the cafeteria to getting the lawns cut. This book has concentrated on the details of the manufacturing function, but it does not require much reasoning to understand that the same concepts apply to many if not most of the things that occupy a manager's work. The striving for excellence cannot stop at the manufacturing floor because the actual manufacturing process does not stop at the manufacturing floor. If the accounting department does not collect the financial data correctly and display them in a form that is immediately useful, it has strayed from the need for excellence and a tremendously useful tool has been lost to the management function. The manufacturing manager may well ask how he can possibly influence a department such as accounting, and of course this may be extremely difficult to do unless there are the same clear communication links between departments as exist within the manufacturing area.

Of course, we are now discussing an issue from Chapter 9. The manufacturing manager has little hope of influencing the remainder of the operation unless there is a clear mandate from top management to accept only excellence in all that is done: not a communique issued and then forgotten, but a living, breathing plan with the full day-to-day support of the people at the very top of the organization. We have gone through a long period of stagnation in the manufacturing area, a period where manipulating money, acquiring other corporations, and similar maneuvers have taken the place of attempting to develop a sound manufacturing base. But we as a nation cannot exist by taking in each other's washing; we have to make products that other people want at a price they are willing to pay. It does appear that changes are coming. More and more frequently we are seeing changes in upper management, with individuals taking charge who understand these truths and who want to develop a strong manufacturing base.

We are also seeing cases where excellence in manufacturing has shone as an example of efficiency and caught the attention of those at the top who have now become interested and eventually expanded the ideas into the entire operation. We cannot change the whole world at once, but by achieving excellence in our own little part of the operation we can demonstrate exactly what can be achieved.

SUMMARY

There is no simple answer to all the questions that arise when we discuss the manufacturing process. There are too many variations in products, in organizations, in companies, and of course in people.

Yet shining through all the confusion of these variations is the guiding light of excellence. In most cases, it provides a clear indication of the path to take. There are a few—a very few—comprehensive rules that we can apply to help us.

- All manufacturing can be looked upon as a repeatable process.
- Develop the process carefully and in detail.
- If the process is not fully recorded you have no process.
- Controlling the process is the only way to guarantee product quality.
- Any variation in the product indicates a variation in the process.
- Gather around you experts whom you trust.
- Listen to these experts when technical problems arise.

- Look for simplicity, be suspicious of the technical gobbledegook.
- Recognize that most people want to do a good job.
- People cannot do a good job unless you train them fully.
- People want to feel they belong, that they are a part of the company.
- People want to have a say in the day-to-day operation.
- Arrange formal communication links, and LISTEN.
- Every person is an individual and needs to be treated as such.

Chapter 25

WHERE DO WE GO FROM HERE?

Forecasting the future is always a dangerous occupation. There is the fascination of the new technologies that promise so much. The optimistic view suggests limitless, pollution-free energy, colonization of the planets, and a futuristic society where all is peace, light, and happiness. On the other hand, the pessimistic outlook implies that our society is doomed, the greenhouse effect will cause monstrous floods and famine, and industry is driven by wicked men seeking only personal gain. The future almost certainly falls somewhere in between these two extremes.

Manufacturing will certainly change. It has been changing ever since the first prehistoric entrepreneur set up a small workshop to make and barter flint tools. The rate of change has accelerated dramatically in the past century until today it sometimes seems that one technology replaces another every year. The technical press encourages that idea, because the new technologies are their bread and butter. I have just read one such article that discusses manufacturing of the future in terms of molecular engineering, world-wide manufacturing, international corporations, lasers, and superconductivity. In other words, reading that article would give a reader from another planet a totally false opinion of the way that manufacturing is developing in the United States or even in the world. Of course it is extremely difficult to forecast the speed with which any of these new ideas will develop into practical manufacturing processes. Many will fall by the wayside and never be heard of again.

It is also extremely difficult to determine if a new technology will replace an older system or merely offer an alternative way of doing the same thing. It is often assumed that the electronics manufacturing technology has totally changed in the last few decades, but there have been only two technical advances that have eliminated their older counterparts. The printed wiring board placed all connections on one plane and made automated assembly and soldering possible; it also provided consistent electrical characteristics in the wiring and reduced assembly labor. This development quickly eliminated the metal chassis, wiring harnesses, and most hand soldering. The development of the transistor, and its offspring the integrated circuit, made the vacuum tube obsolete, except for some very specialized tasks, by reducing power requirements, heat, and size, and offering greatly improved capabilities.

Many other developments have certainly changed to some extent the methods by which modern electronics are manufactured, but there are a great many companies who still fabricate their products using the same methods that have been in existence for twenty years. It seems logical that the other areas of industry will change in the same way; that is, most of the new developments will offer other ways of doing the job but the old ways will still be used in many cases. For example, the machining center has become a popular tool, replacing some of the more traditional machines, but a tremendous number of lathes, drills, and similar machines are still being used in our factories. Many forecasts of the past few years have been incorrect. We have not seen a major change to the use of robots, and the subsequent mass unemployment that was forecast some years ago. The steady and growing use of automation of every kind will undoubtedly continue, but hardly to the degree that had been forecast. Superconductivity has been touted for so long that it is now hardly new idea. Certainly, developments in this technology are announced every now and then, but it is still not in practical use as was sometimes predicted.

Much of the publicity regarding the future of manufacturing technology is based on the large corporations, we have to consider the entire manufacturing spectrum not only the IBMs, the Fords, and the ITTs. A vast range of products are made by the smaller companies employing only a few hundred people or less. They will not disappear; in fact many of the new ideas, methods, and machines will continue to be developed by such enterprises. They are much more flexible than their larger counterparts and often more willing to take chances on novel ideas.

We will see in the future much of the same spread of businesses as we see today. There will be a few large multinational operations which will certainly grow and expand into more and more countries, but there will still be the smaller local companies working very much as they have for the past years, and many of these will be highly successful. What will we see in common with all of these manufacturing operations?

PEOPLE . . . ONCE AGAIN, PEOPLE

No matter how much our operation is automated, people will continue to be the key to success. We have to improve our skills in using people, in motivating them to excellence in all that we do. The successful manager will definitely need to have exceptional skills in this field. As our people become better educated, not only will they be more useful to us but they will also demand that we respect their skills and abilities and offer them a greater part in the overall operation and organization of the company. These changes in the way that we use our people are currently taking place in many of the overseas operations. The level of education is improving and we can no longer look at people in these countries as merely cheap labor to be used like machines.

In Japan the only national resource is their people and every effort is made to educate them, to train them in the latest techniques and technologies, and to use them efficiently. We have to look very hard at the way we do these same things. In fact, industry will have to take the lead in technical education, if, as appears likely, our colleges are incapable of providing the necessary practical training. If we are to encourage our brightest people into manufacturing, where they are undoubtedly needed, we have to give this profession the prestige in society that it deserves, and this relates directly to salary and wage rates. It is not the intent of this book to pursue the question of comparative values, but it always seems strange that the man responsible for producing the products that are the heart and soul of a company is frequently paid less than the accountant or the salesman.

No matter what technical advances occur in the manufacturing arena, the successful manager of the future will have as his primary task the management of people. In this respect it will not have changed, but in detail interpersonal skills will become more demanding as people become more sophisticated, are better educated, and expect to become more and more involved in day-to-day running of the operation.

THE COMPUTER

From the huge expensive mainframe computers of a few years ago we now have desk top personal computers with practically the same performance as their older and much more costly counterparts. Computers for design, computers for testing, and computers for assembly machines are now becoming commonplace. Although each has an important contribution to make to the efficiency of the manufacturing operation, they really become effective when all of these machines are interconnected, using the same data bases, with information readily available to all.

The manufacturing manager of the future will be required to have an excellent understanding of the way that computers operate, what can and cannot be done with them, and how the data is collected and manipulated. He will have to know how they are integrated together into a total system. This integration will have a secondary effect in improving communication between departments. When the designer can see in real time the effect on manufacturing of a design change, he will become much more concerned with the manufacturing process. When the purchasing agent can view the defect figures for the product and see that a particular purchased item is always involved he will be as concerned as the manufacturing engineer. The linking together of computer systems is not easy, but the rewards are much greater than those from each individual computer.

We have discussed the use of computers in the manufacturing process, but we have to remember that this process extends into areas not usually considered as part of manufacturing. When integration of individual computer systems includes these peripheral areas—such as storage, purchasing, quality control, and kitting—the improvements in efficiency can be remarkable. For example, we might consider the assembly of a product containing several hundred parts. They must each be counted as they are pulled from stores, and checked to assure that they are the correct parts and that the right number are kitted. Carrying out this work and recording all of these data manually are costly, time consuming, and not particularly accurate. If these tasks, and the collection of the information, can be controlled by the computer and integrated with purchasing and production data bases, there is the possibility of developing a very efficient materials operation, in which the quantity and situation of all materials are constantly known and updated. Any attempt to operate in the "just-in-time" mode will be simplified by such a materials control system.

Our process control data can also be improved when such items as field failures, test failures, and inspection data can be collected into one data base that is made available to all concerned with the operation. Consider, for example, the value of such information to the designer of the product. This integration of individual computer systems is not simple or easy to achieve, but this is the direction that our process control must go if it is to be effective. There is no doubt that this will be the preferred operational method of manufacturing of the future.

AUTOMATION

The pressure toward excellence in process control makes the development of more and more automation inevitable, and this will place yet more demands on the abilities of the manufacturing manager of the future. When the word "automation" is used, the mind immediately sees large and complicated systems. These will certainly be part of the future factory, but we will also see more and more simple forms of automation—for example, the use of the bar code reader to eliminate visual reading and recording by hand, and the use of sensors to monitor temperatures, pressures, and similar parameters—that remove the operator as far as possible from mindless, continuous operations. These less exotic forms of automation will grow steadily and offer to the smaller companies many of the advantages of the larger systems, not the least being the automatic availability of recorded processing data.

Cost, together with the problems of flexibility, will undoubedbly limit the number of large, totally automated installations. The customer of tomorrow is not likely to accept the philosophy of Henry Ford, that you can have any color you like as long as it is black. We have to comply with the customer's wishes, and the automation must therefore be flexible enough to incorporate the individual design factors that will keep the customer. In turn, these make the automation much more costly. It is almost inevitable that any form of automation will include computer control and the possibility of integration with other computer systems.

As mentioned above, the automation will include more and more of the fringe areas of manufacturing: testing at receiving inspection, controlling the life of materials in stores, packaging the product, handling and distributing materials. The effect of all of these will inevitably bring departments closer together, break down many of the barriers in our organization, and show clearly that excellence in manufacturing is the key to success and that it must be supported fully at all times.

QUALITY

The old philosophies regarding product quality are fast disappearing. The idea that the product should only be good enough to do the job is as out of date as the bi-plane. The belief that inspection can somehow guarantee product quality has been proved to be on a par with a belief in the tooth fairy. Yet these ideas somehow hang around, and the results are still visible in many companies. The manager of the future will view such philosophies as historical fantasies.

The idea of having a "quality control" department as an overall purveyor of quality that can be sprinkled over the product with suitable magic incantations, will fade from view. It will be universally recognized that the quality of any product is only as good as the process by which it is made, and that it is the task of the entire organization to define the correct design, materials, and manufacturing process, and then comply exactly with these definitions. It will become universally understood that manufacturing is not some small part of the operation set apart in a factory building, but that manufacturing is the heart of any industry. Everything else is there only to provide it with the necessary support.

Our customers are also changing, becoming more demanding and more sophisticated. In many areas, price is taking second place to quality and reliability, and this trend is likely to continue as the standard of living improves and the amount of money available to the individual slowly increases.

In the more distant future, we will also have to contend with a static consumer base. Population growth is leveling off in the United States; in some countries it is a matter of public policy to hold down the birth rate. With growing concern over pollution of the environment, it is inevitable that population growth will eventually be recognized as the single most devastating factor. The world population will have to level off or even be reduced if we are to maintain our quality of life. This is obviously a long-term concern but it does suggest that as industry competes for a shrinking market, quality will continue to grow as the dominant marketing feature.

Thus, the manufacturing manager of the future will have to clearly understand the implications of manufacturing to the highest standards of quality and be able to motivate all his people toward these goals.

MANUFACTURING IN THE UNITED STATES

We are seeing a small but significant move of manufacturing from overseas back to the United States, and it seems logical to believe that this move will continue. The drive for quality is pushing our manufacturing methods toward more and more automation with subsequent pressure to more accurately control our processes. Once this happens the labor content of the product is reduced, and the cost of labor becomes less and less important. With automation comes the need for fast and efficient machine maintenance, which can be a major problem overseas. It also requires an increase in the skills of the operators, which in turn calls for better educated people, who eventually will demand higher wages. Thus, in time the so-called "low cost labor" areas will cease to be as attractive as they have been. This trend is already seen in Puerto Rico and Singapore. Both areas have improved the training of their people to provide all of the management and engineering skills necessary to set up and operate a manufacturing plant, not merely to provide cheap labor.

It is logical that this trend will continue. The skills that have been implanted abroad through our overseas factories will provide a base for those countries to develop their own industries, which in turn will inevitably produce more and more competition. If we are to be successful in the international market, we will have to do so through the excellence that we build into our products.

We will certainly see the growth of the totally automated factory, in many cases not because of the requirement of cost or product volume, but because of the demand for excellence in product quality. Of course, only the large operation with the finances to automate will be successful in these fields. This is already the case with the manufacture of semiconductors, and we are beginning to see it in the case of printed wiring boards. There will still be plenty of room for the smaller company—the operation that can be competitive through flexibility, through innovation in the process, or through originality of the product. However, these companies will survive only if they can equal or better the product quality of their larger competitors.

These trends give us a clue as to some of the requirements of the manufacturing manager of the future. He may be running a highly automated operation that relies heavily on machines, on high technology, and on engineers and specialists. He may be running an operation that relies more heavily on the manual skills of his people. Even this operation, however, will include a high percentage of automated process steps. He will have more and more competition, which will in turn demand more and more attention to the excellence of his operation.

ELECTRONICS IN MANUFACTURING

Almost every product uses electronics in some way—either in the product itself or in the machines used to manufacture it. Typewriters, telephones, and calculators were not too long ago mostly mechanical or electromechanical devices, but they are now almost totally electronic. The amount of electronics in our automobiles has risen from a tiny percentage to a considerable part of the total cost. This trend will continue and the manufacturing manager of the future will need to understand this technology. It was not long ago that a knowledge of mechanics was a required skill of anyone in manufacturing, but electronics is fast taking its place.

Even if purchased electronics packages are used in the manufacture of the product, problems with handling and storage may occur, and may not be recognized by the inexperienced manager. If electronics are used in the machines that are a part of the process, test systems, or other manufacturing equipment, the manager who is not at least knowledgeable in the technology will be at a disadvantage in operating his process.

THE PROCESS

No matter what the product, it seems certain that the manufacturing process will become more complex with each change in technology. Products tend to become smaller and lighter, use less materials, yet have many more functions than ever. The 35mm camera was once an expensive masterpiece of mechanical and optical craftsmanship which required the skill of a professional photographer to set up and operate. It is now a comparatively low cost masterpiece of automated manufacturing, electronics, and optics, which can produce excellent pictures without any need for photographic skills. But we must consider the tremendous changes in the manufacturing processes that had to take place to bring about this change in the product.

The case of the camera is not unique; similar examples can be seen in all aspects of daily life. Consider the throwaway items used in medicine today—disposable needles, dressings, and even bedpans. It is only through the tremendous advances in manufacturing technology and materials that these items can be made at a low enough cost to be salable. However, though the advances in manufacturing continue at an ever faster pace, much of the old manufacturing methods remain with us. Manufacturing is changing at an ever advancing pace, but only in isolated areas is there a complete revolution in manufacturing technologies.

The manufacturing manager of the future will always have the pressure of change to cope with, and his success or failure will depend to a great extent on his ability to accept change and manage it effectively. He must be up-to-date with all the applicable technologies, he must be able to sort out the important new items from the mass of information, publicity, and hype that threaten to engulf any manager. Above all, he must understand his own process in every possible detail. He must have the skills and understanding to make the decisions and to provide the leadership that are his prime task.

EXCELLENCE

We have come full circle, and of course excellence has to be at the heart of the manufacturing process: excellence in the relationships with our people, excellence in the organization of our operation, excellence in process control, excellence in everything that we do. When excellence becomes the overwhelming day-to-day objective, then we will have developed a good operation. Anything less than this will at best achieve mediocrity.

A FINAL SUMMARY

This chapter has of necessity been something less than a formally structured document. Repetition has been unavoidable, and sometimes the subject matter must have appeared to be something other than the future of manufacturing management.

Unfortunately, this is the nature of the job. It is almost impossible to clearly define the manufacturing manager's job. It varies from company to company, and from product to product, and will vary even more in the future. However, when we look at where we might be in the coming years, we know that we will have to hone certain skills to razor sharpness if we are to be successful.

- We must have an excellent understanding of people, how they think and behave, and how they can be motivated to excellence.
- We must be competent in the use of computers.
- We must keep up-to-date in all of the relevant new technologies.
- We have to understand the effects of new technologies on our process.
- We should understand at least the basics of electronics.
- We must never forget our struggle toward excellence in everything we do.

Excellence in manufacturing lies at the heart of the well-being of our country. We have the best and most highly skilled workers in the world. Let us provide them with excellence in leadership and management so that we can once again lead the world through our industrial excellence.

INDEX